Advance Praise for Courtney Price Answers the Most Asked Questions from Entrepreneurs

"A valuable guide for can-do entrepreneurs who need practical answers to important questions now! Price presents lively, readable, and effective insights to help start and build successful companies."

Raymond W. Smilor
Vice President
Center for Entrepreneurial Leadership
Kauffman Foundation

"Wow! What a great book—Ask and you shall receive. Courtney Price points the entrepreneur toward success by asking and answering the right questions to grow successful businesses."

Dennis P. Kimbro
Director, Center for Entrepreneurship
Clark Atlanta University

"Hooray! At last a book with real life answers for the how to's of building and growing your business. Dr. Price's book is an invaluable tool and practical guide to success for entrepreneurs everywhere."

Barbara B. Grogen
President and CEO
Western Industrial Contractors
Denver

Courtney Price Answers the Most Asked Questions from Entrepreneurs

Courtney H. Price

McGraw-Hill, Inc.

New York San Francisco Washington, D.C. Auckland Bogotá
Caracas Lisbon London Madrid Mexico City Milan
Montreal New Delhi San Juan Singapore
Sydney Tokyo Toronto

Library of Congress Cataloging-in-Publication Data

Price, Courtney H.
Courtney Price answers the most asked questions from entrepreneurs.
p. cm.
Includes index.
ISBN 0-07-050831-3 (pbk.)
1. New business enterprises—United States. 2. Entrepreneurship—United States. 3. Business enterprises—United States—Management. 4. Venture capital—United States. I. Title.
HD62.5.P648 1994
658.4'21—dc20 94-2310
CIP

1 2 3 4 5 6 7 8 9 0 DOC/DOC 9 0 9 8 7 6 5 4

ISBN 0-07-050831-3

The sponsoring editor for this book was Betsy N. Brown, the editing supervisor was Caroline R. Levine, and the production supervisor was Donald F. Schmidt. It was set in Palatino by McGraw-Hill's Professional Book Group composition unit.

Printed and bound by R. R. Donnelley & Sons Company.

This publication is designed to provide accurate and authoritative information in regard to the subject matter covered. It is sold with the understanding that the publisher is not engaged in rendering legal, accounting or other professional service. If legal advice or other expert assistance is required, the services of a competent professional person should be sought.
—from the declaration of principles jointly adopted by a committee of the American Bar Association and a committee of publishers

This book is printed on recycled, acid-free paper containing a minimum of 50% recycled de-inked fiber.

This book is dedicated to Ewing Kauffman, who in the brief time I knew him made a dramatic impact on my entrepreneurial philosophies and strongly reinforced my belief that hard work combined with treating others as you want to be treated, and richly rewarding those who help create the wealth, are the secrets of personal success, entrepreneurship, and the future of our country.

About the Author

Courtney Price is an internationally recognized management writer, lecturer, and consultant. Her syndicated column, "Entrepreneurs Ask," appears in approximately 350 newspapers nationwide. She has been acknowledged for her innovative Premier FastTrac™ Entrepreneurship Programs, which are now given in 18 states. She is also Director of the Institute of Entrepreneurship of Metropolitan State College in Denver and a scholar-in-residence at the Center for Entrepreneurial Leadership of the Kauffman Foundation in Kansas City.

Contents

Foreword xiii
Preface xvii
Acknowledgments xix

1. Overview of Entrepreneurship 1

1-1 Overview 1
1-2 Smart Entrepreneurial Strategies 3
1-3 Entrepreneurial Trends and Opportunities 3
1-4 Minority and Women Entrepreneurs 10
1-5 Physically Disabled Entrepreneurs 15
1-6 Executive Entrepreneurs 18
1-7 Pitfalls to Avoid 21
1-8 Entrepreneurial Resource Checklist 22

2. The 10 Most Asked Questions from Entrepreneurs 25

1 I'd love to start a new business, but I don't have a great idea. What kind of business should I start? 26
2 I want to open a business in my home. What do I need to do to get started? 28
3 How do I approach a banker to get a loan to start my new business? 29
4 Where can I find a venture capitalist to finance my new venture? 32
5 How do I go about obtaining a patent for my new software program? 33

6 I have already patented a new invention, but need to find a marketing company to distribute my product. Where can I find one? 34
7 How can I increase my sales and find new customers? 35
8 Since I don't have much money to market my business, where should I advertise? 37
9 How can I successfully market my product with a limited budget? 37
10 What kind of franchise should I purchase? 39

3. Starting a Business **43**

3-1 Overview 43
3-2 Smart Strategies for Starting a Business 44
3-3 Do I Have the Right Stuff? 45
3-4 How Does an Entrepreneur Decide What Kind of Business to Start? 49
3-5 What Start-up Factors Should I Consider? 50
3-6 Where Do I Find Help in Starting a Home-Based Business? 54
3-7 What Type of Preplanning Is Necessary? 57
3-8 Should I Locate in a Business Incubator? 61
3-9 How Do I Select a Retail Location? 63
3-10 How What to Consider When Negotiating a Lease 68
3-11 Pitfalls to Avoid 72
3-12 Entrepreneurial Resource Checklist 73

4. Legal Structures for Starting a Business **77**

4-1 Overview 77
4-2 Smart Strategies for Legal Structures 78
4-3 Should I Worry about What Kind of Legal Structure to Choose? 79
4-4 Should I Form a Partnership? 80
4-5 How to Structure Buy-Sell Agreements 83
4-6 Incorporating a Business 84
4-7 How Does a Regular Corporation Differ from an S Corporation? 86
4-8 Should I Form a Limited Liability Company? 88
4-9 Forming a Nonprofit Company 89
4-10 Pitfalls to Avoid 92
4-11 Entrepreneurial Resource Checklist 93

5. Buying a Business **95**

5-1 Overview 95

5-2 Smart Strategies for Buying a Business 96
5-3 Making the Purchase Decision 97
5-4 Advantages of Buying a Business 98
5-5 Disadvantages of Buying an Existing Business 100
5-6 Where to Look for a Business to Purchase 101
5-7 Checklist for Buying an Existing Business 103
5-8 Pitfalls to Avoid 106
5-9 Entrepreneurial Resource Checklist 106

6. Protecting Intellectual Property **108**

6-1 Overview 108
6-2 Smart Strategies for Protecting Intellectual Property 110
6-3 Patents and Inventions 110
6-4 Trademark Protection 117
6-5 Copyright Protection 118
6-6 Licensing Inventions 121
6-7 Trade Secrets 124
6-8 Invention Marketing 128
6-9 Pitfalls to Avoid 133
6-10 Entrepreneurial Resource Checklist 134

7. Venture Marketing Strategies **137**

7-1 Overview 137
7-2 Smart Marketing Strategies 138
7-3 Marketing Research 139
7-4 Developing Your Marketing Strategy and Plan 151
7-5 Expanding Your Customer Base 157
7-6 Advertising and Promotion 160
7-7 Telemarketing 165
7-8 Expanding Your Market through Consignment 168
7-9 Using Sales Representatives 172
7-10 Attending Trade Shows 175
7-11 Pitfalls to Avoid 179
7-12 Entrepreneurial Resource Checklist 180

8. Financing Your Venture **183**

8-1 Overview 183
8-2 Smart Strategies for Financing New and Existing Ventures 184
8-3 Developing a Financial Strategy 185
8-4 Borrowing from a Bank 190
8-5 Venture Capitalists 198

8-6 Private Placements 202
8-7 Taking a Company Public 204
8-8 Tapping Alternative Money Sources 207
8-9 The Small Business Administration 213
8-10 Factoring 218
8-11 Pitfalls to Avoid 223
8-12 Entrepreneurial Resource Checklist 223

9. Selecting the Best Business Advisers **227**

9-1 Overview 227
9-2 Smart Strategies for Using the Infrastructure and Business Professionals 228
9-3 How to Find a Lawyer for Your Business 229
9-4 How to Choose an Accountant for Your Business 235
9-5 How to Find a Reputable Insurance Agent 237
9-6 How to Select and Use Management Consultants 238
9-7 Recruiting and Utilizing a Board of Directors 240
9-8 Establishing an Advisory Board 243
9-9 Pitfalls to Avoid 244
9-10 Entrepreneurial Resource Checklist 245

10. Franchising **247**

10-1 Overview 247
10-2 Smart Franchising Strategies 249
10-3 How to Research and Buy a Franchise Business 250
10-4 How to Evaluate a Franchise Agreement 251
10-5 Purchasing an International Food Franchise 253
10-6 Franchising a Successful Venture 255
10-7 Franchising a New Concept 257
10-8 Pitfalls to Avoid 259
10-9 Entrepreneurial Resource Checklist 260

11. The 10 Questions Entrepreneurs Should Ask But Don't **262**

1 How do I go about writing a feasibility plan to determine if my idea for starting a new business could turn into a profitable business venture? 263
2 What kind of legal structure should I consider for my new business? 266
3 How do I design a plan for financing my business? 267
4 How can I put together a budget that will as accurately as possible measure my start-up costs? 268

5 How can I distinguish my business from others and increase my sales? 270

6 How do I put together a winning management team when I can't pay high salaries to attract and retain a talented staff? 272

7 How do I find a corporate strategic partner to assist me in bringing my invention to the marketplace? 274

8 What kind of business insurance should I get to protect my business? 275

9 How can I strengthen my sales skills as well as those of my staff? 276

10 What skills should I develop to keep pace with the growth of my business? 278

Index 279

Foreword

Have you ever dreamed about starting a business but don't quite know how to go about it? Are you ready to be your own boss, but you aren't sure how to write a business plan? Do you have an exceptional business idea but can't find any money to finance your new venture? Do you think you have what it takes to be a successful entrepreneur?

Or are you currently operating a business but have trouble meeting Friday's payroll? Do you wonder how to attract venture capital? Are you trying to expand your market?

Then this book is exactly what you need. It addresses the typical start-up and growth questions that plague many entrepreneurs. I am continually asked these questions by hundreds of entrepreneurs coast to coast. It all began in January 1990 when Deb Goekin, former business editor and now city editor of the Rocky Mountain News in Denver, asked me to write a weekly column in the business section. Because of the overwhelming response from readers, six months later the column "Entrepreneurs Ask" was syndicated by Scripps Howard newspapers. I was forced to change the mailing address at the end of the column and rent a separate mail box because hundreds of letters from entrepreneurs came pouring in. They asked a variety of questions about starting and growing entrepreneurial ventures. I quickly realized that founders don't know enough about marketing, finance, management, and daily operations. But I knew that these things could be easily learned.

I knew how critical it was to develop, manage, and grow one's own venture, not only for personal success, but also for our nation. I knew that entrepreneurs were struggling for tips, strategies, and information on how to make it all work. I also knew that entrepreneurs were asking the same questions, and many were making the same mistakes. My own entrepreneurial experiences taught me that business is not hard, but lack of information, research, and entrepreneurial skills coupled with problems with the people you hire makes business difficult. Lastly, I knew that if I could share some of my experiences and knowledge along with that of other entrepreneurs I have worked with, I could make a difference. I wanted to share those golden success nuggets that could positively impact the profitability of entrepreneurial companies.

This book comes straight from my own entrepreneurial experiences along with those of others I have consulted with or taught in my Premier FastTrac entrepreneurial training programs or in my roles as Director of the Institute of Entrepreneurship and Creativity at Metropolitan State College of Denver and Scholar-In-Residence at the Center for Entrepreneurial Leadership at the Kauffman Foundation in Kansas City, Missouri. I have written several books on entrepreneurship and reviewed hundreds of business plans. Through the years, I have learned what works and what doesn't work, both the hard way by making many mistakes myself and by teaching and consulting with other entrepreneurs. As management guru Peter F. Drucker wrote in his book *Innovation and Entrepreneurship*, anyone, including workers in a large organization, can learn how to become an entrepreneur. Successful entrepreneurs come in all sizes, shapes, forms, and from all different types of backgrounds.

Millions of people joining this exciting entrepreneurial wave sweeping our nation and the world have identical questions about how to start, finance, or grow entrepreneurial ventures. This book highlights typical venture questions and provides a multitude of suggestions that will increase your innovation, help you develop sound entrepreneurial strategies, better organize your venture, manage growth, and assist you in growing a more profitable company.

You will learn how to better develop and launch new ventures, different ways you can play the entrepreneurial game, how to enter and penetrate the marketplace, and how to evaluate your business ideas so you develop only winning concepts. Entrepreneurial strategies and tactics can be learned. Everyone can develop and enhance their entrepreneurial skills—it is all up to you. Begin your search by reading the answers to the most common questions entrepreneurs have been asking me for the past four years. Successful entrepreneurs have learned, mostly the hard way, that at the core of a profitable business is ongoing research and a never-ending spirit of inquiry of how to get it right. They have learned how to distinguish their businesses from the multitude of mediocre, "me-too," and just-getting-by ventures which comprise the majority of businesses we experience daily. I am convinced that most entrepreneurial ventures fail because of a lack of information, rather than a lack of money.

Join the inspiring and exciting world of entrepreneurship. Release your creative energies, make your dreams into realities, and achieve success by owning your own venture. As Ewing Kauffman told me, teach others how to build and grow uncommon companies where people are treated like you would like to be treated and all share in the wealth created. That's the golden nugget of entrepreneurship. Never forget that information is sovereign. You simply need to know first what to do and then where to go to get the information. Begin here with this book and remember—the greatest job satisfaction, personal development, and freest life of all comes from being your own boss.

Courtney Price

Preface

The United States was founded by entrepreneurs who built our country with small businesses, farms, ranches, and mines. During the Industrial Revolution and after World War II, people began worshipping big business and flocked to the corporate environment, craving stability and job security. At that time, our nation was primarily represented by big businesses, big farms, big ranches, and big mines.

But today, just the opposite is true. Our entrepreneurial roots have begun to take hold and are sprouting up all over. There is an explosion of entrepreneurial ventures driving economic development, reshaping markets, creating new jobs, and playing an important role in our economy and in our society.

Economic evidence is everywhere: entrepreneurship is truly the megatrend of the twenty-first century. Every year *Business Week* selects a subject of transcendent importance and devotes the entire issue to it. In 1993 the special bonus issue of *Business Week* featured how entrepreneurs are reshaping the economy and explained how in today's brutally competitive world, size is no longer the trump card it once was. The issue states that changes in the rules of the business game are putting a premium on the entrepreneurial qualities of small companies. Size, once considered essential for success, is now becoming a liability for many companies.

Small businesses have been the driving force in our economic growth and development since the mid-1970s. For example, between 1980 and 1990, Fortune 500 companies eliminated 3.5 million jobs while smaller companies added 23 million jobs. During 1987 alone, the U.S. Department of Commerce reported that employment in 7 million small firms grew three times faster than in Fortune 500 firms. New business start-ups are dominating our economic growth at the rate of over 700,000 per year—double the rate a decade ago and eight times what it was in the 1950s at the height of the industrial period. Currently, there are about 19 million enterprises in the United States, and it is estimated that there will be 30 million by the year 2000. In 1994, small business is expected to create an additional 1.7 million jobs, while companies with 25,000 or more employees will eliminate about 300,000 jobs. Most of this increase is coming from small ventures with less than 100 employees.

Everywhere, corporations are downsizing, restructuring, eliminating layers of management, and offering attractive early retirement packages to their employees. Workers are fleeing the corporate world in droves to start new ventures and be their own boss. Many feel they have reached the glass ceiling, or are frustrated trying to climb the corporate ladder whose size has been cut in half. The upheavals of corporate America will be with us during the next century and downsizing will be prevalent. Starting a new company has again become a very attractive alternative and a viable career path which has further fueled our entrepreneurial movement. Once burned by a big company, most people decide not to go back, but to create their own venture or work for an entrepreneurial one.

Entrepreneurship is not only a strong trend that continues to gain momentum in our society but it is also a global trend in many eastern bloc nations as well as the new European market, not to mention China and the Pacific Rim countries. Entrepreneurship is empowering nations to become independent and more stable. This entrepreneurial trend not only benefits individual business owners but all of society by creating healthy business environments and self-sufficient people.

Entrepreneurs make it all happen. They are driven and eager to create new ventures in order to bring their ideas to the marketplace. Very simply, they find a need and fill it. Entrepreneurship is a mindset and a total way of life—not just a part-time activity. Today's workers are looking for more self-fulfillment, autonomy, and control over their lives, which entrepreneurial opportunities can provide. They have learned the hard way that they must take control of their professional careers and destinies. Today, the only job security is that which you create. People are realizing that one of the greatest job satisfactions is becoming an entrepreneur.

That is why many of you are jumping on this exciting extrepreneurial wave. Now all you need is a telephone, a desk, a customer, and a business plan. Visions of owning your own business and being your own boss can become realities with proper research, information planning, and entrepreneurial training.

This book provides the practical information you are seeking and lists business resources where you can obtain other critical information. It lists telephone numbers and addresses to help you access the critical information you need. Best of all, this book offers quick, easy-to-find, and common answers to the most typical questions entrepreneurs are asking. It is guaranteed to help you produce results and will become your indispensable entrepreneurial reference guide for achieving success.

Courtney Price

Acknowledgments

To begin with, if four years ago Deb Goekin, city editor of the *Rocky Mountain News* in Denver had not asked me to write a new column entitled "Entrepreneurs Ask," this book, which will help thousands of entrepreneurs grow and develop their new ventures, would never have been written. Deb knew this entrepreneurial wave sweeping our country would be one of the biggest trends during the twenty-first century and would revitalize our economy. Also a big thanks to Don Knox, business editor, who worked with me from the very beginning and helped me shape the direction and focus of my column.

Another key person, who encouraged me to take my idea to New York and introduced me to Betsy Brown, my editor at McGraw-Hill, is Mary Cook, a dear friend and a nationally recognized human resource management writer. Betsy Brown is the best editor I have worked with, whose helpful suggestions and enthusiasm motivated me to complete this book ahead of schedule.

Next, I would like to express my sincere thanks to the many entrepreneurs across the country who sent me letters asking both perplexing and penetrating questions about how to start and develop companies. These questions sent me searching for information and learning much about many different industries and new entrepreneurial techniques.

A special thanks to the hundreds of FastTrac-ers who attended the entrepreneurial training programs I codeveloped and who shared their unique business and learning experiences about how to better grow and manage successful companies.

I also want to thank all the people with special expertise whom I called when I needed additional information to better answer questions from entrepreneurs, especially my partners, Mack Davis and Dick Buskirk. They shared their knowledge as well as their many years of entrepreneurial experiences, which helped shape my thinking. Some of the experts I called upon include Don Margolis, patent attorney, Marilyn Force, banking professional, Sean Mooney, insurance expert, Ted Rice, franchising expert, Judith D. Judd, small business attorney, and my dear friend and colleague, Alys Novak, nonprofit expert and talented writer.

I am particularly grateful to Ray Smilor, Vice President of the Center for Entrepreneurial Leadership, who not only reviewed my book and gave me insightful comments, but also came up with the ingenious idea to include a chapter entitled The 10 Most Asked Questions from Entrepreneurs. This idea led me to develop another chapter, The 10 Questions Entrepreneurs Should Ask But Don't, because I knew that sometimes questions founders (of small businesses) don't ask are as important or even more important than questions they *do* ask. Both of these chapters added+ a key dimension to the book. I would also like to thank Jeff Timmons for his meaningful comments as well as Dennis Kimbro, Jack Stack, and John Bailey. Also thanks to my dear friend and very successful entrepreneur who always keeps me on track, Barb Grogen.

I would, additionally, like to thank my two students who worked with me and researched information they never dreamed might be available at the outset. First, to Laura Vargo who started with me in the beginning and searched for the key information I used to structure the chapters and design the book. Secondly, to Karen Erlandson who continued to work with me even after she graduated because she was so interested and committed to the project. Her devotion and enthusiasm contributed to the writing of this book.

I also want to thank my mom, Catherine Hart, the greatest copy editor I know, who read every chapter and who had sacrificed her own writing career to start and raise our family. Lastly, to my husband, Gordy, whose heart and wisdom, both in business and regarding my career, contributed to many ideas for this book as well as to the columns I write.

1
Overview of Entrepreneurship

1-1 Overview

A rejuvenation of the U.S. entrepreneurial economy is transforming American businesses and the adventurous entrepreneur is now revered as the new American hero. The old American dream of owning and managing one's own business is alive and well—stronger now than ever before. Economic evidence is around us everywhere, making entrepreneurship the megatrend of our times.

Our economy is no longer dominated by giant corporations, which have restructured, downsized, reduced layers of management, and eliminated jobs. Large American corporations are getting smaller and small businesses are getting larger. During the last decade, most of our employment growth has occurred in small entrepreneurial firms. Simultaneously, small entrepreneurial companies have expanded their ventures and created new jobs. When self-employment is included, more than 6 out of every 10 employees work in small firms.

These changes have created many new market opportunities for entrepreneurs to launch or grow their existing ventures. This chapter highlights some of the major trends and hot opportunities in the entrepreneurial trend sweeping our country. Some hot venture opportunities highlighted are in the computer industry, the service sector, ethnic products/services, health care, and biotechnology.

There are many other venture opportunities in delivering various goods and services to your customers' doorsteps. Entrepreneurs are discovering how profitable it is to home-deliver goods and services such as grocery items, videos, books, wine, flowers, and prepared restaurant meals as well as auto detailing, pet grooming, and transporting individuals door to door.

Another major entrepreneurial trend is the emergence of home-based businesses. This trend will continue to grow as our nation shifts from an industrial base to an informational base. Currently, there are 18 million businesses operating out of homes. By the year 2000, it is forecast that one out of every three people will work full time from home. Many of these ventures are service businesses, and the prediction is that more and more businesses will be started in the home. For example, some home-based entrepreneurs are contracting with large corporations for services they no longer provide in house, including computer programming, personnel services, travel management, public relations, and other services to smaller specialized companies.

Because of the growing globalization of our world, trade barriers falling, communications improving, and the time lag between U.S. selling and shipping foreign products disappearing, there are numerous venture opportunities to conduct business internationally. For example, over half the market for technology products is outside the United States.

Women and minority business owners are also at the forefront of entrepreneurship. Currently women and minorities are creating entrepreneurial ventures four to six times faster than any other segment in our society. One reason is that many have reached the "glass ceiling," and the likelihood of being promoted to management and executive levels of management is almost nonexistent. This chapter features how women and minorities can take advantage of government and corporate procurement opportunities as well as obtain disadvantaged business enterprise (DBE) status.

Likewise, there are many entrepreneurial opportunities for the physically disabled, many of whom are discovering that the only way they can do the work they enjoy is by starting a business that accommodates their disability. This trend will continue during the 1990s as many more disabled entrepreneurs start new ventures, often from their homes. Lastly, in today's corporate world, there are more and more entrepreneurial opportunities for talented and motivated executives, particularly those being displaced from their companies. Their skills, expertise, and managerial experience make them prime candidates to launch new ventures.

1-2 Smart Entrepreneurial Strategies

1. Match your skills, contacts, and interests with hot venture opportunities in a growing market when deciding what kind of business to start.
2. Consider adding delivery services to your product/service line to jump-start your sales and increase your market share.
3. Reassure yourself that starting a home-based business and contracting your services with your former employer can be profitable.
4. To determine if your products or services are suitable for exporting, attend an overseas trade show to test the market.
5. Include both English and metric units in your international marketing materials and brochures.
6. After you have been put on a government bidder's list, aggressively market your product/service to buyers and end users.
7. Remember that disabled entrepreneurs advance at a rate of success equal to or a little higher than nondisabled owners.
8. Know that most entrepreneurs who have hired disabled workers find that they give back twofold with loyalty and low absenteeism.
9. Question your desire to become an entrepreneur and assess your business skills, especially if you have recently been displaced from your job.

1-3 Entrepreneurial Trends and Opportunities

Hot Entrepreneurial Opportunities

QUESTION

I graduated from college about 5 years ago and went to work for a large employer in the Midwest. Because of all the corporate restructuring in my company during the past year, I know I will lose my job before the end of this year. Since I have always wanted to be my own boss, what hot entrepreneurial opportunities are around for me to consider in starting a new business?

ANSWER

Many venture opportunities are available in growing markets such as the computer industry, the service sector, ethnic products, health care, and the biotechnology field. The computer hardware and software industry continues to grow and radically change as laptop computers, CD roms, and interactive computer video are becoming standard. Personal computing from anywhere at anytime will become routine, heading us toward a paperless electronic society.

The service sector is another growing area for venture opportunities. The Bureau of Labor Statistics has estimated that by 1995, 9 out of 10 new jobs will be created in the service sector. There are two different types of services—business and personal. Typical business services include bookkeepers, tax consultants, financial consultants, marketing consultants, management consultants, publicists, word-processing specialists, payroll services, computer consulting services, and secretarial services. Technology coupled with the continuous downsizing and restructuring of corporate America has created multiple opportunities for smaller firms to contract with larger companies for business services which were previously performed in house.

Another high-growth segment of business services is medical and small business billing services. Medical billing services transmit medical claims from doctors and dentists to insurance companies. Such services reduce a doctor's overhead and increase cash flow. Also, small service businesses like janitorial services, word processing services, landscape and lawn services, lack the staff to promptly generate invoices and monitor accounts receivable. This coupled with the fact that most entrepreneurs hate billing procedures has made these services ripe for entrepreneurial ventures.

Many opportunities abound in designing and marketing ethnically diverse products and services to various ethnic groups. America is a multicultural country, with people from many different nations living and working together. For example, Asian-Americans are one of the fastest growing, most educated, and affluent ethnic groups in the United States. They are creating new markets for ethnic goods by purchasing products and services unique to their culture. Ethnic medicine is another growing market segment, with an increased focus on special dietary and nutrition needs and medicines related to ethnic illnesses.

Providing personal services is another high-growth industry, with adults spending more hours working outside of the home and experiencing a reduction in the amount of their leisure time. They have increasing needs to purchase personal services such as day care, personal shopping, event planning, wedding planning, and home delivery. Today, there are many more unmet needs of working women such as caring for sick children, transporting kids from school to sports activities, arranging for baby sitting, and keeping medical appointments.

Biotechnology is another growth industry as we expand our knowledge of the human body and other living things at the molecular level. There are many new drugs and therapies focused on life extension and improving the quality of life. Health-care futurist Leeland Kaiser predicts that by the year 2000 hospitals will become body shops where people come in for replacement parts similar to automobile repair shops. The average life span will be 130 years, creating many new markets for our aging population. Likewise, there are biotechnology developments and venture opportunities in the agriculture and food industries.

These are just some of the hot entrepreneurial opportunities. You need to determine where your interests lie and match them to your skills, experience, and contacts. The easiest way to become an entrepreneur and control your own destiny is to parlay the unique talents and enthusiasm you have been giving to your company into your own business.

Cashing in on Home Deliveries

QUESTION

I own an Italian restaurant that has been experiencing a downturn in sales. I was thinking about delivering my meals to my customers as a way to increase my volume. Is home delivery an option I should consider offering?

ANSWER

It is very probable that you can increase your bottom line by offering home delivery to your customers. Many entrepreneurs are making it easier for their customers to purchase and are expanding their market share by offering home delivery services for the goods they sell.

The time crunch has made delivery more attractive to many working families and individuals while giving your customers an extra incentive to do business with you. The biggest users of home deliveries are double-income families with children. Many workers do not want to go out for dinner after they come home from work. They value the time spent at home and are willing to pay extra to have products and services delivered to their doors.

Also consider offering your delivery services to elderly people in your area. This is an expanding market as the number of older citizens and their life spans increase. We have again returned to a convenience-based society where home delivery is a major wave of the future. For example, during the 1930s, many retailers delivered from Good Humor ice cream vans. During the 1980s, the Domino's Pizza policy of guaranteeing delivery within 30 minutes of a phone order made the company an overnight success.

Department stores also made home deliveries before it became too expensive and before women shoppers started driving. Today, most women are employed and drive to work instead of to the store for leisurely shopping. This is one of the reasons that catalogs and home shopping television networks have become so popular. Most women just don't have the time and/or the desire to go out shopping. It is looked upon as a major inconvenience.

During the 1990s, the home delivery trend will steadily increase. Even now, such products as grocery items, videos, books, wine, flowers, and meals are being delivered directly to consumers' homes. There are also a multitude of services being sold and delivered to homes such as auto detailing, pet grooming, and transporting people door to door. Transportation services for elderly people and children are another growing market.

Some chain grocery stores provide delivery and pickup services through the use of telephones, computers, and fax machines. Restaurants have also been discovering the value of home delivery. Studies show that at least 40 percent of all adults order a meal delivered from a restaurant at least once a month. According to some experts, a restaurant that adds delivery service can increase volume by 50 percent and not take away from its eat-in business.

In addition to individual restaurants offering home delivery services, firms have sprouted up that publish menu guides from local restaurants and transmit your orders to them. The meals are then delivered to your doorstep. These companies generally require that a restaurant sell to them at a 25 percent discount.

Businesses delivering services directly to the home often add a $10 to $20 delivery fee. Customers seem willing to pay extra for this convenience. Home delivery services are especially attractive in climates that experience inclement weather.

If you can make it easier for your customers to purchase your Italian food, you could ultimately increase your profit share while creating good will. You have a good chance to expand your market share by delivering and reaching an untapped market segment in your community.

Home-based Business Opportunities

QUESTION

I have two small children at home and would like to return to work. However, with all the corporate downsizing, I think I will have a difficult time finding another data processing job. I am thinking about working at home and contracting with my former employer. What do you think about home-based business opportunities as a viable option?

ANSWER

Home-based business opportunities are significantly increasing as more and more people try to balance work interest with family commitments. Recent studies show that one out of three new businesses in the United States is run from the home. Today, there are over 20 million home-based businesses and by the middle of 1995, there will be approximately 35 million.

John Naisbitt and Patricia Aburdene in *Megatrends 2000*[1] explain that much of this growth is due to the availability and affordability of reliable-technology computers, specialized software, fax machines, modems, and voice mail, along with both 800 and 900 numbers.

Adding to this trend is the number of women, like yourself, who want to work but have small children at home. According to the National Center for Policy Analysis, 70 percent of home-based businesses are run by women.

Both physically disabled people and senior citizens are also discovering the joys of starting their own home-based business. The American Home-Based Business Association reports that 15 percent of home-based businesses are run by retirees. As the average life span in our country increases, so will the number of senior home-based entrepreneurs.

One of the key benefits in starting a home-based business is that it is an inexpensive way to test the market and prove customer acceptance. You can gradually start your new venture and grow it slowly to fit your needs.

By operating a home-based business, you receive the precious gift of time. You will no longer waste time commuting to and from work and will avoid messy traffic jams. You can use your household resources for your business and thereby avoid lease expenses while greatly reducing your child-care expenses. Other benefits include setting your own hours, being your own boss, becoming independent, and reducing your wardrobe expenses.

You should determine whether you are a good candidate for operating a new venture from your home. It takes certain skills, experience, and marketing knowledge to launch and operate a profitable home-based business. Take advantage of the many valuable books and magazines, as well as governmental assistance and college courses, to help you start your own business in your home. Just because the business is being run from your home doesn't mean it should be operated any differently from a free-standing venture.

International Opportunities

QUESTION

I manufacture and distribute western wear and have saturated the market in my area. I tried to expand to other states but ran into a lot of competitors. To increase sales, I am thinking about exporting my products. Is this a good expansion strategy?

ANSWER

Expanding your marketing and sales efforts to foreign markets is often a good strategy, since exporting usually generates higher profit margins for a business. However, more documentation and slightly higher administrative costs are involved. Therefore, you should consider charging more for your products or services abroad than you do in the United States.

Modern technology, communications methods, and speed of travel allow entrepreneurs to better compete in world markets. Time, not distance, is now the important factor in international sales and service. Direct-dial telephone service, the fax machine, computers, printers, and copy machines make it possible to communicate and send information electronically to almost all countries, at a relatively low costs.

Also, the English language has become the language of international business. Most foreign customers have been educated in English as their second language, and can communicate very well, particularly in writing, via the fax machine.

Speed of travel with jet airplanes allows travel to overseas countries in a day or less. Air freight can be delivered in a few days. Modern international standard container shipment by truck, rail, and ocean freighters allows delivery to major countries in a few weeks.

To determine if your products or services are suitable for exporting, consider the following key factors. To begin, if you have vanilla products that are no different from your competitors, it will be difficult for you to be successful exporting. However, if you have created a niche in the marketplace by selling innovative products or services with unique benefits that are distinguishable from your competitors, you have a chance. Your product or service must also have distinguishable features and you must be able to guarantee quality. If your product or service meets these requirements, you could be successful at exporting.

You must also consider government standards and regulations, local customs, electric power requirements, and so on. All these factors will affect your design, production costs, and suitability for exporting.

> ➪ **Courtney's Smart Tip**
> **Design your products so they can be easily modified to meet foreign requirements.**

Your marketing materials and brochures must also be designed with foreign markets in mind. You should show both English and metric units in your literature. Also, use language and symbols that are universal English and not unique to the United States. Then look for expanding markets that are easy to enter such as Canada, Mexico, Northern Europe, Hong Kong, Korea, Singapore, and Australia.

Consider attending or exhibiting at overseas trade shows. This is a great place to gather market research and promote your company name before trying to sell abroad—especially when language and cultural barriers are present.

Seek out exporting assistance in your local community. There are many places that offer exporting help for little or no cost. Start by contacting your local Chamber of Commerce and the international department of your bank. You could also contact your local small business development center (SBDC), a freight forwarder, a local international trade club, or a local entrepreneur group.

Your state Department of Commerce, the Small Business Administration, and the U.S. Department of Commerce also provide exporting assistance. Commercial attachés in U.S. embassies abroad can help you find and meet foreign dealers and representatives. Any of the above can help you or refer you to private consultants and agencies that have expertise in your particular exporting needs. Lastly, there are about 60 world trade centers in the United States that can provide information and assistance for exporting your product.

There are also several hotlines for exporting. The Department of Commerce's Trade Information Center, at (800) USA-TRADE, has a directory of governmental export assistance programs. The Small Business Foundation of America, at (800) 243-7232, offers market analyses, referrals, trade fair information, and assistance in licensing, customs distribution, options, and other areas. It's free, except for customized services that cost from $15 to $40. Lastly, 800-USA-EXPORT offers a fax retrieval service 24 hours a day that covers 50 industries and 78 countries. It has an electronic directory that will help you promote your products and services to buyers and suppliers in Canada and Mexico. Ask for the "Exporter's Kit."

1-4 Minority and Women Entrepreneurs

Special Minority Programs for Entrepreneurs

QUESTION

I am a minority who owns a small printing firm. I am interested in finding out about procurement opportunities. Does the Small Business Administration or government offer any special procurement opportunities for women and minority business owners?

ANSWER

Generally contracting opportunities with the federal government are available to any business, but there are special programs to encourage participation by small businesses, small disadvantaged businesses, and women-owned businesses. Often the government will limit competition for contracts to small or minority-owned firms. There are also an increasing number of awards limited to women-owned businesses. These are called "set asides." Most federal procurement contracts valued under $25,000 are also reserved for small businesses.

To take advantage of these opportunities, become familiar with your local government agencies. All have target goals for contracting with small and minority-owned firms. One of the biggest myths about doing business with the federal government is that all you need to do is to get on a government bidder's list and wait for a call. In reality, the government, like any other customer, does business with people it knows. Therefore, it is essential that you continually market, market, and market your services with the buyers and end users.

There are numerous places to obtain further information and assistance for getting involved with government procurement. Each government agency has a small business specialist available to assist small business owners interested in doing business with that agency. These individuals should be your first contact point to identify a buyer or end user for your product. A useful reference book is *The Entrepreneur's Guide to Doing Business with the Federal Government.*[2]

The Department of Defense also funds Procurement Technical Assistance Centers (PTACs) in most states. Call your local Defense Logistics Agency officer for information or check with your local Small Business Development Center.

Your local SBA office should also have a procurement assistance program. To locate the nearest office, call the SBA Answer Line at (800) 827-5722. Also available to minority firms is the SBA's 8(a) program. This is a business development program that lasts 9 years in which the SBA assists in a firm's business growth. Government contracting is a portion of this program, but any 8(a) firm is encouraged to vigorously pursue commercial business. Participants in the 8(a) program can receive assistance in business plan development, leads on government contracting, and some financial aid, including help with bonding and advance payments under contracts to maintain cash flow during contract performance. The SBA Answer Line can direct you to your local SBA office for more information. Request "Fact Sheet 35," which explains this special program.

> ➪ **Courtney's Smart Tip**
> **8(a) certification is *not* necessary to be recognized by the federal government as a disadvantaged business.**

Federal work is "self-certified," which means that the small or small disadvantaged business owners state they meet the required criteria as outlined by the SBA. Special certification is not needed.

Finally, there are many public utilities and corporations, especially those which have large government contracts, that set annual goals for women- and minority-owned business participation. Each company has a different certification process. Call the small business liaison officer for valuable assistance on how to become a certified contractor. To pursue procurement opportunities, you most likely will have to supply information on your company's ownership, financial backing, history, expertise, a list of clients, and so on. Presenting your business plan is also helpful.

How to Become a Disadvantaged Business Enterprise

QUESTION

I am a minority entrepreneur who has recently started a small travel agency. I heard that I could qualify to become a disadvantaged business enterprise and be eligible for special loans or grants. Is this true and how can I receive this type of certification?

ANSWER

You may be able to become a certified disadvantaged business enterprise (DBE) if your venture meets certain criteria and you submit a completed application form. However, becoming a DBE does not qualify you for special loans or grants. This is a big misconception among many minority and women business owners. The purpose of becoming a DBE is to have the opportunity to compete for various federally and locally funded projects that have certain goals established to award a portion of their work to certified DBEs.

Because of federal legislation, the Department of Transportation provides money through the Federal Highway Administration, the Federal Transit Administration, and the Federal Aviation Administration for state and local transportation projects. A minimum 10 percent of money granted to state and city agencies must be contracted with certified DBEs.

To become a DBE, you must be a small business concern which is 51 percent owned and controlled by one or more minorities or women who are involved with the day-to-day operations and who also meet other eligibility criteria.

First, you must submit an application for certification as a DBE through your local certifying agency. When your completed application is received, it will be reviewed to ensure that all the proper information has been included. DBE certification requires that an on-site interview be conducted. During this meeting you will be asked questions to determine if you are eligible to become a DBE.

After a completed application is received, it takes an average of 60 days to determine if you are eligible to be certified. Once certified, you will be allowed to participate as a DBE on Department of Transportation (DOT) financially assisted projects. Most minority business owners claim that it *is* worth the time and trouble to obtain DBE certification.

A number of public agencies in every state have minority- or women-owned business goals on various governmental projects. Check with your state's Department of Transportation, Transit Agency, and Board of Water Commissioners. Also contact city governments and other local agencies.

To be eligible for DBE certification under DOT guidelines, you must be a citizen or lawful permanent resident who is socially and economically disadvantaged. The following classes of people are presumed to be disadvantaged: black, Hispanic, Portuguese, Asian American, American Indian, and Alaskan Native, women or members of other minority groups, or other individuals found to be economically and socially disadvantaged by the Small Business Administration under section 8(a) of the Small Business Act.

Usually, out-of-state firms must first be certified in their home state before certification can be granted in another state. Proof of home state certification must be included when applying for certification in another state.

DBE firms are subject to an annual renewal process. Renewal applications and financial information must be submitted prior to the certification expiration date. Financial information is required to ensure that firms continue to meet the small business size standards as defined by the Small Business Administration. If ventures undergo changes in ownership and control of the firm, a new application may be required.

If you are denied certification, you may appeal the decision directly to the Secretary of the Department of Transportation or through your state's hearings process. Firms may correct deficiencies in their ownership and control, and then reapply for certification at any time.

Becoming a certified DBE firm allows you the opportunity *only* to bid on certain contracts.

> ➪ **Courtney's Smart Tip**
> **Even when you qualify as a disadvantaged business enterprise (DBE), it is crucial to aggressively market your firm with governmental agencies.**

Since there are many competing firms, obtain further assistance in securing these contracts by contacting the Minority Business Development Center in your region or the National Minority Supplier Development Council, 15 West 39th Street, New York, NY 10018, (212) 944-2430.

Challenges and Opportunities for Women Entrepreneurs

QUESTION

I'm a woman who owns a small retail business, I have found that women face some unique and frustrating barriers and attitudes as business owners. Are there any support organizations that have information or articles which could address my problems and concerns?

ANSWER

Women business owners are attracting considerable attention, and many opportunities are available to this fast-growing group. Women business owners are a driving force in our economy and owned 30 percent of all firms in 1987—a 57 percent increase from 1982. The Small Business Administration estimates that women-owned businesses will increase to 48 percent by the year 2000.

The number of self-employed women working full time at home tripled between 1985 and 1991—from 378,000 to 1.1 million—as reported by LINK Resources, a New York research firm. Women are looking for ways to balance family commitments and professional aspirations.

Despite their increasing numbers, women do experience both more problems and different kinds of problems than men. Women entrepreneurs are more likely to fail than men. Typical barriers include lack of access to capital and a lack of basic business skills, entrepreneurial training, and marketing expertise.

Research has shown that the disparity between women's and men's roles in the business world is rooted in childhood. For example, men and women are socialized differently from the time they are born. Boys are taught to be competitive and encouraged to learn team sports. Girls are taught to follow the rules and avoid risks.

This disparity continues when they become teenagers. Girls tend to lose more of their self-esteem and self-confidence. They focus on their parents, while boys focus on competitive team sports. By the time girls go to college, they are not prepared even to think about running their own business, and most often do not have skills.

Studies indicate that women business owners use less formal and more participative management styles than men. They define their business goals more broadly to include customer satisfaction as well as profit and growth. They start their ventures with less than half as much capital as men.

There are several different resources that could be helpful to you. The National Education Center for Women in Business (NECWB), located at Seton Hill College in Greensburg, Pennsylvania, began in 1993 to promote women and business ownership nationwide. The center is devoted to research, education, and information about women entrepreneurs, who are often overlooked in academic and business circles. This nonprofit organization is headed by Cynthia Iannarelli, Ph.D., who explains that the center's mission is to help women who are currently growing their businesses as well as to help the next generation to be more prepared to become entrepreneurs.

NECWB publishes a free quarterly newsletter containing vital information about women and business ownership. It also offers women-oriented educational programs across the United States, books, and videos. The center also plans to publish a quarterly magazine devoted to the promotion of women and business ownership, with a focus on special issues facing women entrepreneurs.

NECWB is also the first organization in the country to promote business ownership to women with disabilities. During 1994 it is planning to publish *A New Option: Women Business Owners with Disabilities*, a book that features 15 examples of successful women business owners with disabilities. To find out more about NECWB's resources, call (412) 830-4625.

Another resource is the National Association of Women Business Owners based in Chicago. Contact (312) 922-0465. Lastly, Joline Godfrey, in her book *Our Wildest Dreams*,[3] discusses the unique problems facing women entrepreneurs. She is also co-founder of An Income of Her Own, a San Jose, California, company that offers entrepreneurial education to women.

1-5 Physically Disabled Entrepreneurs

Entrepreneurial Opportunities for the Physically Disabled

QUESTION

Recently, I found out that I have a medical condition which confines me to my home and prohibits me from performing my job. I am thinking about starting a home-based business but don't have any experience in small business. Are there any groups that assist disabled people in starting a business?

ANSWER

The only organization I have come across which assists physically disabled entrepreneurs is the Research Institute for Special Entrepreneurs, located in Tucson, Arizona, at (602) 744-8268. It was founded by Jay Krasner, who spent 3 years researching physically disabled entrepreneurs and their needs. The research institute has now attracted the attention of three more nations that are interested in supporting these business owners.

This nonprofit organization serves as a national resource center and offers entrepreneurial training programs for disabled people. The programs range from weekend seminars to longer courses co-sponsored by educational institutions. According to the center, the number of physically disabled people with the profile to become very successful in their own ventures is immense, but many have not been given the chance.

Disabled people go into business for the same reasons that nondisabled people do—to control their own destiny and become their own boss. The ventures they create, like those of all entrepreneurs, are usually related to their past experiences and interests. You need to ask yourself if you have technical skills that can be transformed into products or services that are needed in the marketplace and have the perseverance to succeed as an entrepreneur.

Today, advances in technology have made it easier for millions of people to create new ventures from their garages, basements, and kitchens. Computers, printers, copy and fax machines, and answering services all make running a home-based business possible.

Success rates for disabled founders are no different from those for entrepreneurs in general. Some studies have shown that the success rate for disabled entrepreneurs is slightly higher than that of other business owners. An example is the East Coast female entrepreneur who is in her sixties, bed-ridden, and confined to a wheelchair. She established and operates a successful chain of nationwide child-care centers from her home.

To launch a successful venture, you need to follow the same steps as other entrepreneurs. Start first by researching your industry to determine if there is a market for your venture, if your idea is feasible, and if you can earn a profit. Learning as much about your competition is also important before launching a new venture. You must be able to prove that your concept is sound, has a market, will work, and is worth pursuing.

Obtaining funding is one of the other challenges you will encounter. Disabled entrepreneurs claim that many lenders have viewed making small business loans to them an added risk to the already risky proposition of business itself. However, Jay Krasner declares that lending to disabled people is probably a better bet, since they typically show more grit than their nondisabled counterparts. Entrepreneurs are extremely determined and persevere in the midst of adversity, just like physically disabled people.

Krasner has also started the Foundation for Ongoing Revitalization of Competent Executives (FORCE) for businesspeople stricken with disability in midcareer. Working with Larry Luxton in California, who himself suffers a midcareer disability, the foundation will offer a special program in southern California this fall to midcareer disabled executives who are interested in entrepreneurship.

Hiring the Disabled

QUESTION

I just attended a trade association meeting and learned that I would soon be subject to the Americans with Disability Act (ADA). Where can I find out more information and are there any special programs for hiring disabled workers?

ANSWER

Because nearly two-thirds of all disabled workers are employed by small companies, many business owners are affected by the Americans with Disability Act (ADA), which became effective July 26, 1992. It was designed to eliminate barriers to employment for disabled citizens. While most states have laws that protect disabled people, this is a new layer of federal law which provides for a uniform protection.

Owners are required to make employment opportunities available and to make their workplace more accessible to both customers and employees. The ADA requirements currently regulate employers with 25 or more employees. Owners with 15 to 24 employees have until July 26, 1994, before the regulations apply to them.

Many government programs along with state and federal funds are available for supported employment which gives financial incentives to business owners to hire disabled workers. One popular program is having a job coach accompany a disabled worker to help teach job skills.

You could also access federal on-the-job-training funds which reimburse business owners who hire disabled workers. Employers are reimbursed for 50 percent of the wages for the first 160 hours of employment and 25 percent of the second 160 hours. The purpose of this stipend is to offset the additional time required to train disabled workers. To qualify for federal job-training funds, owners must offer year-round employment and be nonsectarian. They must also intend to employ the person after the training period ends. Most employers have found that disabled workers appreciate the special efforts that owners make to accommodate them and often give back twofold with loyalty and low absenteeism.

Besides hiring the disabled, many owners make use of sheltered workshops which provide a supervised setting for disabled workers to learn new skills and earn a paycheck. Thousands of sheltered workshops operate in cities and towns across the United States.

For more information, contact the President's Committee on Employment of People with Disabilities, which offers technical help and management consulting. Write to the committee at Suite 636, 111 20th Street NW, Washington, DC 20236. Or call the Job Accommodation Network (JAN), whose Committee on Employment of People with Disabilities has a hotline at (800) JAN-7234. Free consulting is available for employers who face specific challenges in accommodating disabled individuals in the workplace.

You could also contact state rehabilitation commissions or private-placement agencies that specialize in rehabilitation. Such sources can be found in the Yellow Pages under "Rehabilitation Services."

1-6 Executive Entrepreneurs

Entrepreneurial Opportunities for Retirees

QUESTION

I am 64 years old and bored. I took advantage of an early retirement opportunity after working 30 years for an insurance company. I have always been interested in running my own business, but don't know what kind of business to start. What do you suggest?

ANSWER

Many retirees are starting new enterprises, since they still want to work but cannot find suitable employment opportunities. They have several advantages over other entrepreneurs such as retirement dollars to invest in a business. Another advantage is having already established a long-term banking relationship with a personal credit history demonstrating credit-worthiness and some available assets to use as collateral.

You have many options to consider about what kind of venture to start. First, examine the skills, expertise, and hobbies you have that are transferable to a business venture. What have you done in the past that either satisfies a current market need or solves a problem for a potential customer? Taking advantages of your skills and interests is the starting point.

Are there contracting opportunities with your previous employers that you could explore? Is there some type of project or new product or service that they might be interested in starting? If so, maybe you should establish a joint venture with them.

Consider the following questions:

Could you start this venture on a part-time basis to test the need and feasibility of your idea?

Could it be started as a home-based business, thus reducing start-up costs?

Are there existing businesses for sale that you might be interested in buying?

Would you be interested in starting a franchise, for which the success rate is much higher than a new start-up venture?

Are there any agreements available through which you could—for a small fee—be licensed to represent an existing product or product line?

Once you have identified a definite need in the marketplace, consider your competitive advantage. Avoid becoming a "me-too" business which just duplicates a successful concept. Determine how you could differentiate your venture, carve a niche, and capitalize on your competition's weaknesses.

Interview owners of existing businesses you might be interested in starting. Ask them questions about the problems they encounter as well as growth opportunities. Contact the national trade association in your industry and ask for information on starting a business in that industry. Or go to work full or part time for a business you are interested in starting.

Another helpful resource is Samuel Small's *Starting a Business After 50*.[4] He provides a popular list of businesses for older entrepreneurs, such as opening a gourmet food store, travel agency, or gift shop or running a delivery service. Finding the right venture is a key to being profitable and successful.

Entrepreneurial Opportunities for Displaced Workers

QUESTION

I just lost my job as an engineer and am having difficulty finding another comparable position. I have always wanted to start my own business. Do you think I could be successful?

ANSWER

Today, more and more workers are being squeezed from the corporate ranks as a result of corporate buyouts, mergers, foreign competition, and reorganizations. Job security is no longer a benefit of being employed by large corporations and many displaced workers are turning to entrepreneurship. If there are no jobs available, why not create jobs by starting a new company?

That is a difficult question to answer, since it depends on your desires and skills. In the 1990s large companies will continue to downsize and restructure. During the 1980s, the 500 largest firms in the United States eliminated 1 million jobs. During the same period, other companies created 18 million jobs. Today many people are discovering what it is like to be without a job and no good prospects for finding a new job.

The reason that many people join the corporate world—to avoid risks and maintain job security—is no longer viable. Gone are jobs for a lifetime. Today, every worker is vulnerable and a possible candidate for a reduction in force (RIF). Many workers are rationalizing that if they are going to take a risk inside the corporation, why not take a risk outside the corporation and become an entrepreneur?

For some, entrepreneurship is an attractive alternative to the corporate rat race and answering to many different bosses. Being in charge of one's own destiny and sharing in the rewards of one's labor are becoming appealing alternatives.

The corporate entrepreneur, like yourself, has many advantages. For example, displaced workers usually receive separation money and over the years have established capital connections and even lines of credit. Experienced managers and professionals have a great deal of business savvy, expertise, and managerial training. Often, their odds of achieving entrepreneurial success are higher than those of other business owners.

To determine if entrepreneurship is right for you, assess the business skills you acquired during your corporate career. Are the skills and experiences you value transferable to a new venture? How much risk are you willing to take? How much money do you want to invest in the new venture and can you get the capital you need? What lifestyle do you want to lead and where?

> ⇨ **Courtney's Smart Tip**
> **Corporate backgrounds are a double edged sword—both a help and a hindrance. They can provide the new entrepreneur with valuable business experience but may foster a bureaucratic management style which would hamper the new venture.**

Your past experience and expertise could be just what you need to launch a profitable business. On the other hand, becoming accustomed to a support staff, sharing in decision making, and having financial resources available will not occur soon as an independent business owner. Many corporate employees have difficulty switching over to an environment where they perform all job tasks, from emptying the trash to marketing a product.

Also consider whether you would miss working for a corporation, having the support of other people and departments, and the daily routines. Question your desire to become an entrepreneur. Is it because you truly dislike working for someone else, or is it just because you have been displaced from your job and are having difficulty in finding similar employment. A good resource is Gilbert G. Zoghlin's *From Executive to Entrepreneur,*[5] which addresses all the hard questions would-be entrepreneurs must ask themselves.

Many executive entrepreneurs find it easier to start a venture closely connected with their former employer and/or its customers. Acting as an independent consultant for your former employer would allow you to keep close ties to the same industry. Other primary options for displaced workers include purchasing a franchise, becoming involved in a family business, and working as a key management team member for a smaller company in the same industry.

If you have the burning desire to become an entrepreneur, capitalize on your years of corporate experience. This experience coupled with your sincere desire to be your own boss can give you great advantages over other entrepreneurs. Displaced workers are beginning to launch new businesses as fast as any other segment in our society.

1-7 Pitfalls to Avoid

1. Starting a new business offering the same services you performed in your corporate job without continually marketing the business and looking for additional clients.
2. Failing to operate a home-based business professionally and treating it as a separate business venture.
3. Exporting products that are not distinguishable from those of the competition.
4. Thinking that if you get on a government bidding list, purchasers will contact you.
5. Assuming that becoming a disadvantaged business enterprise will qualify your venture for special loans and/or grants.
6. Thinking that entrepreneurship is too risky for disabled people.
7. Starting a new business because you have recently been displaced and cannot find other employment.
8. Thinking that your corporate skills are directly transferable to starting a new business.

The Good News. Starting and growing an entrepreneurial venture is an exciting opportunity for all types of individuals, including women, minorities, the physically disabled, and displaced workers. Finding a venture that matches your interests in an expanding market will help you launch and grow a successful business.

1-8 Entrepreneurial Resource Checklist

References

1. Patricia Aburdene and John Naisbitt, *Megatrends 2000,* William Morrow, 1990.
2. Charles R. Bevers with Linda G. Christie and Lynn R. Price, *The Entrepreneur's Guide to Doing Business with the Federal Government,* Prentice-Hall, 1989.
3. Joline Godfrey, *Our Wildest Dreams,* HarperBusiness, 1992.
4. Samuel Small, *Starting a Business After 50, Pilot Books,* 1990.
5. Gilbert G. Zoghlin, *From Executive to Entrepreneur,* AMACOM, 1991.

Further Reading

Books

Patricia Aburdene and John Naisbitt, *Megatrends for Women,* Villard Books, 1992.

Lynie Arder, *The Work-at-Home Source Book,* Live Oaks Publications, 1992.

James B. Arkebauer, *Ultra-preneuring,* McGraw-Hill, New York, 1993.

Jack Stack, *The Great Game of Business,* Currency Books, New York, 1993.

Jeffrey A. Timmons, *New Business Opportunities,* Brock House Publishing Company, Acton, MA, 1990.

Magazines

Home Office Computing
P.O. Box 2511
Boulder, CO 80322-8184

American Demographics
P.O. Box 58184
Boulder, CO 80322-8184

Newsletters

1. Cottage Connection
   Box 14850
   Chicago, IL 60614

   This bimonthly newsletter gives information and tips for the home-based entrepreneur.

2. National Home Business Report
   Brabec Productions, P.O. Box 2137
   Naperville, IL 60565

   This quarterly newsletter offers helpful information for home-based entrepreneurs.

3. Home Business Directory
   Horizon Publications
   324 Wright St., 21-202-PR
   Lakewood, CO 80228

   This is a quarterly newsletter containing home business information.

Exporting Hotlines

1. The Department of Commerce's Trade Information Center, (800) USA-TRADE

   The center will provide a directory of governmental export assistance programs.

2. Small Business Foundation of America, (800) 243-7232

   This agency offers market analyses, referrals, trade fair information and assistance in licensing, customs distribution options, and other areas. It's free, except for customized services that cost from $15 to $40.

3. (800) USA-EXPORT

   This service offers a 24 hour-a-day fax retrieval service that covers 50 industries and 78 countries. It has an electronic directory that assists with promoting products and services to buyers and suppliers in Canada and Mexico. Ask for the "Exporter's Kit."

Contacts

1. American Home-Based Business Association
   397 Post Road
   Darien, CT 06820

   The AHBA is the membership division of the American Home Business Institute, which is a research organization to serve home-based entrepreneurs. AHBA publishes a monthly newsletter, *Home Business Line.*

2. National Association of Home-Based Businesses
   P.O. Box 362
   Owings, MD 21117

   The NAHBB provides seminars and educational materials for home-based entrepreneurs.

3. National Minority Supplier Development Council
   15 West 39th Street
   New York, NY, 10018
   (212) 944-2430

   This agency gives information about procurement opportunities.

4. The National Education Center for Women in Business
   Seton Hill College
   Greensburg, PA, 15601-1599

   NECWB promotes women's ownership of businesses nationwide and offers women-oriented educational programs across the United States, books, videos, and a quarterly magazine.

5. National Association of Women Business Owners
   600 Federal St. #400
   Chicago, IL, 60605
   (312) 922-0465.

   NAWBO supports women-business owners and has many local chapters throughout the United States.

6. The American Women's Economic Development Corporation
   New York, New York
   (800) 222-AWED

   This nonprofit organization assists women in realizing their business potential. It has assisted or trained over 100,000 women during the past 15 years.

7. President's Committee on Employment of People with Disabilities
   Suite 636, 111 20th Street NW
   Washington, DC 20236

   This organization offers technical help and management consulting.

8. Job Accommodation Network's (JAN) Committee on Employment of People with Disabilities
   (800) JAN-7234

   This agency offers free consulting for employers who face specific challenges in accommodating disabled individuals in the workplace.

9. Research Institute for Special Entrepreneurs
   Tucson, AZ
   (602) 744-8268

   This nonprofit organization serves as a national resource center for disabled people interested in entrepreneurship and offers various training programs.

2
The 10 Most Asked Questions from Entrepreneurs

Some entrepreneurs dream about starting a business but don't quite know how to go about it, while others have an existing business that is barely breaking even or just making a small profit. Both categories of entrepreneurs have many questions about the world of entrepreneurship. That is why I was asked to write a weekly column in the business section of the *Rocky Mountain News.*

In the column, entitled "Entrepreneurs Ask," entrepreneurs were asked to send their business questions to me. I was immediately flooded with over 100 letters asking a myriad of questions, from "Do you think I have what it takes to be an entrepreneur?" to "How do I go about writing a business plan?" to "How can I attract venture capital to fund my business?" I continue to be deluged by letters from entrepreneurs across the country asking thousands of questions about starting and operating entrepreneurial ventures. Many ask the same questions over and over again. Here are the "10 Most Asked Questions from Entrepreneurs" who have been responding to my column for the past 4 years. The answers are concise, helpful, practical, and present cost-efficient strategies. They are intended to help entrepreneurs grow more profitable ventures and to positively impact job creation and economic development.

10 Most Asked Questions from Entrepreneurs

1. I'd love to start a new business, but I don't have a great idea. What kind of business should I start?
2. I want to open a business in my home. What do I need to do to get started?
3. How do I approach a banker to get a loan to start my new business?
4. Where can I find a venture capitalist to finance my new venture?
5. How do I go about obtaining a patent for my new software program?
6. I have already patented a new invention, but need to find a marketing company to distribute my product. Where can I find one?
7. How can I increase my sales and find new customers?
8. Since I don't have much money to market my business, where should I advertise?
9. How can I successfully market my product with a limited budget?
10. What kind of franchise should I purchase?

In this chapter, each question is discussed at length.

QUESTION 1

I'd love to start a new business, but I don't have a great idea. What kind of business should I start?

I would do people a great disservice if I tried to recommend what type of venture they should start. People are successful if they are doing what they truly love to do. Entrepreneurs should combine their likes and desires with potential venture ideas.

You do not need a great idea to start a new business. If you wait for that phenomenal new idea to strike, you may never find it. Having the best idea is not the critical element in launching a successful venture. The truth is that many successful entrepreneurs decide to start a new business first and then go looking for a product or service to offer. Seldom does a successful founder start a new venture with a great idea.

➪ Courtney's Smart Tip
It is far better to start a new business because you find an unmet need in the marketplace with a competitive advantage that matches your experience, rather than because you come up with an idea that will revolutionize the marketplace.

Consider many corporate refugees who have spent 10, 15, 20, or more years in the corporate environment and are in the process of starting new ventures because they cannot find comparable jobs. Many do not have a great idea, but search for products or services to offer that match their experience and expertise.

The venture hunt begins by accessing your personal criteria to determine what kind of business will fit your lifestyle requirements. Ask yourself about the type of business that would satisfy you and your lifestyle. Then consider the following list of soul-searching questions.

Entrepreneur's Venture Checklist

1. What do you like to do?
2. What are your interests and hobbies?
3. What are your areas of expertise?
4. Do you have any special skills or talents?
5. What industry are you most interested in?
6. What are your financial needs?
7. How much financial risk are you willing to expose yourself to?
8. Would you be more comfortable with running a small business with few employees or a larger business with many employees?
9. How many years do you want to work?
10. Will your current physical condition withstand the pressures and stresses that come with starting a new business?
11. Where do you want to live and work?
12. How many hours are you willing to work?

Entrepreneurs must identify and evaluate what is important to them in starting a new venture. The key is to assess your personal desires and then decide which business venture matches your personal criteria and represents a significant marketing opportunity. Read several of the entrepreneurial magazines that feature new venture ideas, like *Success, Entrepreneur, INC., Small Business Opportunities,* and *New Business Opportunities.*

Once you have found products or services you want to offer, don't forget to calculate the opportunity costs involved in starting a new venture. Also, determine if you have the right skills for that business. If not, sign up for entrepreneurial courses or seminars to develop your business skills. Reading this book and others like it can also help prepare you for launching and/or growing a profitable venture.

QUESTION 2

I want to open a business in my home. What do I need to do to get started?

There is a growing trend for men and women to start and operate successful small businesses from their homes. Recent studies show that one out of three new businesses in the United States is run from the home. Currently there are over 20 million home-based businesses and by the middle of 1995, there will be about 35 million.

Before starting a home-based business, assess your capabilities and abilities to run a business from your home by taking the following quiz. The more "yes" answers you have, the more likely you are suited to start a home-based business.

Home-Based Business Quiz

1. Do you have adequate living space to devote a section of your home to a business without disturbing your family?
2. Will your family refrain from interfering with you while you work on your business?
3. Are you comfortable operating independently?
4. Can you organize your time well, set aside the necessary hours to run your business, and stick to it?
5. Can you make decisions on your own?
6. Are you a self-starter?
7. Will you leave your home and go out to make customer calls?
8. Do you tend to complete projects on time?
9. Do you have sufficient funds to start a home-based business?
10. Are you willing and able to acquire the right equipment to operate a home-based business?
11. Will your zoning rules and regulations permit you to run a business in your home?
12. Are you willing to research your home-based business idea and write a business plan to make your dream a reality?

> ➪ **Courtney's Smart Tip**
> **Run your home-based business as if it were located in a separate office.**

Next, consider whether the type of business you want to start lends itself to working at home. If location is not important to your venture, then a home base might be perfect. One of the benefits of operating a home-based business is the attendant economies of scale—that is, getting started with minimal capital and overhead expenses. In addition, you have more time to work because you no longer need to drive to and from an office location.

Be sure you establish a network of professional contacts, since running a home-based business can be lonely. Take advantage of the many available home-based resources, support groups, and professional associations. Get a copy of the *Complete Guide to Owning a Home-Based Business*[1] by *Entrepreneur* magazine or *Homemade Money*[2] by Barbara Brabec. Contact the SBA office in your area and obtain a copy of "How to Start a Home-Based Business."

QUESTION 3

How do I approach a banker to get a loan to start my new business?

This is one of the most frequently asked questions by entrepreneurs who have the misconception that a bank is the first place you should go to finance a new venture. Just the opposite is true. Most first-round financing for new ventures comes from family and friends. When looking for start-up capital, first talk to your family, friends, and relatives about investing in or loaning you money for your venture. Next, look to some of the alternative sources of financing discussed in Chapter 8.

Many entrepreneurs do not realize that the available sources of capital change dramatically depending on the stage and rate of the venture's growth. Most debt and equity financial sources are not available until the venture progresses beyond the early stages of growth.

Commercial banks do need and want small business clients. By the same token, owners need the support of banks and their services to deposit checks, process credit card transactions, obtain lines of credit, and so forth. Therefore, establishing a banking relationship is extremely important to all entrepreneurs. However, it is difficult to obtain a small business loan unless you have a significant amount of initial equity money, including both a primary and a secondary source of repayment. In addition, banks prefer to lend to businesses that have at least a 3-year operating history, with accompanying financial statements. *Banks lend almost exclusively to existing businesses with identifiable cash flow and capital.* Typically a loan officer will require the following documents before considering a loan request.

Banker's Lending Checklist

1. Current interim balance sheet and income statement
2. Cash flow projections
3. Pro forma balance sheet, income statement, and cash flow
4. Fiscal year-end financial statements
5. Three-year historical balance sheet, income statement, and cash flow statement
6. Business tax returns for past 3 years
7. Current accounts receivable
8. Current accounts payable
9. Inventory, furniture, fixtures, and equipment lists
10. Business plan
11. Current personal financial statement
12. Personal tax returns for past 3 years

Generally, a start-up venture is able to provide only a business plan, pro forma or financial statements, a personal financial statement, and personal tax returns. Bankers know that the younger the company, the riskier the investment. Remember, banks and risk do not mix. Bankers feel that start-ups have little if any proven capability of a strong management team much less an ability to generate sales and subsequently pay off short-term debt.

➪ **Courtney's Smart Tip**
Establish a banking relationship before you ever need to borrow money. Finding the right banker is more important than finding the right bank.

The first step in establishing a banking relationship is to get a referral for specific loan officers at several different banks. Ask your referrals to call ahead and let the loan officer know that you will be calling to set up an appointment. The following checklist of questions is provided for you to use when interviewing and selecting the right banker.

Checklist Questions to Ask Bankers

- What type of commercial loans does the bank make? Do they prefer loans under $500,000? Over $1 million? Do they secure loans by assets of the company, such as accounts receivable, equipment, or inventory? Or do they prefer to use real estate and personal assets of the owner? Do they offer term loans that amortize, or revolving lines of credit?
- What type of repayment options are available? Interest only for 6 to 12 months? Principle and interest payments due monthly, quarterly, or semiannually? One-year term? Five-year term?
- What criteria are considered when the loan is first submitted? What documentation is required?
- Ask what documentation will be needed when the loan matures and you wish to renew?
- What will be the interest rate and all other fees?
- Are the interest rate and fees open to negotiation?
- What determines rates and fees?
- How long does the process usually take from application to closing?
- What other business services does the bank offer? What types of deposit accounts are offered and how is interest paid? Does the bank offer credit card deposits? Are money bags supplied to make deposits in? What are the related fees?
- May the applicant (or applicant's attorney) review all loan documents prior to signing them?
- Does the bank have an advertising program where businesses can put ad coupons in the statements mailed to bank customers?
- Ask if the bank can use your services.
- How long has the bank been open? Under its current management?
- How long has the loan officer been with the bank? In banking? Determine if he or she understands your business and its needs.
- Find out how, in the event of a temporary downturn in your business, the bank will work with you.
- If the bank would be unable to help you at such a time, could they recommend a bank that might be able to?

An excellent resource for start-up financing is Lawrence W. Tuller's *When the Bank Says No!*[3] It contains an extensive appendix for financing assistance.

QUESTION 4

Where can I find a venture capitalist to finance my new venture?

Very few start-up businesses can qualify for venture capital funds. Most research shows that less than 14 percent of investments made by venture capitalists are in start-up ventures, and most of these investments are for new product development. Venture capital firms are not a good source of financing for start-ups.

To begin with, a very limited number of venture capitalists are interested in funding raw start-ups. Although venture capitalists frequently invest in high-risk ventures, usually through an equity purchase, they look for a 20 to 30 percent annual return on their investment—and, if successful, 10 times their investment in about 5 years. They are interested in the strong cash flow and profits that a business can generate. Like bankers, they prefer to see several years of operating history before they consider investing. They also have stringent criteria for their investments and fund less than 1 percent of the deals that come across their desks.

For their financial help, venture capitalists usually get a healthy percentage of ownership in the business. It is not unusual for venture capitalists to take up to 75 percent ownership of a start-up, high-technology venture. They want a hand in managing the company, usually through active participation in management decisions and/or through board seats—either as directors or as advisers.

In addition, they prefer to invest in companies that will go public within a reasonable time period, usually 5 years, at a share price high enough to give the venture capitalist a significant gain on the investment and an exit. Last, they usually invest in certain types of industries like computer hardware, electronics, and health care.

If you think your start-up business can qualify for venture capital, look in the Yellow Pages, *The Wall Street Journal,* and *Venture* magazine. To better understand the venture capital world read *Venture Capital at the Crossroads*[4] by William D. Bygrave and Jeffry A. Timmons. You can also get a listing of venture capital firms from the National Venture Capital Association, 1655 North Fort Meyer Drive, Suite 700, Arlington, VA 22209.

Instead of looking for a venture capitalist to fund your new business, look to informal sources of venture capital, such as family, friends, private investors or angle networks (groups of independent investors interested in lending to entrepreneurs), professional advisers, business acquaintances, successful entrepreneurs, customers, suppliers, and prospective employees. It has been estimated that over 95 percent of capital for new businesses comes from these sources.

QUESTION 5

How do I go about obtaining a patent for my new software program?

Many investors do not understand the field of intellectual property, the need to become more familiar with it, and how to protect their ideas. Overall, there is much confusion about how to protect intellectual property and the differences between a patent, trademark, copyright, and trade secret. Determining the form of protection to pursue is critical before marketing your invention. See Chapter 6 for more detailed information on different types of intellectual property and how to obtain protection for them.

To begin with, software programs cannot be patented, only copyrighted. A patent may be obtained for a new and usable process, machine, manufacture or composition of matter, or any new and useful improvement. A patent gives the inventor the right to exclude others from making and selling the product for 17 years, provided that maintenance fees are paid every 3½ years. Patents keep others from using or selling the patented invention and are in a sense a legal right to litigate against those who infringe on the patent.

To apply for a patent, you must file an application with the U.S. Department of Commerce, Patent and Trademark Office, Washington, DC 20231. Although you can do much of the legwork yourself, I strongly recommend that you consult with an intellectual property attorney to assist in this process. Become knowledgeable about the process before you begin. Also read *Patent It Yourself*[5] by David Pressman.

If your creation involves any written or artistic matter which includes a symbol, word, shape, or design, you can qualify for protection under trademark law. Trademarks are used by a manufacturer or business to identify goods and to distinguish them from other goods. Service marks are slogans or phrases used in the sale of advertising of services as opposed to products. A trademark can be easily obtained by attaching the letters TM to your mark (or SM for a service). It is advisable to register with both your state and federal trademark offices. Unlike patents, trademarks have an indefinite life when used properly. Federal trademarks are issued for a period of 10 years and can be renewed if still in use. For the appropriate forms and information to register a trademark federally, write to the Patent and Trademark Office, Washington, DC 20231.

A copyright includes any book, poem, speech, recording, computer program, statue, painting, label, cartoon, dramatic or musical work, pantomime, choreographic work, motion picture, video, map, game board, packaging design, or instructions. Copyrights offer legal protection just like patents and trademarks, but are much easier and less costly to obtain. To give notice of your copyright write "Copyright," followed by the year the work is completed, along with your name or company name. You can also use © as an alternative to writing "Copyright." It is advisable to register your copyright with the U.S. Copyright Office, Washington, DC 20559.

Trade secrets include techniques, designs, materials, processes, and formulas that are not known by the public and can be licensed the same way as a patent. Trade secrets last as long as you keep them secret. To qualify as a trade secret, the information must have economic value and be a secret; also, you must attempt to protect it. It is strongly recommended that you stamp all such information "confidential" and use a confidentiality or nondisclosure agreement for information you consider to be a trade secret.

To remember the differences between patents, trademarks, and copyrights, think of Coca-Cola:

- The artwork on the can or bottle can be copyrighted
- The way it is expressed can be trademarked
- The formula for Coca-Cola can be patented

Martha Blue's *Making It Legal*[6] includes an extensive section on patents, trademarks, and copyrights.

QUESTION 6

I have already patented a new invention, but need to find a marketing company to distribute my product. Where can I find one?

Don't bother looking for one. The problem with most invention marketing companies is that they promise you the moon but deliver little. Many of these companies advertise in entrepreneurial and invention magazines looking for investors with novel ideas who want to take their invention to the marketplace.

For an initial fee, usually $500 to $800, these companies will research your invention to determine its marketability. You will receive a boilerplate research report which indicates an exceptional potential for your invention that will bring in thousands of dollars and make you rich and famous.

Next, these companies will entice you to send in more money—this time between $2000 to $8000—to produce an in-depth report on how to market and sell your invention. The second report, like the first one, promises a huge success and forecasts spectacular earnings for the invention.

The problem is that few, if any, invention marketing firms deliver on their claims. According to *The Wall Street Journal*, less than 1 percent of investors ever get a penny from their inventions, despite the high fees they paid up front. Many of these companies are being investigated by the Federal Trade Commission. See Chapter 8 for further information and hints on how to investigate invention marketing firms.

> ⇨ **Courtney's Smart Tip**
> **Research the market potential for your invention. Write a business plan to determine if the invention could be profitable and then learn how to market your product yourself.**

QUESTION 7

How can I increase my sales and find new customers?

Add sales to your business by first concentrating on developing and expanding your current customer list. Many entrepreneurs spend the majority of their time looking for new markets instead of trying to cultivate their current customer base. They make the mistake of responding to the many different market segments without successfully penetrating any of them. Also, they forget the 80/20 rule: 80 percent of sales come from 20 percent of customers. Your marketing goals should be to concentrate on the 20 percent who generate most of your business. Remember that new sales and spinoff products or services often come from customers and employees.

Pinpoint your best customers and then work at increasing their individual orders. Here are the advantages of developing your own customer list:

1. It is probably the most inexpensive marketing strategy you can use.
2. You can increase your ability to accurately measure the results of your marketing efforts.
3. You can zero in on this target market and personalize your message.
4. You will receive the highest response rate from this group.
5. You can experiment on different marketing strategies and receive feedback on what works best.
6. You can increase your sales to proven customers.

Seasoned entrepreneurs have been compiling their own mailing lists of current and potential customers since opening their ventures. Research your customer base and develop a detailed customer list containing such information as your customers' backgrounds, how they discovered you, purchasing history, buying preferences, and specialized needs. Look for common customer characteristics and purchasing trends. Use the following tips to increase your sales.

Smart Customer Marketing Tips

1. Send postcards announcing an upcoming sale.
2. Send an informal newsletter or a "For Your Information" memo to keep customers informed about new products/services or special offerings.
3. Send a fax about a special promotion.
4. Send a direct mailing about items customers might be interested in purchasing.
5. Call customers at various times during the year when they make their biggest purchases.
6. Experiment with coupons.
7. Send an attractive promotional one-page flyer.
8. Follow up after customers have purchased from you to determine if everything was satisfactory.
9. Visit customers at their offices and ask about how you could improve your product/service.
10. Take people out to lunch to keep them informed about your business and to inquire about their future needs.
11. Send a thank-you note after people have purchased from you.
12. Ask your customers for new customer referrals.
13. Ask your best customers for testimonial letters you can use to solicit new customers.

The more you find out about your current customers, the better able you will be to increase the amount of business you get as well as receive referrals for new customers. Develop creative ways to stay close to and continually communicate with your customers. See Chapter 7 for more information.

QUESTION 8

Since I don't have much money to market my business, where should I advertise?

First, consider whether advertising is the best market penetration strategy for your business. Many entrepreneurs take the easy way out and just place an ad in a newspaper or magazine without first determining whether that type of advertising will bring in more sales. Using ads and mailing brochures is a lazy marketing strategy that usually does not bring about desired sales. You may reach many people, but how many will take action and purchase your product or service? Ask yourself if advertising is the best marketing method to use.

According to *Marketing Without Advertising*,[7] more than two-thirds of profitable businesses operate successfully without advertising. There are several reasons that advertising may be inappropriate for your business:

- It may not be cost-effective.
- Directly reaching your target market is more important than reaching a large audience.
- Advertising may not establish a sound customer base with repeat sales.

Instead, develop a sound marketing plan which evaluates several different market penetration strategies and the costs of each; then identify which types of media should be used to obtain the greatest amount of response and sales. Each type of media has its own particular strength and should be selected for its ability to meet your marketing goals and fit your marketing budget.

Entrepreneurs have been experimenting with many new marketing tools during the last decade: bumper stickers, postcard decks, buttons, T-shirts, contests, skywriting, 800 telephone numbers, personal letters delivered via overnight mail, movie and theater advertising, and so forth. There are many choices.

Start by analyzing each market penetration method and determining which ones will reach your target customers, whether you can use the method properly, and whether you can afford it. Read Chapter 7 to get more ideas about developing a marketing plan. Another resource to help plan your marketing strategy is *Guerrilla Marketing*[8] by Jay Conrad Levinson.

QUESTION 9

How can I successfully market my product with a limited budget?

Be creative and develop a marketing plan. Begin by developing a marketing plan that includes identifying your best target markets and then developing a strategy for penetrating each. First, study your markets and determine who your best customers are or could be. Prepare individual profiles on all your current customers, listing important demographic and lifestyle information.

Next, identify your target markets. Prioritize them according to profitability, size, and the share of your market they represent. Pick the markets that will produce the most sales and are easiest to penetrate. Then observe your competitors to determine what kinds of marketing tools they utilize. Look at which marketing methods work well and which kinds do poorly. Try to learn from others' mistakes. Attend your industry trade shows and professional meetings. Ask other owners what works well for them and which pitfalls to avoid.

Consider the various market penetration methods available:

Direct sales force
Manufacturing representatives or sales agents
Lead blockers
Trade shows
Consignment sales
Media advertising
Flyers
Signage
Direct mail
Telemarketing
Infomercials
Distributors
Franchising
Licensing
Exporting
Interactive computer disks

Look for cost-saving ways to use each of the above market penetration methods. For example, buying remnant space in magazines can reduce your media costs. Writing feature stories about your business is another, cost-free way to obtain media coverage. Look for other innovative marketing tools. Evaluate each market penetration method and its costs. Then match these strategies with your markets.

Successful entrepreneurs use multiple market penetration methods. They begin by trying to determine which methods will be most successful and then experiment with a few. Your market research will indicate which methods are likely to be the best ones for you to pursue. Remember that your market penetration methods will change as your business matures.

Finally, write a marketing plan that outlines realistic short- and long-term goals. Include a marketing calendar. Stick to your marketing plan; evaluate its effectiveness and the results of your marketing efforts. Revise your plan accordingly. Flexibility is important. Remember, most entrepreneurs severely underestimate the amount of money it takes to successfully penetrate just one target market.

QUESTION 10

What kind of franchise should I purchase?

Franchising is becoming one of the hottest new entry strategies for entrepreneurs. This is especially true in light of the increasing number of corporate refugees who have lost their jobs but have substantial separation packages. Many of these displaced workers purchase franchises as their entry strategy.

Purchasing a franchise eliminates many of the headaches associated with starting a new venture from scratch. Also, proven franchises offer lower risks of failure than unproven franchises or new start-up businesses. *Inc.* magazine has reported that 38 percent of start-up businesses fail within the first year, while less than 4 percent of franchises experience failure in the first 12 months.

However, I could not recommend a specific franchise operation for an entrepreneur. Considerable due diligence should be exercised in evaluating and choosing a franchise before ever entering into a franchise agreement.

First, visit your library to review franchise handbooks that contain information about existing franchises and their parent companies. Write for a copy of the *Franchise Opportunity Handbook,* published annually by the Superintendent of Documents, U.S. Government Printing Office, Washington, DC. It is extremely helpful and contains more extensive information on franchises than any other publication. The handbook costs about $10.

Next, ask the librarian to assist you in locating some of the electronic databases that contain financial information and disclosure statements on franchises. It is critical that you evaluate the financial strength of the parent companies. These databases contain annual reports, quarterly financial statements, and other detailed financial information.

While at the library, obtain copies of anything written about the franchises you are interested in pursuing. Also examine the various magazines that publish annual listings of franchise opportunities. For example, each year *Inc.* magazine publishes a list of the 100 best franchise operations.

During your evaluation process, compare the different front-end fees, royalty payments, expenses, and so on. Franchising can offer an easier alternative to starting a new business, but entrepreneurs must carefully assess and analyze each opportunity.

> ➪ **Courtney's Smart Tip**
> **Most entrepreneurs think that purchasing a franchise is a "turnkey" operation. In reality, much due diligence, research, and up-front work is necessary.**

Potential franchisees who think this is a "slam-dunk" business venture have been misled. Instead, finding the right franchise to purchase, locating a site, negotiating a lease, finishing the tenant space, obtaining the equipment, putting together the management team, and hiring the right staff take much time and effort. Read Chapter 10 for more detailed information on how to evaluate different franchise opportunities.

Entrepreneurial Resource Checklist

References

1. *Entrepreneur* magazine, *Complete Guide to Owning a Home-Based Business,* Bantam, New York, 1990.
2. Barbara Brabec, *Homemade Money,* Betterman Publications, White Hall, Va., 1992.
3. Lawrence W. Tuller, *When the Bank Says NO!,* Liberty Hall Press, Blue Ridge Summit, Pa., 1991.
4. William D. Bygrave and Jeffry A. Timmons, *Venture Capital at the Crossroads,* Harvard Business School Press, Boston, 1992.
5. David Pressman, *Patent It Yourself,* Nolo Press, Berkeley, 1988.
6. Martha Blue, *Making It Legal,* Northland Publishing, Chicago, 1988.
7. Michael Phillips and Sallie Rasberry, *Marketing Without Advertising,* Nolo Press, Berkeley, 1990.
8. Jay Conrad Levinson, *Guerrilla Marketing,* rev. ed., Houghton Mifflin, Boston, 1993.

Further Reading

Books

Arden, Lynie. *Work at Home Sourcebook,* Live Oak Publications, Woodland, Calif., 1992.

Burstiner, Irving. *The Small Business Handbook,* Prentice Hall, Englewood Cliffs, N.J., 1989.

Clark, Scott A. *Beating the Odds,* AMACOM, New York, 1991.

Coleman, Bob. *The New Small Business Survival Guide,* W. W. Norton, 1994.

Edwards, Paul and Sarah. *The Best Home Businesses for the 90's,* J. P. Tarcher, Los Angeles, 1991.

Edwards, Paul and Sarah. *Making It on Your Own! Surviving and Thriving on the Ups and Downs of Being Your Own Boss,* J. P. Tarcher, Los Angeles, 1991.

Frohbieter-Mueller, Jo. *Stay Home and Mind Your Own Business,* Betterway, Whitehall, Va., 1989.

Smith-Kern, Coralee, and Tammara Hoffman Wolfgram, of VGM Career Horizons. *How to Run Your Own Home Business,* NTC Publishing Group, Lincolnwood, Ill., 1990.

Woy, Patricia A. *Small Businesses That Grow and Grow and Grow,* Betterway, Whitehall, Va., 1990.

Contacts

1. Home-Based Business Information
   Association of Home Businesses
   6645 SW Terri Court (40)
   Portland, OR 97225-1054

   This organization provides support for home-based business owners.

2. New Mexico Home Business Association
   537 Franklin
   Santa Fe, NM 87501

   This area-networking group supports education for home-based business owners.

3. The Association of Home-Based Businesses
   P.O. Box 10023
   Rockville, MD 20844

   This association serves 90 home-based business owners in Maryland, northern Virginia, and Washington, DC.

4. National Association of Small Business Investment Companies (SBIC)
   618 Washington Bldg.
   Washington DC 20005
   (202) 833-8230

   This association, sponsored by the SBA, provides loans to small business.

5. Procurement Automated Source System (PASS)
   Procurement Assistance
   Small Business Administration
   1441 L Street NW Rm 628
   Washington DC 20416
   (202) 653-6938

Through this agency, the SBA facilitates and promotes small business procurement opportunities. It brings together federal agencies, major contractors, and entrepreneurs.

6. Small Business Administration—Publications
   P.O. Box 15434
   Fort Worth, TX 76119

   This organization offers free and low-cost booklets to help entrepreneurs develop budgets, personnel policies, and business plans.

7. Small Business Innovation Research Program (SBIR)
   Office of Innovation, Research and Technology
   Small Business Administration
   1441 L St. NW
   Washington, DC 20416

   This agency provides seed funds for research and development grants.

8. U.S. Government Printing Office
   Superintendent of Documents
   Washington DC 20402
   (202) 783-3228

   This office prints hundreds of thousands of documents and booklets which help entrepreneurs start and operate their ventures.

9. National Business Incubation Association
   One President Street
   Athens, OH 45701

   This association is a support organization for incubators and publishes an incubation newsletter.

3 Starting a Business

3-1 Overview

One of the most frequently asked questions I receive from my readers is "What kind of business is easy to start and guaranteed to be successful?" It is impossible for me to offer a winning business idea, since launching a successful venture is so dependent on the entrepreneur. Other entrepreneurs want to know where to look for a novel idea that will revolutionize the marketplace. Most successful ventures come, not from novel ideas, but from gaps in the marketplace or problems that people encounter. Prospective entrepreneurs should begin by assessing their abilities, business acumen, motivations for getting into business, and proposed business strategy. It is critical for them to evaluate their talents, skills, experiences, and contacts, and then to determine if these could be translated into a successful venture.

Another frequently asked question is "Do I have the right stuff to start and run my own business?" Many prospective entrepreneurs are perplexed, since they recently lost a job or are going nowhere in their current position. They are seriously thinking about starting a business of their own. They are a little frightened of taking a risk and failing. The risk of starting a new venture is significantly reduced by thoroughly researching an idea and proving that there is both a market for the product or service and potential customers who want to purchase it.

Others frequently ask about how to start a home-based business, wondering if it is possible to operate a business from their home, and what type of licenses are required. Still other readers inquire about whether it makes sense to locate a new venture in a business incubator. There are advantages and disadvantages to both approaches for starting new ventures.

Sometimes, readers ask me to recommend a consultant to do all the legwork and research their business concept to determine if it is feasible. Some ask me for consultants who could write a business plan for them. I caution readers that it is critical to research their business idea and learn about the flaws in their business concepts and the weaknesses of their venture idea. They will not discover the venture's pitfalls if they hire someone else to write their business plan. Besides, most entrepreneurs cannot afford to pay someone to write their plan. It would cost too much, since it takes many hours of research and "pounding the pavement" or talking to everybody from potential customers to suppliers to determine if the idea is feasible. In addition, founders should develop and write their own business plan. It is a learning experience and the best way to determine if the venture idea is worth pursuing.

Readers often question whether it is even necessary to write a business plan. Why can't they just open their doors for business? In most instances, they have just talked with a potential lender or investor who wants to review their business plan before deciding whether to approve a loan request or invest any money in the venture. The importance of writing a business plan cannot be overemphasized. Developing one is the first step in deciding whether to start a new venture. Practically every person in an entrepreneur's infrastructure—i.e., support system—will ask to review the business plan before getting involved with a venture.

This chapter includes the questions that readers of my column ask most frequently about start-up issues. I hope you find this information helpful to use in deciding whether to start a new business.

3-2 Smart Strategies for Starting a Business

1. In determining whether to start a new business, analyze your personal criteria, interests, knowledge, and skills.
2. Be sure to prove that there is a market for your new idea before embarking on the venture.
3. Remember that your experiences and know-how are key to starting and operating a successful venture.

4. Be aware that starting a new venture from scratch takes time, market research, seed capital, and a sound business plan.
5. Before starting a new venture, conduct a feasibility analysis to determine whether to pursue your business idea.
6. Consider becoming a creative imitator versus trying to find a unique idea for starting a new venture. Imitators often have a tremendous advantage over innovators. Imitators already know there is a demand for the product or service.
7. Study the strengths and weaknesses of potential competitors. Improve upon their weaknesses and avoid trying to compete against their strengths.
8. Looking for a market gap or solving a problem for potential customers will produce sound venture ideas.
9. Become a trend spotter. Look for trends that are just beginning to unfold and take advantage of your "window of opportunity" by getting to the marketplace quickly.
10. Write a business plan to prove your venture concept and develop your business strategy while researching the industry and your competition.
11. Consider the advantages of locating your new venture in a business incubator if location is not important to your business concept.
12. Operate your home-based venture as if it were in a separate business location. Be professional at all times.
13. Carefully research and evaluate potential retail locations by studying the trading area, reviewing customer demographics and traffic patterns, talking to other tenants, and contacting a competent commercial real estate company.
14. Always negotiate the terms and conditions of a commercial lease for your venture.

3-3 Do I Have the Right Stuff?

QUESTION

I am in a dead-end sales job and seriously thinking about quitting and starting my own business. But I don't know if I have the disposition or the right characteristics to become a successful entrepreneur. I am not a big risk taker, but I am self-motivated. How can I determine if I have the right stuff to start my own business?

ANSWER

The most common entrepreneurial traits include a strong desire to be your own boss, the drive to implement your ideas, and a thirst to control your own destiny. Entrepreneurs are inordinately determined to be successful and persevere in the midst of adversity. They thrive on ambiguity and prosper in a world that is confusing and has few answers.

> ➪ **Courtney's Smart Tip**
> **If you cannot accept and operate in the ambiguous world of entrepreneurship, you would be wise to avoid it.**

Running your own business is an ongoing puzzle, a long series of problems to be solved. If you do not like constantly solving a multitude of problems, then an entrepreneurial career might be difficult. Much of your time will be spent troubleshooting, pinpointing problems that are plaguing the business, and trying to solve them. As soon as you solve one problem, others spring up.

Almost invariably, successful entrepreneurs have the creative capacity to recognize and pursue opportunities. They possess strong selling skills, and are both persuasive and persistent. They persuade others to lend them money, work long hours, buy new products or services, and sell them on favorable terms. They are constantly promoting their company, its products or services, and new ideas. Entrepreneurs are visionary and get others excited about and committed to their vision.

Entrepreneurs have high energy levels, are impatient, and can't sit still for a minute. They continually think about their business and how to increase market share. Most have experience in the type of venture they start and are confident about launching and operating the firm. Research shows that the role of experience and know-how is central to successful venture creation. If you lack experience, consider working as an apprentice for someone in a business similar to the one you want to start.

Overall, successful entrepreneurs develop essential business skills, know-how, and contacts. Evaluate your talents. Question whether your skills, contacts, and experience are transferable to the business idea you want to pursue.

What about support needs? Many people are surrounded by staff ready to support their activities and are accustomed to having people attend to their needs. Entrepreneurs do not have the luxury to hire staff support, especially when starting a venture. Instead, they wear many different hats from opening the mail in the morning to emptying the trash at night. They do everything that needs to be done by themselves.

Risk is involved in any entrepreneurial venture. Entrepreneurs take calculated risks and reduce the risk factor by thoroughly researching their business concepts, industry, and market. One way to reduce risk is to start small—at home—and test your business concept. Test your idea by asking potential customers to buy it. Don't ask your friends if they think your venture idea will work. Instead, ask customers to give you a "letter of intent" to purchase. This forces potential customers to seriously think about whether they would really buy your product or service. If you are unable to obtain a "letter of intent," you may not have a viable idea.

The *Do-It-Yourself Business Book*[1] by Gustav Berle has a 20-point test that measures an individual's entrepreneurial quotient and provides a checklist for measuring entrepreneurial characteristics. Don't let the lack of some of these characteristics, or money, or time keep you from achieving what is important to you. If you have the drive to research the industry and your market and write a business plan, you have significantly increased your chances of starting and operating a successful venture.

QUESTION

I am looking for a business idea with high success potential. Where can an aspiring entrepreneur find a good business idea?

ANSWER

Examining some entrepreneurial myths can lead to discovering a good business idea.

Myth 1. The best product or service will be successful. This myth comes from Ralph Waldo Emerson's frequently quoted statement that if you build a better mousetrap, the world will beat a path to your door. Ralph probably would not have made a successful entrepreneur. Thousands of potential entrepreneurs have been sidetracked, even ruined, by taking Emerson's advice to heart.

Unfortunately, just the opposite is true. Regardless of the superiority of your product or service, customers do not beat a path to your door. Producing the best-quality item does not guarantee market share. It simply means you may have an edge over your competition. Successfully penetrating your market is key. The entrepreneur who demonstrates this superior mousetrap to the world, and convinces people to buy it, is successful.

Myth 2. At the core of every successful new enterprise is a novel idea or invention. Granted, a completely original idea or new technology has a good chance of succeeding. The fact is that very few new business ideas are truly novel. Instead, they are modifications or improvements of already-existing products or services. Many aspiring entrepreneurs make the mistake of searching for a completely new idea and never find one. Focus on improving or enhancing proven venture ideas. Inventors design new products, but entrepreneurs seek out new opportunities anchored by customer needs, a competitive edge, and good timing.

Myth 3. Great ideas make successful ventures. There is an enormous difference between good ideas and "do-able ideas." Ideas that are feasible may have a potential market. Entrepreneurs observe new trends and market opportunities. They continually listen to customer concerns and complaints. Potential ideas come from customers who are willing to tell you about the deficiencies and inadequacies of the existing product or service. What do people want that they cannot find? What are they unhappy about? What new products or services are they excited about? Discovering customer dissatisfactions is a great way to find a new venture idea.

Idea Resource Guide

Use your experience factor to generate new business ideas. Many studies reveal that the common denominator among successful start-ups is the founders' knowledge of the marketplace, new technology, and the industry in which the bulk of their apprenticeship and managerial experience has been acquired.

Read. Successful new venture ideas come from a multitude of sources, such as trade magazines, patent magazines, business books, journals, and newspapers. Look for emergent themes, changing values, and new habits.

Observe demographic changes. Research local, national, and worldwide demographic trends that might identify new markets. Examples include the growth of the Hispanic population, the increasing numbers of working women, the "graying of America," and new opportunities in foreign markets. Read *American Demographic* magazine.

Monitor society, industry, and market changes. Are people's tastes, routines, lifestyles, or habits changing? Pick up a copy of *Megatrends 2000*[2] or *The American Forecaster Almanac,*[3] published annually, to learn about emerging trends.

Talk to your industry contacts and editors of your association journals. Venture ideas can come from suppliers, wholesalers, and distributors who have an acute awareness of strengths and weaknesses of existing products. Ideas also come from competitors whose products or services can be improved upon.

Attend a trade show. Over 60 percent of those attending a trade show are there to buy. Trade shows covering the industry you are interested in may provide a wealth of potential do-able ideas.

The real challenge for the entrepreneur is (1) to look for venture opportunities, (2) to identify do-able ideas, and (3) to implement those ideas with a proven market and growth potential.

3-4 How Does an Entrepreneur Decide What Kind of Business to Start?

QUESTION

I am 31 years old, employed in a dead-end job with a large company, and bored stiff. I don't think I can be happy unless I am able to work for myself and be my own boss. What kind of business should I start?

ANSWER

After working in dead-end jobs, some people realize they have a desire to be their own boss and start a new venture. But they can't decide what type of business to start. If they find an attractive opportunity, they wrestle over whether it will be successful. Unfortunately, it is impossible to recommend a successful business idea to another person. Finding a good business start-up opportunity is directly related to the personal criteria of the individual, his or her interests, knowledge, experiences, and skills, and whether there is a market for the venture idea.

You need to identify the personal criteria that are important to you in starting a new venture. For example, will the purpose of the enterprise be to provide you and your family with a good living? Is the goal of the venture to provide a job for you and other family members? To what extent will the enterprise simply be a personal money machine? If creating wealth is not your goal, you can look at deals that offer other opportunities. Will the business offer you the lifestyle you are comfortable with? It is important to pursue a business venture that will accommodate the lifestyle you desire.

How important is power? Would you be more comfortable operating a venture or taking directions from others? Some people crave power while others find it distasteful.

How old are you and how many hardworking years can you look forward to? If you are in your thirties, you can undertake ventures that might be more difficult for someone older. If you want to move quickly because you are aging or plan to retire you will need to find a venture that you can launch and grow quickly. At times it may be necessary to look for an injection of outside capital or find a management team that will speed up your rate of growth.

Are you healthy? Can your physical condition withstand the pressures and stresses associated with starting a new venture? Or will spending long hours daily on your venture during the first several years hurt your health? Health considerations will dictate what type of business an entrepreneur can undertake.

What role does—or will—your family members play in the business? Will they work in it? Will they eventually take it over? These decisions will affect the type of venture you start and your business strategy.

Where do you want to live and work? How many people work hard all their lives so they can retire to Hawaii, Arizona, or Florida? Why not locate your business in one of these areas and get there quicker?

Do you plan on investing any money in the venture? Decide early on about the extent to which you are willing to expose yourself to financial risk. Many entrepreneurs refuse to invest much money in their own ventures. Instead, they use their brains and somebody else's money. Your attitudes about these personal criteria will determine which type of venture you should pursue. Whatever business you decide to start—be passionate about it.

3-5 What Start-up Factors Should I Consider?

QUESTION

I am getting ready to start a new retail shoe store. I have started to check out what kind, how many, and where my potential competitors are located. But how can I differentiate my shoe store from others in my same geographic area?

ANSWER

Researching and learning as much as possible about your competition is an excellent strategy to follow before launching a new enterprise.

Unfortunately, not enough entrepreneurs obtain this type of data before they start their businesses.

Many astute entrepreneurs creatively model their products or services after their competitors'. Imitators have a great advantage over innovators. Imitators know that there is already a demand for the product or service. They can observe how their competitors have run their businesses. Innovators often have great ideas, but do not know if anyone will ever buy the product or service. They are forced to prove their market and establish demand from potential customers—all of which requires more up-front money.

Costs tend to be much lower for imitators than for innovators. Imitators do not have to pay all the high research and development costs, market testing costs, and educational marketing costs. Developing and testing a new product or service requires a long lead time before the market can be tapped.

A better approach is not only to creatively imitate your competitors but also to improve upon their weaknesses. Identify what they do well and the areas they need to improve on. Learn from both their successes and their mistakes. Shy away from their expertise, especially if you might have a difficult time matching or exceeding it. Instead, build upon their weakness by positioning your business a little differently. Carve a niche that none of your competitors has addressed. Think about other services your customers would like to receive. Look for gaps in the marketplace and consider the expertise you have to fill these gaps. Successful ventures are frequently created because entrepreneurs find potential customers who are looking for products or services that no one else is providing.

Track the products and services your competitors offer. Which ones have they recently added or deleted? What new products or services are they beginning to offer? What are their best-sellers?

Examine the pricing policies of your competitors. What types of discounts, if any, do they offer? How much market share does each one have? Find out the average percentages of gross margin and net profit for your industry. How do your competitors stack up? Can your new venture compare favorably? How many of your competitors (and which ones) are profitable?

Find out how much money your competitors spend on marketing and advertising. Where do they advertise and why? What types of sales support, brochures, flyers, or other promotional material do they use?

Be wary if you find too few or too many competitors. Finding too few competitors may mean that there is limited consumer demand and a small market. Finding no competitors may indicate that there is no market for your product or service. Finding too many competitors may signify an oversaturated market in which price cutting and lower profit margins abound.

Skillful adaptation, imitation, and "nichitizing" take research and time. But this knowledge is essential to develop your marketing strategy. One big mistake is misreading what your competitors are trying to do. Anticipate their reaction to your new business. Be as knowledgeable about your competition as possible before launching your business. Develop both offensive and defensive marketing tactics.

QUESTION

I have recipes for good dill pickles, sweet pickles, pickle relish, and an excellent spaghetti sauce that I would like to sell to a large manufacturer. I don't have the funds to market them myself, or the time to do it. What do you recommend?

ANSWER

Probably, you should continue making your pickles and spaghetti sauce for friends and enjoy them yourself. You may have great ideas for several new tasty food products, but you may not have anything worth selling at this stage.

There are millions of recipes for these types of products, and hundreds of varieties are already in the grocery stores. Why would someone want to buy yours and pay you a royalty each time a jar of your pickles or spaghetti sauce is sold? Unfortunately, many aspiring entrepreneurs have great ideas, but nothing proprietary to sell. You could copyright your recipes. However, someone could just substitute a few ingredients, and then you would have nothing of value to sell.

Customers purchase food items for both the taste and the name. Usually, they buy the name first and the taste secondarily. You do not have an established, recognized name, like Heinz or Kraft. Recognition in the marketplace will be difficult to achieve. Even if your spaghetti sauce is better than Paul Newman's spaghetti sauce, customers will most likely choose his product. Why? He has a recognizable name that sells in the grocery stores.

Most investors, other entrepreneurs, and larger manufacturing companies do not buy ideas. Instead, they buy proven concepts that have established sales in the marketplace. Consider the following questions:

- Have you thought about a name for your products?

- Have you thought about carving a distinctive niche for your products?
- What distinguishes your pickle products and spaghetti sauce from others in the market?
- What is unique and different about them?
- Why should a customer switch from buying Heinz dill pickles to yours?
- What steps have you taken to protect your proprietary interests—i.e., your recipes?
- How will you mass-produce these products?

  How much will it cost you?

  Can you competitively price your products?

  Who will carry your products?

  How will you obtain shelf space in grocery stores?
- How will you market these products?

  Will you use coupons?

  What types of licenses and governmental approvals will you need to obtain before making and selling food products?

There are hundreds of questions like these that need to be researched and answered before you can produce and sell these items yourself, or find someone to purchase and sell your products.

If you are serious about building your pickle products and spaghetti sauce into a business, you should first write a feasibility plan that proves your concept, and proves that your business ideas could be feasible and profitable.

A feasibility plan includes an executive summary and a description of the product or service, market, price and profitability, and plan for further action. Obtain a copy of *The Entrepreneur's Planning Handbook,*[4] which will take you through the phases of writing feasibility and business plans. Ideas are usually not sold, but proven business concepts with sound business plans could be sold and marketed. (See section 3-7 below.)

> ➪ **Courtney's Smart Tip**
> **Without researching the feasibility of your concept and developing a feasibility plan, it will be difficult or almost impossible to obtain a potential investor or corporate partner.**

3-6 Where Do I Find Help in Starting a Home-Based Business?

QUESTION

I want to start a computer business, but I have two young children who need care at home. Where can I find help in getting organized and started on a home-based business?

ANSWER

Home-based businesses continue to boom. There are a multitude of opportunities for entrepreneurs interested in starting these ventures. Experts predict that by the year 2000, 50 percent of all business will be operated out of the home. Today, about 90 percent of new businesses start in the home.

Important considerations for starting a home-based business include zoning restrictions, business licenses, insurance, equipment, and structure. Every city and/or county has established its own set of zoning rules and regulations. Call your local planning or zoning department and ask about existing restrictions in your area and about zoning rules.

If you find restrictions that prevent you from starting a home-based business, consider going to your town council meeting and trying to change the law or contacting your elected officials. Another option is to apply for a zoning variance.

The number and types of licenses you will need to start your home-based business vary in different states. Usually, you will be required to obtain a local business license and register your venture's name with the county clerk. You might also need to obtain a state or federal license. Typically, a small fee is charged for each type of license, and each one must be renewed periodically. Securing a resale certificate or seller's permit allows you to buy inventory at wholesale prices.

Insure your home-based business against theft, fire, and other losses. Your standard homeowner's or renter's insurance policy will not cover business-related accidents, lawsuits, damages, or losses. Obtain a rider or endorsement that covers potential losses. Purchase business insurance for property and liability, automobile insurance for employees who will be driving while working for you, and workers' compensation insurance for losses due to work-related accidents. You might also want to secure a separate rider for your equipment.

> ➪ **Courtney's Smart Tip**
> **Buy a business owner's policy (BOP)—a comprehensive insurance plan to protect your business against unforeseeable losses.**

Acquiring the right equipment is key to running a home-based business. Obtaining a personal computer and printer will save many hours of time, and help to organize your business. Also, consider buying or leasing a fax machine, perhaps one with a copier. Last, an office telephone answering machine or voice messaging is essential to operating a home-based venture. Having a dedicated line for incoming calls and adding a call-waiting feature allows you to service your customers and leave home without missing important calls.

Having a specially designed area for your work is important. You need privacy to be productive and to conduct your business professionally and without interruption. If possible, try to separate your work area from your living area. If it is impossible to make a complete physical separation of your business from your home life, try to attain some psychological separation by occasionally removing yourself from the work and taking minivacations. As your business grows and takes more space in your home, consider moving to an outside location. The challenge is to continually increase profits while keeping the volume of work at a level that can be handled by family members or outside contractors.

Contact the National Association for the Cottage Industry (NACI), which supports home-based entrepreneurs with specialized information and resources. Members receive a newsletter, *Cottage Connection*, which keeps home-based business owners apprised of new industry trends and techniques. Another popular newsletter to consult is Barbara Brabec's *National Home Business Report*. For more information see "Contacts" in the Entrepreneurial Resource Checklist at the end of this chapter. Finally, there are several books about setting up and operating home-based businesses. Find copies of *Complete Guide to Owning a Home-Based Business*[5] and Barbara Brabec's *Homemade Money*.[6]

QUESTION

Last fall I lost my accounting job and have had no luck in finding another one. In January, I began working in my home and doing taxes for individuals and small businesses. However, I don't seem to budget my time well, and I work harder while accomplishing less. Do you have any suggestions?

ANSWER

When you drive to the office each day, it is easy to separate your professional and personal life. When you work at home, these two lives clash.

Here are some tips on how to better manage your time. First, separating your home and workspace is essential to being productive. Keep your work documents together and organized so you don't waste time looking for something that isn't where it ought to be. Explain to other members of your family that your work documents must be kept separate and should not be disturbed.

Develop a work calendar or use a day timer to schedule your time. Establish daily goals of what you want to accomplish and make lists. Put the most important tasks at the top of the list. Follow the 80/20 rule: 20 percent of what you do will yield 80 percent of the results. Concentrate on this 20 percent. Lists save time and mental anguish. Also, checking off the tasks you have completed is a great spirit lifter.

Keep a time sheet for a month to determine what percentage of your day is being spent on various tasks. You can't begin to control your time if you don't know how you spend it. Try to cluster like jobs to save time.

Plan ahead by setting deadlines and then sticking to them. Always schedule a little extra time for important tasks instead of rushing to complete a job or meet a deadline. Rushing will cause you to make mistakes unnecessarily.

Maintain as regular a work schedule as possible. Decide what times of day you are most productive and set aside these times for your most challenging work. Try to start off at the same time each day, and when your workday is over, forget about the business so you can enjoy your personal life. Schedule back-to-back appointments when you leave the house so you don't waste extra time traveling.

Guard against family and friends stealing your time. Be firm about keeping the hours you have set for yourself. Family members can be great distractors and time wasters. Instead, set aside separate time for family activities or visits.

Reward yourself for completing a major job by indulging in something you love. Tell yourself what a great job you did. Remember, constantly working at home can be very lonely and isolating. Be sure to schedule times for seeing others. Stay in touch with your industry and its leaders. Attend a professional meeting or go to a trade show. Look for new trends and market opportunities.

Homemade Money[6] by Barbara Brabec and *Working from Home*[7] by Paul and Sarah Edwards are helpful resources. Also, the Small Business Administration has several good booklets on starting and running a successful home-based business. Successful entrepreneurs, whether working in an office or working at home, learn how to control their time instead of letting time control them.

3-7 What Type of Preplanning Is Necessary?

QUESTION

I want to start a catering business but work full time, go to school at night, and have only one day off. Therefore, I have no time to research the market before I open my doors for business. I cannot quit my job, since I am my sole means of support. Do you know of any inexpensive consultants who would do the necessary groundwork for me?

ANSWER

No. There are many small business consultants who could help you get started, but since you are so stretched for time and money, you probably would run out of both before opening your doors for business.

Consider working for a catering company that might be interested in selling the business at a later date. Look for a partner who has the time and money, and whose skills balance yours. Contact the catering industry association for leads. Launching a business from scratch takes time, market research, seed capital, and a sound business plan—all of which you lack.

Although the catering business is one of the easiest to start, it is beset by stiff competition, poor management, improper market testing, and lack of sufficient capital. The failure rate is shocking. Many industry experts claim the reasons for this high failure rate include poor planning, not running the venture as a business, and failing to carve a distinctive market niche.

Being an excellent cook is just one ingredient for operating a successful catering venture. Experience in the industry—coupled with enough cash to get through the first year and differentiating your services—is your biggest challenge. Discovering a promising idea that matches your expertise and has potential for success is the starting point. Although you already have the idea, 90 percent of the work involved in launching your new enterprise remains, and it is unrealistic to find someone to do the rest.

Your next step is to conduct a feasibility analysis to see if your catering idea could be profitable. A feasibility analysis consists of researching your business concept—its workability, marketability, and profitability—and assessing your capability. A feasibility analysis can prove to you, and others interested in your concept, that your catering venture is economically feasible and could earn a profit. The analysis will help you guard against an unworkable concept that does not fit the market, takes too many resources, cannot compete with other companies, and is not worth your time and effort.

Choosing the business you want to start and then making it work takes considerable research, trial and error, and refinement. Analytical checking and market testing are crucial. Finding competent help is a starting point. You must be willing to do much of the legwork, follow through, and test the market yourself.

QUESTION

I have a great idea for starting a new business, but my banker is insisting that I have a business plan before proceeding with the loan request. Do I really need to write a business plan? Are there small business consultants who would write a business plan for me?

ANSWER

Entrepreneurs constantly fight the battle of writing good and sound business plans that will attract financing for their new ventures. Most often they delay writing business plans because they are uncertain of how to write and prepare the planning documents essential to operating a successful venture. A business plan forces you to consider every facet of your proposed business and places funding decisions on paper, where they can be evaluated and considered by everyone involved.

On the basis of my experience reading thousands of business plans, I suggest that you begin with the following outline, or one similar. It is not necessary to include all 10 sections listed. The outline should give you an idea of what information to include, depending upon the exact nature of your proposed venture. For example, if your venture is a service business, you would not include a production plan. Also, there is nothing sacred about the order of these sections, although this order is commonly used and preferred in the entrepreneurial world. It is more important for the plan to flow logically.

Outline of a Business Plan

- Cover page
- Table of contents
- Summary and executive overview
- Management and organization

- Product or service plan
- Marketing plan
- Financial plan
- Operating and control system
- Growth plan
- Appendix

This outline was taken from a book I co-authored entitled *The Entrepreneur's Planning Handbook*[4]. The book features a question-and-answer format. After answering the questions in each section, you will have essentially written your business plan. The book also provides formatting tips and lists subtitles for each section. Other recommended books for writing a business plan include *How to Prepare and Present a Business Plan*[8] and *Business Plans That Win $$$.*[9]

Developing financial statements for the business plan is a difficult task. Your accountant or bookkeeper can help you develop these documents. But it is still necessary for you to study your industry and market carefully. This research forms the basis for making realistic and meaningful projections. You might also consult the *Business Planning Guide,*[10] which has a lengthy segment on developing the financial section for the business plan. Refer to *Robert Morris Studies,*[11] available in most libraries, when preparing your financial documents. This reference book lists industry statistics and financial ratios for every industry.

There are companies or consultants who will prepare your business plan. However, most of the benefit of writing a business plan is lost if another person writes it. Sitting down and developing the plan, section by section, forces you to think critically, evaluate, and plan. Without exception, entrepreneurs who have written their own business plans report that they were compelled to rethink many aspects of their venture when it became apparent that there were some serious flaws in their thinking. Most entrepreneurs cannot afford to pay someone for all the hours it takes to write a professionally prepared plan. If a consultant offers you a "good deal to write a business plan," beware. Either the quality of the plan will be lacking or the consultant is donating time free of charge!

If you still have trouble developing your business plan, ask your local college or university about courses on writing a business plan. Or you could call your local chamber of commerce or small business development center about support services for writing a business plan. The best news about developing and writing your own business plan is that once you have been through the process, additional plans take half the time to write. Also, you have learned valuable planning skills that will be critical to your success as an entrepreneur.

QUESTION

I am a technical writer and wish to set up a company to contract my services. I have many samples of my work but need to find the means to write for others on a steady basis. How can I market myself? What prices should I charge? For years I doubted the viability of a writing career. Now it is time for me to find out. What advice do you have?

ANSWER

Many entrepreneurs have commendable technical skills that can be transformed into different services that potential customers might need. The catch is to determine if you could make a living as a technical writer. Having the necessary experience and expertise is only the first step. Whether you can attract potential customers and charge enough for your work to earn a profit will determine if you should start this type of business.

Even though your initial business idea involves only yourself, writing a business plan will be valuable. A business plan forces you to consider every facet of your proposed business and puts the decision of whether to proceed on paper, where you can objectively evaluate your chances of success. Other benefits of writing a business plan include attracting financing and advisers, developing strategies and plans to grow your business, and determining the prices you should charge. Discovering what your competition is charging and what the market will bear will dictate your rates.

Identifying fatal flaws is another key benefit of writing a business plan. Often entrepreneurs do not identify these flaws until the business has been launched, and then it may be too late. They scramble around trying to overcome unanticipated obstacles. Uncovering serious flaws before you begin gives you the lead time you need to prevent these flaws from becoming disasters.

To begin with, you must search for flaws in your market analysis. You must be able to articulate who will purchase your services, how you will penetrate the market, and why you will be successful with your marketing strategy. If you cannot justify a large enough target market for your services, there is no reason to proceed.

To test your business plan's feasibility and soundness, have it reviewed by knowledgeable outside sources, such as investors and lenders. Frequently, entrepreneurs feel this detailed planning is not essential, since they will be the only ones involved in a venture. But you would be surprised at how many single-owner enterprises turn into multimillion-dollar ventures.

Contact your local college, university, or small business development center for assistance in writing a business plan. You might want to call one of the major accounting firms and ask for a set of business planning brochures, usually available at no cost.

3-8 Should I Locate in a Business Incubator?

QUESTION

I have heard a little about business incubators that offer shared services with adaptable space that entrepreneurs can lease on flexible terms and at reduced rates. How do I determine if I should locate in one, and where can I obtain further information?

ANSWER

Business incubators were started in the 1970s, and today there are over 400 in the United States. (California, Oklahoma, Texas, Indiana, and Mississippi are experiencing the fastest growth rate.) The goal of business incubators is to launch new ventures and improve their chances of success by providing low-cost space, overhead, and ancillary administrative services.

Most business incubators are private, nonprofit organizations sponsored by government, nonprofit, university-related, or privately sponsored agencies whose mission is to spark job creation and economic growth in the community. What distinguishes incubators from shared office space is free in-house management consulting and technical consulting. Essentially, they offer shared support services such as financial, managerial, technical, and administrative.

No two business incubators are alike. Their orientation depends on the particular needs of the region where they operate and their mission statement. Incubators are driven by local economic needs. Thus, if technology transfer is of prime importance, the business incubator facilitates this mission. Incubators can be technology-based, service-based, retail-based, or manufacturing-based. For example, kitchen incubators have sprung up in such locations as Spokane, Washington, San Francisco and Arcata, California, and Sandpoint, Idaho. Kitchen incubators provide support services to start-up catering ventures and other companies that prepare "specialty" foods like salsa, cookies, breads, burritos, and soups.

Interestingly, incubators are opening at faster rates in rural areas than in suburban and urban locations. Nearly 26 percent of the country's incubators are located in rural areas, and 42 percent of these opened in the past 2 years. The largest number of business incubators are urban facilities (62 percent), while 12 percent are suburban incubators.

The benefits of locating in an incubator include affordable rental space on flexible terms, elimination of building maintenance responsibilities, sharing of equipment and services, access to various types of financial and technical assistance, and networking. On the average, incubators offer rents 15 percent to 50 percent below market. Locating in an incubator gives a start-up venture legitimacy, a business address, a functional location, and access to an entrepreneurial resource network. Basic secretarial and bookkeeping services are part of the rental package, and an array of office equipment is available, including computers, printers, and fax machines. As the new venture grows, additional space can be leased. Most incubators try to graduate businesses within 2 to 3 years.

Another benefit is the networking with other entrepreneurs who conduct business in the incubator facility. They begin sharing ideas, referring customers, participating jointly on specific projects, and experiencing personal enrichment and growth as business owners.

The potential disadvantages of an incubator are geographic limitations, poor neighborhood image, and the public's perception of the incubator's location. Incubators vary according to their mission, services, costs, and managerial expertise.

Before locating in a business incubator, investigate whether the incubator has an established track record. Determine how successful its previous tenants have been. Interview both the director of the incubator and several key tenants to discover whether this is the right setting for your new venture. To find various types of business incubators, contact the National Business Incubation Association, One President Street, Athens, OH 45701, (614) 593-4331.

QUESTION

I have recently developed a new and different software package that I want to market to educational institutions. I have limited capital and cannot afford to waste time or money getting my package to market. I know that this software will be very successful in the marketplace. Could I find help in a technology-based incubator?

ANSWER

Obtain the assistance of one of the many U.S. technology-based incubators by contacting the National Business Incubation Association at (614) 593-4331. Technology incubators were specifically established to help entrepreneurs with innovative ideas and technologies to commercialize their products and grow entrepreneurial ventures. The origin of such incubators can be traced to research parks and to experimental innovation centers.

A technology-based incubator can help you with marketing your software products, finding manufacturers and suppliers, and identifying sources of potential financing. The rent may or may not be a bargain, but the incubator is likely to offer such sophisticated services as computer assistance, library, labs, technical equipment, and even faculty involvement. Some of the best marketing and management expertise in the country may well be in university-based technology incubators. Many of these incubators are spinoffs of academic research projects and most are rooted in science and technology. Their major goal is to translate the findings of basic research and development into new products or technologies.

For example, tenants in the Rensselaer Polytechnic Institute's Incubator Center in Troy, New York, offer large networks of contacts and alumni in the government and business communities. In return, the university may take an equity interest in the firm.

Most incubators subject applicants to a rigorous review process and require a detailed business plan. Interested new tenants should make an appointment to determine if their business ideas fit the incubator. Tenants must demonstrate that they have enough finances to carry them through the start-up stages. Those who meet the incubator's criteria will be asked to complete an application and submit a business plan along with 2-year cash flow projections. A board of business professionals usually reviews application packages and decides whether to accept or reject them.

3-9 How Do I Select a Retail Location?

QUESTION

I am in the process of starting a small vacuum repair service business. I live outside of Denver, but I would not mind opening up my new store somewhere in the city if the location was right. What criteria should I consider in choosing a location for my business?

ANSWER

There is no ideal location. In most cases there are just compromises. You must compromise some ideas for the sake of finances or your personal preferences. But that's the fun of being an entrepreneur. You can put your business where you want it, as long as you can afford the space.

Several different factors need to be considered before a specific location is chosen. The decision will depend on whether the business is a service or involves manufacturing. Since your venture is a service business, I will discuss the factors you should consider in selecting a retail location.

First, the location of retail stores is an art unto itself. The value of a piece of property depends almost entirely upon its location.

> ➪ **Courtney's Smart Tip**
> **For the retailer, the key to business success rests in the selection of a good location. A particular location can make or break a retail business.**

You should consider the following factors before deciding on a specific area of the city to open up your business.

1. *State of incorporation.* Since the majority of retail businesses are incorporated, you must decide in which state to incorporate. The corporate statutes of most states are similar, but there are some differences that may be important. For example, some states give stockholders more rights than others. The laws of the state in which you incorporate establish the ground rules under which you must operate your business.

Delaware is a popular state for incorporation because its laws allow management maximum control over the business with a minimum of interference from minority stockholders. If you incorporate in a state other than the one in which you are doing business, you must file as a "foreign corporation" in the state in which you are doing business. The matter of determining the state in which you should register as a foreign corporation is complex, may have tax consequences, and requires legal counsel. If you are doing business in several states, legal counsel might advise setting up separate corporations in each state. The general rule to follow is to incorporate in the state in which the business will be operating.

2. *Taxes.* The success of the southern states in attracting new businesses demonstrates the effect that low taxes have on locational decisions. In some situations, however, you may be better off paying higher taxes and selling more goods for a higher price. There are many places to locate and enjoy tax relief, but you may have difficulty generating a profit there.

3. *Costs.* The best location for your business may be in the newest local mall. But the cost of the space may prohibit you from locating there. You may be forced to go where you can afford the rent or where you can operate more efficiently.

4. *Security.* Many retailers avoid certain areas of a city because they fear for their safety and property. Customers might also be leery to drive to these types of locations. Choose a site where you will feel both comfortable and secure.

5. *Availability.* Many entrepreneurs locate where there is available space at the time they wish to open. Expediency does have its virtues, but consider the long-term effects of your immediate decision. Don't be shortsighted.

6. *Infrastructure.* Sometimes location decisions are based on selecting an area where there is a large infrastructure that is ready to help you get into business and serve your continuing needs. For example, computer businesses often locate in an area where materials and parts are readily available.

7. *Personal considerations.* The location of your business may depend on how far you want to drive to and from work each day. Family commitments may prohibit you from locating in a more desirable area that requires considerable driving time. Your personal happiness is an important factor as well. Once you have considered these elements, it is time to focus on the selection of a specific area for your retail location.

QUESTION

I am in the process of opening a frozen yogurt store and need some advice about selecting a retail location. What factors do I need to consider?

ANSWER

After deciding on the general area for your business, consider the following nine major factors to select your retail location.

Smart Tips for Selecting a Retail Location

1. Determine the trading area.
2. Look up the demographics of your trading area.
3. Observe traffic patterns.
4. Evaluate the ease of entry and exit.
5. Evaluate available parking.
6. Study community growth patterns.
7. Pinpoint the competition.
8. Look for an "anchor store."
9. Contact a reliable commercial real estate company.

1. *Determine the trading area.* Every location has a trading area from which the venture derives its business. The trading area may be only a few blocks surrounding the store or it may have a 5-mile radius. Each type of store draws customers from varying distances. To determine your particular trading area, start by locating on a map your potential site and your competitors' stores. Everything being equal, customers trade at the most convenient place. If location is important to your business, survey the license plates of cars parked in or around your proposed location to determine where they come from.
2. *Look up the demographics of your trading area.* Determine the sizes of the families living in the surrounding area and the average family income. This information will be helpful in forecasting the sales potential for the proposed location. Can the people living in your area afford your product? Evaluate the buying habits and profile of potential customers in your trading area.
3. *Observe traffic patterns.* Where does the traffic come from and where is it going? Are cars just zooming by on the way to or from work? Is public transportation accessible? Ask nearby residents about their buying habits. Approach a local merchant to find out where his or her customers come from. Don't be fooled about the number of cars passing by your site hourly. Vehicular traffic may not stop at this location. The key is to assess the quality of the people exposed to your proposed site, not just the quantity. Both are important, but the quality outweighs the quantity.
4. *Evaluate the ease of entry and exit.* Are there any major freeways, one-way streets, traffic patterns, or other physical characteristics of the area that directly influence where people go to shop? Some locations appear to be excellent, but on closer inspection prove to be quite difficult to get to. Keep in mind the principle of convenience.
5. *Evaluate available parking.* Does the location you are considering have enough accessible and convenient parking? Is the location so busy that customers cannot find a parking place? Adequate parking is essential to selection of a good location site.
6. *Study community growth patterns.* You might want to consider locating in an area targeted for significant growth and expansion, as opposed to situating in a well-established center. To obtain a prime space, you may need to anticipate the direction of growth in an area and locate a store in this path before adequate sales volume is realized. Smaller merchants usually need immediate sales volume and cannot risk betting on growth. You must have sufficient money to wait until the market develops.

7. *Pinpoint the competition.* Is there any competition located close to your proposed site? You may want to locate your store near a competitor with an established clientele which you hope to attract. Or you may want to locate where there is no close competition to capture the market in the immediate area.
8. *Look for an "anchor store."* Retailers often locate in shopping centers where there are popular "anchor stores," such as established chains. You can live off of the existing traffic flow and offer a selection of goods the shopper cannot find in the anchor stores. Entrepreneurs can use the promotional efforts of larger stores to help build their traffic and customer base.
9. *Contact a reliable commercial real estate company.* Some real estate companies have trained salespeople who are familiar with the availability, traffic patterns, demographic information, and busy centers in your city.

Selecting a location is one of the most critical elements to your success. Base your decision on facts, rather than on subjective perceptions. Research the area well. The rewards your business will reap are the direct result of the time you spend today investigating various available locations.

There are also several pitfalls to avoid when selecting a retail site. Entrepreneurs are often too eager to get the door open. They want the business to be open right now. Selecting a retail location is a complex process that often takes considerable research and much time.

First, you get what you pay for. The bottom line is that good locations cost more money than less desirable locations. Many retailers simply do not have the money to invest in a good location. There are three main factors that contribute to operating a successful store: location, location, location.

Rents are not a function of costs; they represent how much money can be earned from the space. A small location in a large shopping mall can cost more than a larger space in a smaller mall. However, large shopping malls attract more people per square foot than do smaller malls. Entrepreneurs pay for the people the mall delivers to their door.

Remember the Law of Landlords: They are in business to make money. Often they are reluctant to risk the successful image of their shopping center or mall by renting to an unknown retail operation when they can obtain prospective tenants from a host of well-known, established national retailing organizations. Some landlords may not want to risk renting their space to you. They may fear that your business will eventually fail, leaving their lease virtually unenforceable. You must compete with large retail chains for prime space.

Beware of "deals." Don't get lured into a vacant store location by landlords seeming to offer the bargain of the century. They may offer you a few rent-free months until you get settled or a lower-than-average price per square foot. Be careful of space that is consistently vacant. Maybe the location is tucked away in the corner of the shopping center. The store could not be seen unless the sign fell on a passing customer. Find out which other tenants have occupied the space and for how long a time. Don't fall prey to such great deals. Instead, thoroughly research the center.

Be careful of unsubstantiated claims. Landlords are anxious to rent available space in their centers and tend to be overly optimistic about the virtues of their location. Verify every piece of information they give you. Talk to other tenants in the center. Ask lots of questions about the location, customers, traffic, and the policies enforced by the landlord. Locate other business owners who closed their shops to determine what problems they encountered.

Researching any site location is essential. In-depth research can mean the difference between selecting a really superior site or finding one that merely appears to be good. You can learn much about the feasibility of a location by both subjective and qualitative observation. Ask yourself these questions:

- Is the area prospering? A close look will tell you if many homes are for sale. What is the condition of the homes in the immediate area? Are there many children around?
- Are the residents prospering? Look over the places of employment. Notice the clothes people wear, the cars they drive.
- Are local shopping centers and entertainment attractions thriving? What is the traffic flow around this area? What time of day is the traffic count the highest?
- Do people seem to be spending their disposable income at these shops? Are they just walking around or are they making purchases?

The *Census of Business* and the *Census of Population* are excellent sources of data. Also check the *Survey of Buying Power,* which usually contains more current data than the other two sources. These books are available as references in most libraries. Remember, location is the key to any successful retail endeavor.

3-10 What to Consider When Negotiating a Lease

QUESTION

I have decided to open a dry-cleaning business in a new shopping center. I have selected the location, and I'm confident there will be enough traffic and potential customers to make my business successful. I am getting ready to negotiate a lease with the landlord. Can you give me any tips?

ANSWER

Negotiating a lease with a landlord is similar to negotiating the purchase of a car. Get as much information as you can in advance of your negotiations.

Determine competitive prices and market conditions in your area. Ask other tenants in the shopping center, as well as other business owners, about the terms and conditions of their leases.

You may want to consider working with an experienced real estate broker who specializes in commercial leases. Leases can be extremely technical. They're difficult to interpret. A broker can help. Usually a broker's fee is paid for by the landlord.

Second, realize there are no standard leases. Most landlords or rental agents will say they use only a standard lease that cannot be altered.

> ➪ **Courtney's Smart Tip**
> **One common rule in entrepreneurship is that "everything is negotiable," especially when it comes to leases.**

This principle is really applicable when there is an over-built commercial real estate market.

It is helpful to have your business attorney look over your lease before you sign. Make sure you understand all the conditions in the lease. The money spent on a legal opinion is money well spent.

Smart Tips for Lease Negotiations

1. Negotiate the length of your lease.
2. Negotiate one or two renewal options.
3. Negotiate the initial lease rate with a renewal rate.
4. Understand all the conditions concerning your monthly rental.
5. Determine whether a gross or net lease is better for your business.
6. Find out about every tenant obligation in the lease.

1. Negotiate the length of your lease so it will allow you to remain in the same location for a reasonable length of time yet give you flexibility if the business is unsuccessful. Most shopping center leases run 2 to 5 years.
2. Negotiate one or two renewal options in your lease. After the initial term of your lease expires, it should be your option to stay or to leave if business is not meeting projections.
3. Negotiate the rate of the initial lease along with a renewal rate. When the occupancy rate is low, many landlords offer free initial rent as an incentive.
4. Be sure you understand the conditions concerning your monthly rental. Landlords may ask for annual increases. If this is the case, negotiate a reasonable and competitive rate. If you can agree to a fixed annual increase, you will know exactly what your rent expense will be in subsequent years. Be careful not to agree to an annual increase that may rise above the market rate in later years.

> ⇨ **Courtney's Smart Tip**
> **Agree that the rent may be raised according to the cost of living in your area, as determined by government statistics.**

5. Determine whether the lease will be a gross or net lease. With a gross lease, the landlord pays for taxes, insurance, janitorial services, and utilities. This is more advantageous for entrepreneurs. Net leases means tenants are partially responsible for these expenses.
6. Find out your exact obligations as a tenant. Once into a lease, you may find you are responsible for trash or snow removal.

QUESTION

I own a beauty shop located in a medium-sized shopping mall. I have been there for almost 6 years. It is now time to renegotiate my lease, which I feel is too high, especially with all the vacancies in this shopping mall and others in the same area. I have no renewal options in my current lease. How can I negotiate a lower monthly rental? Also, I'm thinking about increasing my space and possibly moving into a larger space next door to my shop, a space that has been vacant for 6 months. Do I have a better chance of lowering my monthly rental fee if I expand?

ANSWER

In today's commercial rental marketplace, the business owner is in the driver's seat, not the landlord. Thus you should be able to renegotiate a lower lease, especially if you are thinking about increasing the size of your shop. Do your homework first before approaching the landlord.

First, determine how many customers come to your shop each month. You'll want to establish how much traffic your shop generates for the mall. You might even consider asking your customers to fill out a short questionnaire about whether they shopped in the mall before or after they came to your shop. Find out how many customers your shop has drawn and the average amount of money they spend on purchases. Gathering this type of information will be most helpful in demonstrating how much business your customers bring to the other mall merchants.

Next, talk to the other merchants in the mall and find out the terms of their leases. Determine if their leases are comparable to yours. Mention that you are considering moving to another location if you are not able to renegotiate your lease. Through the grapevine, your landlord will become aware that you are unhappy with the terms of your current lease and thinking about moving.

Then contact other landlords at locations you think would be appropriate for your shop. As a rule, if you stay within a 3- to 4-mile radius, you will not lose customers. Find out what other malls are charging for the same space. Ask other tenants in the malls about the terms and conditions of their leases. See if you can get a better deal at another mall.

Now you are ready to schedule a meeting with the landlord. Be up front and tell the landlord that you feel the terms and conditions of your lease are too high. Mention that you are thinking about moving your shop if you cannot negotiate a lease that you feel is fair. Tell the landlord that you have already priced comparable space in other malls and that some of those locations look very attractive. Mention how much money you could save by renting space at another mall.

Explain how much business your customers do with other merchants in the mall and how a move by you would be a loss to the other businesses. Show the landlord the results of the questionnaire your customers completed.

Then discuss the possibility of renting the larger, vacant space next door. Tell the landlord that you would be willing to pay the same monthly rental for the larger space. Explain that if you move, the costs of remodeling the new space will reduce your profits. Ask for a few months' free rent until you are able to build up your business. Don't be afraid to ask for what you think is fair.

Try to renegotiate the percentage of gross sales you currently pay the landlord. If you move to a larger space and increase your sales, your payments will be much higher. See if you can get the landlord to reduce the percentage you now pay.

Last, be prepared to move to another location if you are unable to negotiate a reasonable and competitive rate. If it is a renter's market, it is a good time to renegotiate your lease.

3-11 Pitfalls to Avoid

1. Don't think that all good ideas are opportunities and will make successful ventures.
2. Don't let others tell you what kind of business you should start.
3. Don't conclude that lack of competition means you have a wonderful opportunity. It might mean there is no market for your product or service.
4. Don't search for a business concept that will revolutionize the world.
5. Beware of friends and family telling you what they think of your business idea.
6. Don't start a business that does not match your image and personal goals.
7. Don't open a "me-too" venture—a direct copy of an existing business.
8. Don't fool yourself into thinking that good food recipes are easy to sell and market.
9. Don't forget about securing the required licenses for starting a home-based business.
10. Don't overlook business insurance for your equipment and inventory—even if it is a home-based business.
11. Don't start a business without writing a business plan.
12. Beware of business consultants who offer to write your business plan for a reasonable price.
13. Don't assume that all business incubators offer the same level of management expertise and consulting services.
14. Don't try to save start-up costs by locating your retail business in a less desirable location.
15. Don't get lured into a vacant store location by a landlord who offers an unbelievable deal.

The Good News. If entrepreneurs are willing to exercise a little patience, thoroughly research their venture idea along with the potential market, and write a feasibility and/or business plan, their chances for success will be greatly improved. Learn from other entrepreneurs in similar industries by studying their successes and failures. If you lack business experience, read entrepreneurship books and take an entrepreneurship course or seminar. Business is not risky, but starting one without researching your industry and strengthening your entrepreneurial skills is.

3-12 Entrepreneurial Resource Checklist

References

1. Gustav Berle, *Do-It-Yourself Business Book,* Wiley, New York, 1989.
2. John Naisbitt and Patricia Aburdene, *Megatrends 2000,* William Morrow, New York, 1990.
3. Kim Long, *The American Forecaster Almanac,* American Demographics Books, Ithaca, N.Y., 1994.
4. Dick Buskirk, Courtney Price, and Mack Davis, *The Entrepreneur's Planning Handbook,* PEP, Denver, 1991.
5. *Entrepreneur* magazine, *Complete Guide to Owning a Home-Based Business,* Bantam, New York, 1990.
6. Barbara Brabec, *Homemade Money,* Betterway Publications, White Hall, Va., 1992.
7. Paul and Sarah Edwards, *Working from Home,* J. P. Tarcher, Los Angeles, 1990.
8. Joseph R. Mancuso, *How to Prepare and Present a Business Plan,* Prentice-Hall, Englewood Cliffs, N.J., 1983.
9. Stanley Rich and David Gumpert, *Business Plans That Win $$$,* Harper & Row, New York, 1985.
10. Daniel H. Bangs, Jr., *Business Planning Guide,* Upstart Publishing, Portsmouth, N.H., 1992.
11. *Robert Morris Studies,* Robert Morris Associates, Philadelphia. (Published annually)

Further Reading

Books

Clark, Scott A. *Beating the Odds,* AMACOM, New York, 1991.
Edwards, Paul and Sarah. *Making It on Your Own!: Surviving and Thriving on the Ups and Downs of Being Your Own Boss,* J. P. Tarcher, Los Angeles, CA, 1991.

Levinson, Jay Conrad. *555 Ways to Earn Extra Money*, Holt, 1991.
Price, Courtney, Richard Buskirk, and Mack Davis. *Program for Writing Winning Business Plans*, 2d ed., PEP, Denver, 1991.

Magazines

American Demographics, P.O. Box 58184, Boulder, CO 80322-8184

Cottage Connection, P.O. Box 14460, Chicago, IL 60614

Home Office Computing, P.O. Box 2511, Boulder, CO 80302

National Home Business Report, P.O. Box 2137, Naperville, IL 60567

Contacts

1. Small Business Administration (SBA)

   The local SBA office in your area will provide you with a list of government agencies, trade associations, chambers of commerce, or other professionals or counselors.

2. Small Business Development Centers (SBDCs)

   Contact one of the small business development centers (SBDCs) in your area to assist you in starting a new venture. SBDCs are university-affiliated advisory centers located in more than 500 cities and are a partnership of the SBA, the local university, and the local state government. SBDCs provide many free management consulting services to existing and new business owners. They also offer training workshops and have business information resource services. Counselors will match your needs with existing resources and identify both fee-paid consultants and volunteers who have expertise in your specialty area.

3. Small Business Institutes (SBIs)

   The SBA operates small business institutes on about 500 college campuses in every state. SBIs are staffed by instructors and students trained to provide counseling to entrepreneurs. Call the SBA's toll free answer desk at (800) 827-5722 to find the SBI nearest you.

4. SCORE

   The Service Corps of Retired Executives provides free, confidential counseling for entrepreneurs. SCORE has about 385 offices and an equal number of satellite or branch offices. It also offers small business workshops for a nominal fee. Local SCORE offices are listed in the blue government section of the phone book, under Small Business Administration; or call (800) 827-5722.

5. National Association for the Cottage Industry (NACI)
   P.O. Box 14460
   Chicago, IL 60614

NACI supports home-based entrepreneurs with specialized information and resources. Members receive the newsletter "Cottage Connection," about new industry trends and techniques.

6. "National Home Business Report"
   Barbara Brabec Productions
   P.O. Box 2137
   Naperville, IL 60567

   This quarterly home-business publication is dedicated to helping small home businesses grow and prosper.

7. Local Colleges and Universities

   Many colleges and universities offer entrepreneurial courses or workshops on writing a business plan. Ask about business plan writing courses or workshops.

8. Chambers of Commerce

   Many local chambers of commerce offer workshops and/or seminars on how to write a plan. Call the chamber in your area.

9. National Business Incubation Association
   One President Street
   Athens, OH 45701
   (614) 593-4331

   The National Business Incubation Association can provide information and resources about any type of business incubator located in the United States. The association also publishes a useful newsletter.

10. Census of Business
    U.S. Bureau of the Census
    Washington, D.C. 20233

11. Census of Population
    U.S. Census of the Population
    Washington, D.C. 20233

12. National Association of Small Business Investment Companies (SBIC)
    618 Washington Bldg.
    Washington DC 20005
    (202) 833-8230

    This association, sponsored by the SBA, provides loans to small business.

13. Procurement Automated Source System (PASS)
    Procurement Assistance
    Small Business Administration
    1441 L Street, NW, Rm. 628
    Washington DC 20416
    (202) 653-6938

Through this agency, the SBA facilitates and promotes small business procurement opportunities. It brings together federal agencies, major contractors, and entrepreneurs.

14. Small Business Administration—Publications
P.O. Box 15434
Fort Worth, TX 76119

This organization offers both free and low-cost budget booklets to help entrepreneurs develop budgets, personnel policies, and business plans.

15. Small Business Innovation Program (SBIR)
Office of Innovation, Research, and Technology
SBA
1441 L St. NW
Washington, DC 20416

This agency provides seed funds for research and development grants.

16. U.S. Government Printing Office
Superintendent of Documents
Washington DC 20402
(202) 783-3228

This office prints hundreds of thousands of documents and booklets which help entrepreneurs start and operate their ventures.

4 Legal Structures for Starting a Business

4-1 Overview

Typically, entrepreneurs launch new ventures without much forethought about which legal structure is best for their enterprises. They don't stop to consider key issues about ownership, control, liability, management, decision making, and capital. Yet these key issues directly affect income taxes and the future success of the venture.

The three major forms of business ownership are the sole proprietorship, partnership, and corporation. If the entrepreneur owns and operates the business as an individual and does not have large capital needs, the informality of a sole proprietorship may be appropriate. This is true only if business liability is not an issue or sufficient liability insurance has been purchased to protect the founder. During the last two decades, the limited partnership has become popular because the *control* of the venture is minimal and there are no stockholders.

Of prime importance to a new venture is assessing financial needs, legal risks, and liability. Overall, the corporate structure provides liability protection that founders need. If corporate profits are paid out in salary and/or commissions, the problem of double taxation can be avoided. In addition, the corporate structure makes it possible to raise capital that would be extremely difficult, if not impossible, for an entrepreneur to raise. For these reasons, most entrepreneurs select the corporate structure.

It is not unusual for entrepreneurs to create a corporate shield, but act as a sole proprietor. They neglect to follow corporate requirements and fail to hold board meetings, take minutes, file a corporate report with the Secretary of State every 2 years, and follow other procedures.

Some choose to form S corporations to avoid the double taxation involved with incorporating. However, while the S corporation may be ideal for new ventures and for businesses that are losing money, it may not be the best legal structure when profits are realized.

To avoid the requirements of a corporation, some entrepreneurs select the partnership form, in which owners pool their resources and share control. Others choose to operate as a limited liability company, which combines the advantages of a corporation and a partnership.

Still other entrepreneurs start charitable nonprofit organizations, designated as 501(c)(3), which qualify for exemption from federal income tax. With a nonprofit organization, the entrepreneur identifies a need in the community which is currently not being addressed. An example is an organization that solicits contributions to form a loan pool for minority and female business owners who have difficulty accessing capital.

Selecting the legal structure for an enterprise is a critical decision that takes considerable forethought and planning. The decision should always be discussed with an accountant, since ever-changing tax laws affect business owners differently according to their personal financial situation.

4-2 Smart Strategies for Legal Structures

1. Evaluate and select the most appropriate business structure for your new venture, taking into consideration ownership issues, liability, tax ramifications, and your ability to raise capital.
2. Consider working with a potential partner on a trial basis before giving away equity.
3. Incorporate your business and limit your liability by protecting your personal assets.
4. Don't conduct business without limiting your personal liability or obtaining liability insurance.

5. Keep separate records for your business, regardless of the type of legal structure you choose.
6. Preserve the corporate shield by following all the corporate rules, regulations, and reporting requirements.
7. Don't become a general partner if you have the majority of personal assets. You are jointly liable for all the debts of the business regardless of how the partnership agreement defines ownership.

4-3 Should I Worry about What Kind of Legal Structure to Choose?

QUESTION

I have just started a carpet-cleaning business and was wondering if I should remain operating as a sole proprietorship. Also, do I have to file any special papers for my new business?

ANSWER

The form of organization you choose to operate your venture is crucial to your strategic planning and potential success. Do not make the mistake of ignoring a legal structure for your business, assuming it is not that important. Then, the law assumes that your business is a sole proprietorship—meaning that you and your business are legally one and the same.

A sole proprietorship is the easiest legal structure to start (and terminate), since there are relatively few formalities and legal restrictions. Also, you have complete control of the business and are the sole recipient of any earned profits. For tax purposes, the IRS treats you and your business as one, and your reporting goes on the Schedule C of your 1040 tax form. If the business ends up losing money, you can deduct these losses on your tax return against any other income that you may have earned during that year. For these reasons, the sole proprietorship is the form most used by small businesses.

In a sole proprietorship, you are fully liable for all business debts and actions. If your business is unable to meet its financial obligations, creditors can pursue your personal assets, including your home and car. Your personal assets are not protected from lawsuits. You can lessen the risk of liability in the case of physical loss or personal injury by purchasing business owner's insurance.

Another major obstacle in operating as a sole proprietorship is your ability to raise capital. If you borrow money for your business, the bank will usually require you to sign personally for the money and pledge your personal assets. You will be required to make periodic loan payments regardless of whether your venture is making money. Therefore, risking your personal assets is an important factor to consider.

Another disadvantage of running a business as a sole proprietorship is that the life of the business terminates with the life of the proprietor. Obviously, severe problems can arise here with estate planning and disposing of the business. Also, the sole proprietor cannot deduct many expenses which are deductible to corporations, like defined-benefit pension plans, insurance expenses, and health benefits. Last, it is difficult to attract good management to a sole proprietorship, and this can severely hamper the business' growth and performance.

Since you have already begun your business as a sole proprietorship, you need only file whatever licenses are required in your area. If you are operating the business under a name other than your own, you must register the business as a trade name with your state's revenue department.

> ➪ **Courtney's Smart Tip**
> **Given the realities of the business world, the corporation is the best legal structure for those entrepreneurs who intend to grow their business and raise money from outside sources.**

Key considerations in choosing a legal form of business include your income and tax implications, your ability to raise capital, and your need to limit your liabilities. If you are in business alone and will not need much capital, then maybe the informality of a sole proprietorship might be appropriate.

4-4 Should I Form a Partnership?

QUESTION

I started a small limousine service a couple of years ago. My business has grown substantially and I now have four limos. However, as my business has grown, my capital has shrunk. I can't borrow any more money from the bank and am thinking about getting a partner who has some money to invest. Is this a good strategy to follow? Will I need to become a corporation, or will becoming a partnership be better?

ANSWER

What are you really looking for—a true partner who will share investing in and operating your venture or an investor? If you are just looking for an investor, you don't need a partnership. If you are looking for someone who will contribute money and share in the management of the business, then consider forming a partnership.

A partnership is a tricky proposition. Finding someone with cash, similar goals, the expertise you need, and a style you can work with is difficult. It is akin to finding a marriage partner. You must choose wisely or bear the consequences. Many partnerships end up in disaster under the pressure of a crisis. Crises and chaos are typical environments in entrepreneurial ventures. Conflict seems inevitable when the founder has a need for autonomy.

The advantages of taking on a partner include companionship as well as the enhanced ability to raise money and recruit and motivate key people. The disadvantages include losing control of your venture, losing wealth, being stuck with other owner(s), and having to account to others. The most common reason that entrepreneurs add partners is to raise money; acquiring needed expertise is secondary.

Issues that need to be addressed include deciding who will contribute the most money; how much equity you will give up for additional investment; what kind of exits will be available; who will make the spending decisions; who will sign checks; and who will hire, supervise, and fire staff.

> ➪ **Courtney's Smart Tip**
> **Select a partner who complements your skills and then structure a partnership agreement that addresses both the division of ownership and buyout provisions.**

Try to find a partner who complements your strengths and weaknesses rather than one who has a similar background to your own. Look for someone who specializes in your weakest area. Seek out someone you can trust, are compatible with, and can communicate with easily. Be sure to evaluate whether a potential partner exhibits the ability to compromise.

Be wary of partnering with family or friends. Most often you will end up gaining a partner but losing a friend. Consider a trial period before settling on a partner and giving ownership in your venture.

Many investors consider a venture team more advantageous than a single founder. They like to see a balance of talents among the members of the management team. There are many functional areas involved in operating a business, and it is unlikely that someone will be highly competent in all aspects of the venture. Instead, strengthen your business by either adding partners or hiring staff who will balance your management team. Entrepreneurial wisdom affirms that it is very difficult to run a business on your own.

If your business is currently a sole proprietorship, you could become a partnership immediately. The terms do not have to be written down, especially if you become equal owners. However, it is better to have the terms of the partnership detailed in a formal agreement.

There are two legal forms to consider: the general partnership and the limited partnership. In a general partnership, the owners are liable for all business debts, even if the partnership agreement specifies a certain split in profits. Each partner is 100 percent responsible for all liabilities. Personal assets of the partners may be attached to cover the partnership's liabilities.

In a limited partnership, there is one general partner who runs the business and remains personally responsible for all the partnership's debts. The limited partners are liable only up to the amount of their investment in the business. They do not contribute to the day-to-day operation of the venture. Limited partnerships are created by filing a certificate of limited partnership with the state secretary of state.

If one partner dies or withdraws, the partnership terminates. For tax purposes, the income of the business is considered the income of the partners. The partners are individually responsible for the taxes on their personal income tax return. Profits and losses may be divided in any way agreed to by the partners. If the partners are operating the business under a name different from their legal names, the business must be registered as a trade name with the state department of revenue.

Incorporation is another option to consider. It requires formal paperwork and documentation, but offers the advantages of limiting the owners' liability, existing as a separate entity from the individual owners, and generating certain tax options. The corporate structure is usually more attractive when partners share control and management of the venture. Most founders wisely elect the corporate structure as their business grows.

4-5 How to Structure Buy-Sell Agreements

QUESTION

Should entrepreneurs always include a buyout agreement in their legal structures?

ANSWER

Yes. There should always be a buyout agreement, whether you have formed a partnership or a corporation. Clashes between partners are inevitable, and some provision should be made for separation if the dispute cannot be resolved. Either the partnership agreement or the corporate bylaws should stipulate that any owner must sell back shares at a predetermined price upon separation. This is known as a buy-sell agreement.

It is also recommended that the buy-sell agreement include a "shoot-out clause" stipulating that a partner who wishes to buy out another must offer to sell at the same price at which he or she wants to buy. Then the other partner must agree either to sell at the offered terms or to buy at those same terms.

The trick with this type of agreement is how to price the shares. There are two approaches you can take. The first is to set a predetermined price that is agreeable to the partners. The problem here is that as the venture grows, the value of the shares will change. The other approach is to agree to make a yearly evaluation determining the price of the shares for that year. The evaluation could be made by the partners or by an outsider, or it could be arbitrated.

> ➪ **Courtney's Smart Tip**
> **Develop a provision regarding how and when the shares of the venture will be priced for buyout.**

The buy-sell agreement also makes provisions for a death of a partner. Typically it provides for redemption by the company of that person's share, possibly paid for by a life insurance policy carried by the company. Or it provides for cross-purchase of the person's shares by the surviving partner(s), possibly paid for by insurance carried by the surviving partner(s). The best arrangement depends largely on tax considerations. Consult your lawyer and accountant about a buy-sell agreement suited to your particular situation.

A valuable adjunct to the buy-sell agreement is key partner life insurance, which provides money for the company to buy out the shares of any partner who dies. An advantage of purchasing this type of insurance is that the premiums are tax-deductible expenses for the company.

Consideration should also be given to insure key employees of the business whose loss could have substantial financial consequences. The loss of a key person could mean the loss of key customers, loss of services or special skills provided by that person, or loss of capital. Many entrepreneurial ventures purchase key employee life insurance, which pays compensation to a business on the employee's death, or key employee disability income insurance, which pays compensation caused by permanent and total disability.

Normally the company owns the policy and is the premium payer and the beneficiary. Sometimes a business and key employee will agree to split the premium payments. A key employee must agree to the company's purchase of the insurance on his or her life. If the key employee is terminated, the company may continue the policy in force, surrender the policy for its cash value, or sell it to the employee. Contact your small business insurance agent for more details on purchasing key person insurance. A consumer education organization in your area may also provide insurance information to business owners.

4-6 Incorporating a Business

QUESTION

I have been thinking about starting a gift basket service business and was wondering if I should incorporate. What do you think?

ANSWER

Let's look first at the various advantages and pitfalls of becoming a sole proprietor. When you operate as a sole proprietorship, all the profits are yours, as well as all the losses. The liabilities are also yours, which means they are unlimited and a major disadvantage in this litigious age. This form of business provides no shield for your home, car, or other personal possessions.

Further, operating a sole proprietorship makes it difficult to raise money from lenders, since if anything happens to the owner, the venture could go down the drain. Sole proprietors borrow funds either on their personal signature or on collateral. Life insurance is usually required to cover the amount of the loan in case something happens to the founder. Owners are severely restricted in their ability to raise money, and growth is limited. The death of the founder of the business.

For these reasons and others, most entrepreneurs are advised to incorporate their ventures. A corporation is a lega that exists separate from its founders. It is created by filing artic incorporation with the state secretary of state. The company is own by its shareholders and run by a board of directors elected by the shareholders. You can become a one-person corporation, the sole shareholder, and the only director. However, you cannot be both the president of the corporation and the secretary. You must appoint another person to act as the secretary, but you are not required to give this person any ownership.

Three primary characteristics distinguish a corporation from other legal structures. First, a corporation limits a stockholder's liability to the amount of investment in the business. Second, if shareholders are active in operating the business, they are considered employees and must be paid a reasonable wage subject to both state and federal payroll taxes. Finally, a corporation must pay tax on income as a separate legal entity. If profits are distributed to shareholders as dividends, these profits are subject to taxation as part of the shareholders' income.

Corporations shield shareholders from the claims of creditors and contractual relationships—unless the shareholders sign personally instead of as officers of the corporation. The corporate shield does not relieve any shareholders from personal negligence, civil wrongs, or torts.

> ⇨ **Courtney's Smart Tip**
> **Preserve the corporate shield by strictly following all the legal requirements and reporting procedures.**

Great care must be given to protect the corporate shield and keep the affairs of the corporation at arm's length. This means the shareholders must adopt bylaws, file separate corporate tax returns, hold regular shareholder meetings, record minutes of the proceedings, maintain corporate records, and file a report with the state every 2 years. Following these procedures takes time, effort, and money.

Compliance with all such requirements is mandatory to maintain the corporate shield and receive limited liability protection. For example, shareholders should always identify themselves as officers of the corporation and keep the affairs of the corporation separate from their personal lives. Shareholders should never pay corporate debts person-

sonal debts from corporate funds. If
edures to keep the corporate shield
ld be protected.
rating as a corporation is double taxa-
s a tax on its profits and those receiv-
lividends are taxed again. A way to
any yearly corporate profits in salary
urs seldom pay corporate dividends
rrent tax law, the tax advantages are

resources available for making the job of incorporating easier is the *Do-It-Yourself Incorporation Kit*[1] by S.J.T. Enterprises. Also, check with your state about a business start-up kit for owners. Many states provide these kits free of charge.

4-7 How Does a Regular Corporation Differ From an S Corporation?

QUESTION

For the past 6 years I have been running my gardening business as a sole proprietorship. Because my business is growing, I am thinking about incorporating to protect my personal assets. Should I form a regular corporation or an S corporation?

ANSWER

Whether you should form a regular corporation or an S corporation depends on your financial condition, your assets, and your tax bracket. The S corporation was designed for the lower-income enterprise, since profits or losses are reported on a shareholder's 1040, as in a partnership. Income or losses pass through the corporation to the shareholders in the same form as they are in the corporation. Few entrepreneurs operating small companies ever pay out corporate dividends.

S corporations are not actually separate legal structures, as are corporations, but constitute a special tax status granted by the IRS. S corporations do not pay corporate income tax; rather, expenses and income are divided among its shareholders. Shareholders report profits and losses on their personal income tax returns. You need to find qualified tax counsel to answer your specific question and take advantage of the tax law's provisions.

Most entrepreneurs form S corporations to avoid the regular corporation's double taxation. This should not be the primary reason for forming an S corporation.

> ⇨ **Courtney's Smart Tip**
> **Avoid double taxation by taking corporate profits as salary and/or paying bonuses or commissions.**

There are several restrictions on the organization and activities of an S corporation. First, it must be a domestic corporation. It may only have one class of stock—common stock—issued and outstanding. However, common stock can be issued with or without voting rights. An S corporation may not earn more than 25 percent of its gross receipts from passive investment income (royalties, rents, dividends, interest, etc.) during any 3-year period. It must have a tax year that ends December 31. It cannot have more than 35 shareholders, and all shareholders must be citizens or residents of the United States. Lastly, all shareholders must agree to elect S corporation status.

To become an S corporation, you must file articles of incorporation with your state's secretary of state before applying to the IRS for S status. Then your corporation should file Form 2553, Election by a Small Business Corporation, to indicate it chooses S corporation status. Generally, the election must be filed by March 15 to be effective for the current tax year. The S corporation status remains in effect until the shareholders revoke the choice or until the corporation no longer meets the qualifications. If the corporation reverts back to be taxed as a regular (C) corporation, it must wait a full 5 years to once again make the S election.

While the S corporation can be ideal when the venture is losing money, problems may occur when profits are realized. Stockholders must pay income taxes on these profits while no cash is passed on to pay the taxes. This is one compelling reason for obtaining qualified tax counsel to assist in the S corporation decision.

Before you decide to become an S corporation, give careful consideration to the amount and type of income your company might generate in the future, other income or losses you might earn independent of the company, and whether you plan to sell either the assets or the entire company in the foreseeable future. An S election can be a viable tax-saving device in certain circumstances. It provides a way to operate the business as a proprietorship or partnership for tax purposes and still benefit from the protection of the corporate shield.

For more information about S corporations, obtain a copy of the *Internal Revenue Service Publication 589—Tax Information on S Corporations* by calling (800) 829-3676.

4-8 Should I Form a Limited Liability Company?

QUESTION

Some of my business associates are thinking about buying a business and are considering a limited liability company. What are the pros and cons of this type of entity?

ANSWER

The limited liability company (LLC) is neither a corporation nor a partnership. It is a relatively new type of business entity which, when properly structured, combines the benefits of liability protection afforded to shareholders of a corporation with the favorable tax treatment provided to partnerships and their partners.

In many states, LLC owners are called members, and people who operate the business are called managers. Managers are elected by members. (There must be at least two members to form an LLC.) The exact number of members may vary among states. Corporations are usually eligible to become members of an LLC.

The principal advantage of an LLC is that, unlike a C corporation, it pays no federal income taxes. Instead, as in a partnership, the income or loss of the LLC is passed directly through to its members and reported on their respective tax returns. The principal advantage over the partnership is that, unlike general partners (in both general and limited partnerships), the members' liability for the debts of the LLC is limited to the extent of their investment in the business. In addition, in an LLC all owners may participate in management, a right once available only to general partnerships. Lastly, the LLC offers the same limited liability of the corporate structure.

Because of these advantages, along with flexibility, the LLC may be a better choice of legal structure than the S corporation. It is not subject to the cumbersome and often confusing rules relating to electing S corporation status. S corporations are inhibited by strict limitations on who may be shareholders (only U.S. citizens, resident aliens, and certain types of trusts). S corporations are also limited to issuing only common stock and the allocation of profits and losses must be proportionate to shareholders' ownership. In contrast, the LLC provides tremendous flexibility in distributing and allocating profits and losses.

Forming a LLC is like forming a limited partnership. Articles of organization must be filed with the state secretary of state. In addition, there must be an operating agreement, akin to a partnership agreement, which spells out the details of how the business will be operated and how the profits and losses will be shared. Consult a business attorney to prepare the LLC's articles of organization and operating agreement.

The LLC has disadvantages as well. Unlike the corporate arrangement, unanimous written consent of all members is required to admit new members or to transfer a member's interest, since this structure is treated like a limited partnership. Additional restrictions are imposed on transfers of interest and upon an LLC's ability to continue if a member withdraws. These restrictions are tax-driven, since they provide the pass-through tax advantage of a partnership.

It is not clear whether states that do not yet have LLC legislation will respect the liability protection afforded to its members. Approximately 20 states have enacted LLC legislation and it is becoming more widely accepted. Other states are slowly adopting the LLC status and many others have legislation pending.

Another disadvantage of the LLC relates to legal costs. It is more expensive to start an LLC, since there are no standard documents to use as a model. The operating agreement must be tailored to each venture and requires the services of an experienced attorney. There are no "boilerplate" kits available, as there are with corporations.

Despite its disadvantages, the LLC is a good planning tool. It is an attractive legal structure because it creates tax savings, shields businesspeople from personal liability, and provides almost unlimited opportunity to participate in the management of the venture. Its simplicity and flexibility make it attractive to closely held businesses which operate in a state with LLC legislation. This legal entity is ideal for many real estate ventures, oil and gas, and mining businesses.

> ➪ **Courtney's Smart Tip**
> **As your business grows, change your legal structure to accommodate changing tax laws and the individual situations of your members. Always consult with a tax accountant and/or business attorney first.**

4-9 Forming a Nonprofit Company

QUESTION

I want to start a day-care center and I am interested in incorporating as a nonprofit business. I want to fund my venture from tax-deductible donations or by applying for a grant. What do I need to do to become a nonprofit corporation?

ANSWER

First, research whether it is likely that private individuals, foundations, and/or corporations would consider making charitable donations to your nonprofit corporation. Today, the demand for charitable donations is extraordinarily high and increasing. Competition for funding abounds among nonprofit corporations.

Question whether your venture will be seen as meeting a critical need in the community and therefore deserving of contributions. True, day-care services are vital in most communities, but your venture will be serving relatively few residents and thus may not attract enough funds. Fundability is a key question that must be answered before proceeding.

Developing a constituency of potential donors takes considerable time and effort. Michael Seltzer's *Securing Your Organization's Future*[2] offers a comprehensive workbook approach on how to acquire funding for nonprofit corporations and how to identify potential donors. Two good funding resources are your state's community resource center and Junior League. Also, check to see if you have a state association of nonprofits or a council of foundations. The United Way agency in your city could assist you with contacting such organizations.

Obtaining funding for nonprofit organizations is a challenge. You must write a sound and professional proposal to be considered for funding. This can be a long process, since many donors review proposals only at certain times during the year. Their response is not immediate, and it may take from 6 to 18 months to secure funding.

Consider direct-mail solicitation. But remember that it takes time to build a constituency. Response rates tend to be low, averaging 1 to 2 percent.

Once you determine that your venture provides a needed service in the community and that it is feasible to obtain funding, you can begin the process of forming an independent 501(c)(3). This organizational structure qualifies your venture for exemption from federal income tax and enables donors to make their donations tax-deductible.

You can register as a nonprofit corporation with your secretary of state. Registration does not grant your corporation tax-exempt status. A separate application must be made to the IRS. Numerous forms and documents must be created and completed. The IRS fees depend on the size of the proposed project. In addition, it takes from 3 to 6 months to receive the 501(c)(3) designation. Call your local IRS office to determine how to obtain your application packet.

Because of the technicalities and complications involved in obtaining 501(c)(3) status, legal assistance for nonprofits is essential. Contact an attorney who specializes in nonprofit incorporation and taxes. The cost ranges between $2000 and $5000. You can reduce these expenses by doing much of the legwork yourself and having your attorney review your efforts.

Contact some of the organizations in your state or community that provide both management consulting and training to nonprofit corporations.

QUESTION

Because of the special problems female entrepreneurs experience in securing a loan for their ventures, I am thinking about starting a company that would provide funding for them. Could my venture be started as a nonprofit organization?

ANSWER

Your venture could be organized as a nonprofit corporation, known as a 501(c)(3), if you can establish that financial assistance for female entrepreneurs is needed in your community. This IRS classification is for organizations that provide a charitable service to the community for one or more of the following purposes: religious, charitable, scientific, testing for public safety, literacy, educational, fostering of national or international amateur sports competition, and prevention of cruelty to children or animals.

Nonprofit organizations qualify for exemption from federal income tax and are not prohibited from making a profit, only from distributing the net income to members, directors, or officers.

There are two steps in becoming a 501(c)(3) nonprofit corporation. First, you should apply for incorporation in your state, delivering articles of incorporation and paying the required filing fee. If the articles conform to the law, you will receive a certificate of incorporation. Second, to make your enterprise exempt from income tax, you must file for tax-exempt status with the IRS. You will need to submit Form 1023 plus a variety of other materials such as articles of incorporation, bylaws, and budgets along with a nonrefundable IRS filing fee.

You can prepare your own articles of incorporation and bylaws or contact a lawyer who specializes in nonprofit corporations. Many local and national organizations have start-up packages at little or no charge and offer seminars on incorporating as a 501(c)(3).

Prepare as much of the required documentation as possible and then meet with a lawyer and/or public accountant to review and finalize your work. This way you can reduce much of the expense involved.

Since it is not always easy to determine whether your venture idea will meet state and federal requirements for nonprofits, you may want to schedule an initial meeting with the lawyer to determine whether to proceed. Depending on the amount and accuracy of the paperwork you provide, the complexity of your venture, and other factors, the total costs to incorporate and obtain tax-exempt status for a 501(c)(3) could reach $5000.

Another option is to form a strategic alliance with an existing nonprofit organization that is currently providing similar services to female entrepreneurs. The advantage of pursuing this strategy is that the nonprofit will have already established a service track record and philanthropic relations. Therefore, it will be easier to raise the funds you need to operate your venture. Today, newly established 501(c)(3) organizations have a difficult time competing for and securing the decreasing amount of charitable funds available. It's the old chicken-and-egg theory—it is hard to raise funds without having already been in operation and funded.

Another advantage of working with a nonprofit is that you can utilize the experience, expertise, and contacts of the existing organization. Establishing a 501(c)(3) is a complicated and expensive process. Getting initial funding is the major challenge, since charitable funds are limited. The funding community prioritizes what it considers to be the most critical needs. Regardless of how meritorious your idea is, if your venture is not perceived as a critical need, obtaining funding might be impossible.

4-10 Pitfalls to Avoid

1. Choosing business partners who do not complete your strengths and weaknesses.
2. Not thinking through the ownership issues, management concerns, liability issues, and tax consequences of the various types of legal structures for your venture.
3. Failing to require a written partnership agreement that specifies all the agreed terms of the business.
4. Operating as a sole proprietorship when the venture has potential liabilities you would be personally responsible for.
5. Mixing personal and business expenses on your financial statement.

6. Paying corporate debts personally and/or signing personally on corporate business.
7. Piercing the corporate veil by disregarding the rules, regulations, and requirements for maintaining the corporate structure.
8. Using an attorney who does not specialize in nonprofit incorporation and taxes.
9. Emphasizing a community service which is already being provided by another nonprofit.

The Good News. Entrepreneurs can benefit from spending the required time and effort to research the right legal structure for their venture. Legal structure and tax implications affect all founders differently, depending on their personal situations. Carefully consider all the alternatives and seek advice from the infrastructure about what kind of legal entity to form.

4-11 Entrepreneurial Resource Checklist

References

1. S.J.T. Enterprises, *Do-It-Yourself Incorporation Kit,* Lakewood, Ohio, 1991.
2. Michael Seltzer, *Securing Your Organization's Future, A Complete Guide to Fundraising Strategies,* Foundation Center, New York, 1987.

Further Reading

Books

Howell, John Cotton. *Forming Corporations and Partnerships,* 2d ed., Liberty Hall Press, Blue Ridge Summit, Pa., 1991.

McQuoum, Judith. *Inc. Yourself,* Harper Business, New York, 1992.

Nicholas, Ted. *How to Form Your Own Corporation Without a Lawyer for Under $75.00,* Enterprise/Dearborn, Chicago, 1992.

PSI Successful Business Library, *The Essential Corporate Handbook—For Small Business Corporations,* Oasis Press, Grants Pass, Ore., 1992.

Sanderson, Steve. *Standard Legal Forms and Agreements for Small Business,* Self-Counsel Press, Bellingham, Wash., 1990.

Sitarz, Daniel. *The Complete Book of Small Business Legal Forms,* Nova Publishing, Carbondale, Ill., 1991.

Magazines

Chronicle of Philanthropy, P.O. Box 1989, Marion, OH 43306-4-89 (800) 347-6969.

Contacts

1. State Department of Revenue

   Register your company's trade name with your state department of revenue.

2. State Secretary of State

   File articles of incorporation, limited partnerships, and limited liability company (LLC) documents with the state secretary of state.

3. Internal Revenue Service

   All forms of legal structure, except sole proprietorships with no employees, must obtain a Federal Employer Identification Number (FEIN), which becomes your federal tax ID number. If you are a sole proprietorship with no employees, your federal ID number is your social security number.

4. Start-Up Kits

   Many states have small business start-up kits that contain all the necessary information you need to start your venture. Check with your secretary of state.

5. Council of Foundations
   1828 L. Street, NW, Suite 300
   Washington, DC 20036
   (202) 466-6512

   This organization has publications, information, referral services and workshops for nonprofit organizations and grant makers. Check to see if your state has a council of foundations listing nonprofit support organizations in your area.

6. Nonprofit Management Association (NMA)
   315 W. 9th Street, Suite 1100
   Los Angeles, CA 90015
   (213) 623-7080

   This association is dedicated to the improvement of management of nonprofit organizations. It sponsors annual conferences and offers a variety of other services for its members.

5
Buying a Business

5-1 Overview

The entrepreneurial trend is here to stay for at least the next 20 years. However, there is a new model of entrepreneurship emerging—the buyout entrepreneur. This is the individual who buys a business rather than starting one from scratch. Many entrepreneurs are finding that big returns come from the growth and revitalization of existing businesses.

The number of businesses for sale is increasing as well as the number of buyers including corporate acquirers, larger corporations (both U.S. and overseas) that are looking for smaller companies that will provide innovative products in new markets. In addition, the impact of downsizing by larger corporations will be felt for years. Today, corporate refugees are more receptive to becoming entrepreneurs and a good proportion find buying a business more appealing than launching a new one.

The often-quoted statistic that 6 out of every 10 new businesses fail during the first 5 years represents the risk that is involved in starting a new venture. Overall, a successful business needs an operating history of 5 to 8 years to sufficiently prove its concept, market, prices, location, and management.

In a start-up venture all operational aspects are unknown. There is a high degree of uncertainty in starting a new venture from scratch. Some entrepreneurs estimate that they will break even in six months.

However, it might take 18 to 24 months, during which time they need unanticipated operating capital. Typically penetrating a market takes two to five times as long as originally projected.

However, buying an existing business is different. One can equate the differences to those of buying a house versus building a house. With a new house, owners worry about everything—similar to the worries of starting a new business. With the purchase of an older home, however, less risk is involved—likewise in the acquisition of an existing business. When you purchase an ongoing business, there is an existing reputation, customer base, suppliers, equipment, leases, and cash flow. The infrastructure and management team are also in place.

Many entrepreneurs are more successful as turnaround artists—building ventures rather than starting them. They are not creator types with ideas that could revolutionize the marketplace. Instead, they recognize good business opportunities and make an existing venture more profitable. One successful entrepreneur claimed that he had only 2 failures out of 10 ventures—the two businesses he started from scratch. The other business successes were all ventures he had purchased and grown.

Buying an existing business is a good entrepreneurial strategy when you have thoroughly evaluated and analyzed the business opportunity. It may take up to a year to find the right purchase. It is also a wise strategy to match your interests and industry experience with an opportunity to purchase a business.

5-2 Smart Strategies for Buying a Business

1. Reduce the time involved in planning, organizing, and launching a new start-up by buying the right business.
2. Negotiate with the seller to carry back debt and give you good terms so that the business can generate enough cash to buy itself back in five years.
3. Ask the seller to continue working in the business for three to six months to help you make the transition and provide training.
4. Seek outside help from accountants, lawyers, and bankers to assist you in assessing opportunities to purchase a business.
5. Always ask for audited financial statements for the past 3 to 5 years.

6. Hire a business owner of a similar business outside of your competitive area to help you evaluate purchase opportunities.
7. After analyzing historical sales and profits, prepare your own projections of future profitability and growth potential.

5-3 Making the Purchase Decision

QUESTION

I have a choice between purchasing a business that has been in operation for several years or starting one of my own. Which route would you recommend?

ANSWER

Many entrepreneurs feel that purchasing an existing business is like buying a used car. You inherit all the problems and headaches that someone else has caused. However, purchasing a business can be an attractive alternative to starting one of your own. There are six good reasons for buying a business instead of starting one from scratch. They include time, finance, existing operating systems, lower risk, management training, and lower asset costs.

Starting a business from scratch takes considerable time and effort, usually requiring several years to get it to a level of being profitable. You can own a profitable business from the beginning by purchasing it. Buying an existing business is a quick way to obtain ownership of a mature business that is generating profit.

What if the business you are interested in purchasing is losing money? Should you still consider purchasing it? Buying this type of venture is still a quicker way to get to profitable operations than starting a new business. Turning around a business can be both a profitable and a rewarding experience. Many failing businesses are just poorly managed. An astute entrepreneur may be able to immediately generate a profit.

Perhaps the most compelling reason for buying a business is to make use of the seller's invested capital. Most sellers ultimately finance a large part of the sale to help sell the business and to obtain a higher selling price. Sellers are the purchaser's biggest financing source.

Typically, the seller's money is the lowest cost of funds available. Sometimes, the seller will finance the entire transaction if he or she has faith in the buyer. Many times, the seller does not need cash immediately but instead wants assured income.

Most sellers will ask for all cash up front. However, they often have to give more lenient terms to make the sale. It all depends on the buyer's persuasive powers and the seller's alternatives and needs.

Remember, the selling price of the business is not the most important aspect. Instead, the terms for purchasing the business are key to making the deal work. Also, bankers and other lenders are more willing to lend to an established business with several years of performance to evaluate. It is a known quantity.

> ➪ **Courtney's Smart Tip**
> **Terms are everything when buying a business; the selling price is not.**

The entrepreneur who starts a business spends considerable time, money, and effort building an organization and developing an effective operating system. The buyer of a business already has one in place and can avoid the pitfalls of start-up.

Most often, some changes are needed. It is usually easier to make changes in the operating systems than to begin from nothing. Some of the value of an existing business comes from the fact that it is a "going concern." All its parts are functioning. One of the most valuable parts of the operating system is the venture's current customers. Customers are gold. It takes a substantial amount of time and effort to build and maintain a good customer base.

Another important part of a venture's operating system is its sales force and distributing system. It is one of the most significant values of an existing business that does not appear on any balance sheet. A well-trained sales force combined with an effective distribution system is a most valuable asset and one well worth acquiring.

5-4 Advantages of Buying a Business

QUESTION

I am going to be laid off in the next several months and I have an opportunity to buy a rental business that a friend of mine owns. Is this advisable?

ANSWER

Overall, the risks associated with entrepreneurship are less in buying a business than in starting a new business. There are many advantages of buying an existing business, especially if you know the owner and his or her business. Consider these advantages of purchasing a business—lower risk, management training, and lower asset costs.

It is often easier to assess the risks involved in buying a going business than those inherent in developing a new venture. You can evaluate a known quantity with an existing location, current customers, staff, suppliers, and a reputation. The first 2 years of any business are the riskiest. Survival is key during this period and the failure rate is the highest. It can take 2 or 3 years to reach the breakeven point with a start-up and another 5 years to become stable and successful.

Two major factors help limit risks. First, the buyer has better information on both the operating characteristics of the venture and its established market than the entrepreneur would have with a start-up enterprise. Much of the market speculation and sales forecasting are eliminated, since the business already has a track record. Therefore, better and more accurate forecasts can be made.

Second, and perhaps more important, the buyer can usually invest fewer dollars when purchasing an existing business. This relates back to the seller financing the majority of the venture. The more the seller is willing to carry back as debt, the more he or she can expect to sell the business to a prospective buyer.

As previously mentioned, this is usually the least expensive cost of funds available. Negotiated terms can be better than those available from any other type of lender. The buyer should be more concerned with how the purchase can be structured than with the actual price involved.

Management training provided by the seller is another advantage of buying an existing business. Often, the seller will teach the buyer how to run the business. Much inside knowledge and expertise can be exchanged. Consequently, the buyer of an existing business may not have to learn those important start-up lessons the hard way. In addition, a financially involved seller is motivated to hold the buyer's hand for a longer period of time.

Finally, it is usually cheaper to acquire assets by buying a business

> ➪ **Courtney's Smart Tip**
> **Ask the seller to work with the new owner for the first 6 months after the sale.**

than it is to purchase them new. You can often purchase the building and equipment for 10 to 20 percent of what it would cost new. Some businesses are purchased just for their location or for the lease they have with the building owner.

Frequently, the assets of an existing business are not worth much, except as to how they are used in that particular business. Thus, an entrepreneur may be able to get into this type of business with less capital than by starting a new venture. In essence, you are purchasing used equipment at an attractive price. This happens more often when you acquire a firm that is in trouble.

An entrepreneurial tip to remember is that the business success a seller has achieved costs the buyer more money. Likewise, business failure costs the seller money.

5-5 Disadvantages of Buying an Existing Business

QUESTION

I have an excellent opportunity to buy a business from someone who is moving. Because of the business's existing client base and positive cash flow, I think this would be a good investment for me. What should I look out for?

ANSWER

Many businesses for sale aren't worth buying. The advantages of buying a business usually outweigh starting one from scratch. However, there are some disadvantages of buying existing businesses that you should consider before deciding to buy.

There are many businesses for sale that should be avoided. Primarily, these businesses can be grouped into the following categories: (1) inadequate market potential, (2) serious competitive problems, (3) technological problems, (4) disadvantageous cost characteristics, (5) seller backing out, and (6) nothing worth buying.

Let's take a look at each of these disadvantages. First, many businesses are not going anywhere because there is nowhere for them to go. The founder is doing everything possible and the business is still losing money. Essentially, the market potential is just not there.

Second, the business is experiencing serious competitive problems. The market is saturated with similar-type ventures, and the cost of the product has become very price-competitive. There are just too many businesses chasing after the same consumer dollar. It is a cutthroat industry where it is difficult to enter into the marketplace.

Some businesses become technologically obsolete. Would you purchase a business that makes silent movies or 78 rpm records? Sometimes the product can no longer compete technologically in the marketplace because of new inventions.

Astute entrepreneurs may realize that they are losing their technological edge. They quickly place their business for sale before this situation becomes apparent to the general public. In acquiring any business with a technology base, take great care to assess what is happening to the technology in that industry. Are new products being tested that will replace yours? It is essential that you determine whether or not the business has the ability to compete in the new technological arena.

It is also difficult to make money if your competition has a cost advantage over you. You will always be vulnerable to price wars. Moreover, your cost disadvantage comes right out of your profits. Unless you have an idea of how to rectify the cost problem, be careful.

Sometimes you will negotiate with a seller for several months. Then, just as you get ready to sign the deal, the seller notifies you that he or she has decided not to sell the business. Often, sellers become too emotionally attached to let go of the venture. Yet you have spent considerable time and money performing due diligence, doing research, securing financing, and negotiating the deal. In addition, you have paid legal and accounting fees that are unrecoverable, plus the incalculable opportunity costs.

Lastly, there are some businesses that are just not worth buying. They are going nowhere fast. Their products may be inadequate and/or defective. The inventory is old and outdated. The business is on a downswing and experiencing a negative cash flow. Overall, it is difficult to find one good feature about the business, except the sales price. When this situation occurs, it is easier to start a new venture than purchase an old one.

Be careful when you find an owner who is trying to sell the business in a short period of time. He or she may be trying to bail out quickly before the market turns sour. When speed replaces price as the primary goal, beware. You might be able to get a good deal, but the business is or will become unprofitable.

5-6 Where to Look for a Business to Purchase

QUESTION

I am a corporate refugee who is looking for a business to buy. I don't want or feel qualified to start one from scratch. Where do you suggest I look?

ANSWER

Avoid a hasty decision and try not to get too excited about a good potential until you have spent enough time evaluating a potential business and analyzing its marketplace. Many experts say that you should count on spending at least a year to find and evaluate a business that you would like to purchase. Use the following guidelines as a starting point in your search.

1. *Newspapers.* The easiest place to start looking for a business to buy is in the classified section of newspapers under "Business Opportunities." The Sunday edition usually has the most listings. Look in the "Mart" section of *The Wall Street Journal* on Wednesdays and Thursdays. *The New York Times* Sunday edition contains several pages of diverse businesses for sale. There are also specialized business opportunity newspapers, such as *The Business Opportunity Journal.* Check with your librarian for similar publications to review.
2. *Industry trade magazines.* Many industry magazines and trade papers contain a classified section with business opportunities that are industry-specific.
3. *Banks.* Some banks, such as the First National Bank of Maryland, publish newsletters of business opportunities. Call (800) 842-BANK. There may be a charge for some of the newsletters and/or catalog listings. You may also ask banks in your area if they have lists of businesses for sale. Bankers can be helpful in your search and establishing a relationship with them early on is a must. It might not be long before you'll be asking them for lending assistance to help finance your venture.
4. *Business professionals and members of the infrastructure.* Talk with attorneys, accountants, venture capitalists, investment bankers, insurance agents, salespeople, and other members of the entrepreneurial infrastructure. These professionals often know of business opportunities that are never advertised.
5. *Business brokers.* Brokers have extensive lists of businesses for sale. They work for business owners and are paid a commission to market and sell businesses. A business broker's fee typically runs between 5 and 10 percent of the purchase price. Your response to an ad may very well be to a business broker. Try to negotiate a "buy-broker agreement" in which the broker agrees to seek out companies for you. Look in the Yellow Pages of your telephone directory for listings of business brokers. You can also obtain a brokers' list of those who belong to the International Association of Business Brokers by calling (617) 369-5254.
6. *Business owners.* Look for businesses you might be interested in purchasing and contact the owners. Ask them if they are interested in selling. On the average, about 3 out of every 10 calls attract

some interest. If owners are not interested in selling, they might be able to refer you to someone else.

7. *Chambers of commerce.* Some chambers of commerce maintain buying and selling services for businesses in their area.
8. *SBA and state or county economic development agencies.* These organizations frequently know of businesses for sale and can give you referrals.
9. *Trade sources.* Check with suppliers, vendors, distributors, manufacturers, and trade associations about potential businesses for sale. They are excellent resources for industry-specific businesses.
10. *Business bankruptcy listings.* Most local business journals publish a list of businesses that have filed for bankruptcy. If you feel you have skills to become a turnaround artist, these listings may produce good leads.
11. *Friends.* Your friends have a wide network of contacts. Let them know what kind of business you are looking for and ask them to notify you of any opportunities they discover. You might want to consider offering an incentive to get people to give you qualified leads. Paying people for their time and effort is a good business practice.

When answering an ad, present yourself as a fully qualified person so you will receive a response back. You will probably be asked some qualifying questions to see if the owner or broker wants to continue the process. This list is a starting place and demonstrates that there are many sources for you to tap during your search. A successful search requires diligence and hard work.

5-7 Checklist for Buying an Existing Business

QUESTION

I have recently taken an early retirement benefit and received a cash bonus. I have been thinking about buying an office supply store instead of looking for another job. What factors should I consider before buying this business?

ANSWER

There are personal considerations as well as business factors to analyze and evaluate when thinking about buying an existing business.

Identify your personal goals for purchasing the business. Will the business you are considering match these goals?

Think about your expertise. What are your strengths and weaknesses? Do they complement the venture? Will your knowledge and skills be of help in operating the business? No one is strong in all areas of entrepreneurship.

Consider your lifestyle. There is prestige in owning your own business. Does this business fit your status and image needs?

Decide about location. Is the location convenient for you and does it have enough traffic flow? Is the location convenient to your target customers?

Determine the location history. How long has the office supply store, for example, been in that location? Have other businesses failed and frequently turned over in that location? Sometimes a location carries a stigma and should be avoided. On the other hand, sometimes entrepreneurs purchase existing businesses just for the location and the lease.

Look at the surroundings and physical conditions. Is any remodeling needed? If so, estimate the costs for such remodeling.

Consider your financial needs. How much money do you want to make? How much money will you need to purchase the business?

After identifying your personal criteria, make an in-depth venture analysis. You will need assistance in investigating the office supply store from various business experts including an accountant, an attorney, and a banker.

> ➪ **Courtney's Smart Tip**
> **Hire a successful owner of a similar venture in another community, someone who is not a competitor, to consult with you. The owner's wealth of experience can help you detect areas of concern that you might otherwise overlook.**

Ask for historical and projected profit and sales figures. Ask for the past 3 to 5 years of audited balance sheets, income statements, and cash flow statements. Have your accountant review them.

Review the venture's operating ratios. How do they compare with industry ratios from the Robert Morris studies, which is a reliable source of statistics and financial ratios on every industry? If there are significant deviations, ask the owner to explain identified differences.

Ask for a list of current assets and liabilities. Examine the age and condition of assets. Evaluate debts and other liabilities. Are there any pending legal actions? Count the number, amount, and ages of the receivables. Review how many receivables were written off as uncollectible each year for the past 3 years.

Review corporate tax returns. Remember that a seller won't exaggerate the business's worth to Uncle Sam. If the seller cannot provide financial information for the past 3 years, this is an indication that something is amiss.

Run a background check. Contact the local better business bureau to determine if customers have filed a complaint about the business. For a fee, Dun & Bradstreet will give you an estimate of the worth of the business. Look for a local office in the Yellow Pages.

Assess the current staff. You are buying not just the company but also the employees. Who are they? Is there good chemistry among them? Do they appear to be ethical and honest? Check their personnel files and look for any disciplinary actions and poor evaluations.

Evaluate local economic and political conditions. What are the industry trends for this business? Is the market increasing or decreasing? What is the growth potential? What is the competitive environment? Is the market overcrowded with competition?

Meet with customers. Determine their level of satisfaction with the business. In any walk-in business, always talk to customers who come into the store. Also, talk to former customers and find out why they are no longer buying from this store.

Choose the right seller. The owner should be both cooperative and willing to disclose all the financial and personnel, customer, and legal information related to the venture. If the owner is resistant to sharing this information, you have reason to be concerned.

These are just some of the key issues to raise and information to analyze when considering purchasing a business. A good reference book is C. D. Peterson's *How to Leave Your Job and Buy a Business of Your Own.*[1]

Evaluating this information is only half the equation. It is important to use a combination of both research and intuition in deciding whether a business is right for you and whether you should make an offer to buy it. Although it may be a good acquisition opportunity, you need good management skills and business experience. Remember, all that glitters is not gold.

5-8 Pitfalls to Avoid

1. Purchasing a business without thoroughly evaluating the venture and its financial statements.
2. Accepting nonaudited financial statements.
3. Purchasing a business with a shrinking market.
4. Purchasing a business in an industry with many competitors.
5. Thinking you can manage the business better than the owner without any prior business experience in the industry.

5-9 Entrepreneurial Resource Checklist

References

1. C.D. Peterson, *How to Leave Your Job and Buy a Business of Your Own*, McGraw-Hill, New York, 1988.

Further Reading

Books

Goldstein, Arnold. *The Complete Guide to Buying and Selling a Business*, Wiley, New York, 1993.

Gordon, Douglas F. *How to Profitably Sell or Buy a Company or Business*, Van Nostrand Reinhold, New York, 1981.

Knight, Brian, and the Associates of County Business, Inc. *Buying the Right Business at the Right Price*, Upstart Publishing, Portsmouth, N.H., 1990.

Kohl, John C., Sr., and Atlee M. Kohl. *The Smart Way to Buy a Business: An Entrepreneur's Guide to Questions That Must Be Asked*, Woodland Publishers, Irving, Tex., 1986.

Mancuso, Joseph R., and Douglas D. Germann, Sr. *Buying a Business for Very Little Cash*, Prentice-Hall, Englewood Cliffs, N.J., 1991.

Tuller, L. *Buying In: A Complete Guide to Acquiring a Business or Professional Practice*, McGraw-Hill, New York, 1990.

Magazines

The National Review of Corporate Acquisitions
Tweed Publishing Co.
23 Main Street
Tuburon, CA 94920
(415) 435-2175

Business Ventures Magazine
Elsevier Science Publishing Co., Inc.
655 Avenue of the Americas
New York, NY 10020
(212) 989-5000

Contacts

1. International Association of Business Brokers
   POB 704
   Concord, MA 01742
   (617) 369-5254

   This association provides lists of business brokers who have been certified as business intermediaries and belong to their association.

2. First National Bank of Maryland
   (800) 842-BANK

   The corporate finance division of this bank publishes a quarterly list of companies that are up for sale and provides a listing of financing sources for $350 a year.

3. World M&A Network
   717 D Street NW
   Washington, D.C. 20004
   (202) 628-6900

   This organization publishes *The Network*, a 100-page magazine that includes a listing of sellers, buyers, and financing information for $335 a year.

4. Robert Morris Studies
   Robert Morris Associates
   1616 Philadelphia National Bank Bldg.
   Philadelphia, PA 19107
   (215) 665-2858

   A valuable source of industry statistics and financial ratios on every industry. Available in most libraries.

6 Protecting Intellectual Property

6-1 Overview

Entrepreneurs have millions of great ideas that are commercialized every day, but many don't consider protecting their intellectual property, which can be extremely valuable proprietary rights and assets. Intellectual property covers patents, trademarks, copyrights, trade secrets, and trade names. Astute entrepreneurs not only protect their intellectual property, but they also may be able to obtain an injunction against infringement and compensatory damages. The costs associated with obtaining such protection are well worth it.

The amount of time, the associated costs, and which agency to register your intellectual property with to obtain protection for intellectual property differs. Registration for patents and trademarks can be made by filing an application with the U.S. Patent and Trademark Office. The greatest benefit of a patent is the U.S. government's grant of the right to exclude others from making, using, and selling the invention in the United States for 17 years from the date of issue, so long as it is maintained. Patents and pending patent rights can be licensed for royalty payments, and are also assignable for valuable consideration.

NOTE: Don Margolis, Boulder, Colorado, patent attorney, contributed and reviewed many of the comments on intellectual property.

Many inventors fall prey to paying invention marketing companies high up-front fees for commercializing their inventions only to discover that they have been taken advantage of. Most of these companies are great on promises, but short on delivery. Few inventors ever earn a penny from these companies. Inventors should avoid using them or should diligently research them ahead of time.

If your idea includes any written or artistic matter which includes a symbol, work, shape, or design, and you use this mark as a brand name, service mark, or trade dress, then using the trademark letters is strongly recommended. A common law trademark can be obtained easily by using the mark with the goods or services. By using the letters TM or SM, you can show your clear intent to use your idea as a registered mark. You can also register it with state or federal trademark offices. Trademarks are an important marketing tool for distinguishing the owner's goods from those of competitors. They add value to a venture as intellectual property and assist in raising capital.

A copyright is the legal right to control specific uses of art, sculpture, books, music, motion pictures, videotapes, photographs, software programs, or other types of creative material. It is a low-cost procedure administered by the U.S. Copyright Office. According to the current copyright law, a copyrightable work is automatically protected from its creation whether it is marked or not. However, it is best to include a copyright notice on the material in the form of the full word "copyright," the abbreviation "copyr," or the small circle ©, along with the year of completion and the owner's name.

Trade secrets are any proprietary information used in the course of business to gain an advantage in manufacture or commercialization of products or services. They can be formulas, devices, patterns, techniques, customer lists, sales forecasts, databases, manufacturing processes, or compiled information that has a specific business application. They must have economic value, they must be secret, and the owners must take steps to attempt to protect them. Trade secrets are an important part of an entrepreneur's intellectual property, and often owners either are not aware of these rights or just don't bother to protect this proprietary information which is critical to operating their ventures.

Protecting intellectual property takes time, effort, and money, but is well worth it. Finding an experienced intellectual property attorney to assist you in protecting your proprietary rights is essential.

Caveat. All government fees quoted are correct as of this writing, but may be (and probably will be) increased annually. When submitting fees to the government, avoid the delay and disappointment of having your papers rejected on the technicality of an improper fee.

6-2 Smart Strategies for Protecting Intellectual Property

1. Use a log book to document and describe in detail your invention recording your ideas in ink. Then date and sign these pages as you go along, mark them "confidential," and have at least one noninventor witness and date them as "read and understood."
2. Conduct a novelty search to determine if your idea or a related idea has already been patented at a library with a patent depository, or engage a patent professional (not a marketing company) to provide such a search.
3. Protect your ideas by having others sign a confidential disclosure agreement before you disclose them.
4. Protect your customer lists by treating them as a trade secret and requiring employees and agents to sign a confidential information agreement.
5. If you have an innovative or a high-technology invention, consider trying to license it to an established company, and collect royalties.
6. Establish a working relationship with a potential licensee before sending a blind solicitation letter or confidential disclosure agreement.
7. To protect your invention while marketing it, after filing a patent application, use the words "patent pending" to warn others not to start to copy your product during the patenting process.
8. Use the symbol TM or SM to show trademark or service mark ownership.
9. Use a copyright notice to alert others that your material is not public domain.

6-3 Patents and Inventions

How to Protect a Patent

QUESTION

I have developed several patentable ideas for new products. I would like to know how to protect these ideas before I apply for or receive a patent, since I know this will be a very expensive process. I understand that if I don't protect my rights they could later be lost. How should I proceed?

ANSWER

Keeping a patentable idea confidential until a patent is obtained is not an easy process. Protecting your patent rights is extremely important, especially before taking any ideas to the marketplace. The following steps will assist you in protecting your patent idea.

1. Reduce your idea to writing and drawings, in ink if appropriate, by preparing clear and concise descriptions of the invention. Photographs may be used. Sign and date these documents.
2. Immediately mark all the documents confidential. Each page should contain the word "confidential" on them. It is your responsibility to inform people that your idea is secret and confidential. Your state's trade secret laws will provide you with the necessary protection; but even then do not disclose trade secrets indiscriminately or to people whom you do not trust.
3. Find at least one person who is technically competent to understand your idea. Have this person sign and date a statement indicating that he or she has read and understood your idea. Make sure you inform this witness that your ideas are confidential.
4. Obtain a confidential disclosure agreement for valuable protection against the misuse of your idea. Essentially such a document officially informs someone who is about to receive information about your idea that it is being disclosed in confidence.
5. Have the confidential disclosure agreement signed and dated by each party that you share your idea with—at least until the patent application is on file.

Legal advice is warranted at this stage from an experienced competent patent attorney. You can obtain confidential disclosure agreement forms from your attorney or in the *Entrepreneur's Resource Handbook.*[1] Or you can find a credible form in the back of the book *Patent It Yourself.*[2]

A confidential disclosure agreement is a simple contract that any judge can look at to determine if there has been a breach of contract. An inventor has a stronger and more enforceable position when a confidential disclosure agreement has been signed.

The reason to involve a patent attorney at this stage is to determine if your idea is patentable, before you spend additional dollars. An inventor needs to have a novelty search done before applying for a patent. You can do much of the legwork yourself and work with your attorney to develop a specific business strategy. Even if it is determined that your idea is not patentable, you may be able to license your valuable, confidential trade secrets and know-how.

If you apply for a U.S. patent, it is a good business strategy to continue to keep your business ideas confidential until there is some good financial reason to make them public. Even though legally you do not have any enforceable right without a patent, maintaining your idea as confidential gives you the power to control it until there is a need to make it public or until the patent is issued.

Lastly, using a confidential disclosure agreement and maintaining the invention as confidential gives you some bargaining power when approaching other parties about their ideas. If a company accepts your idea, you might be able to negotiate to have the company pay some or all of your patent costs.

How to Apply for and Acquire a Patent

QUESTION

I am an inventor who has perfected a working prototype of a very unusual mobile. How can I patent and market a new product without a proven track record and without money? It is my first invention and I would love to make a living in this manner. Can you give some good advice to us poor, starving inventors?

ANSWER

These questions are typical of many inventors interested in securing a patent and getting their product to the marketplace. The first step is to write a letter to the U.S. Department of Commerce, Patent and Trademark Office, Washington, DC 20231. This office will send you some information and brochures about the patenting process. Or you can call the Public Service Center at (703) 557-INFO for information about the filing process. You can also write for a copy of the book *General Information Concerning Patents,* available for $2 from the Government Printing Office, Washington, DC 20402.

A mobile may or may not be patentable. Even if your invention is patentable, you might consider obtaining a copyright for such a visual arts product. You should write to the Registrar of Copyrights, Copyright Office, Library of Congress, Washington, DC 20559. Ask for Form PA or VA and other necessary information concerning a copyright. You will be required to fill out the proper form, send in a processing fee of $20, and provide two sets of photographs of your mobile. Such a copyright will cover only the specific form of your mobile, not the functional or operational aspects. Therefore, you might be better protected by a patent, if you can qualify for one.

You can obtain a patent by yourself or use a professional patent attorney. If you choose to try it on your own, refer to *Patent It Yourself.*[2] This is an excellent book for better understanding the whole patenting process. The next step is to undertake a novelty search to determine whether your concept or a closely related concept has already been patented. Again, you can conduct the search on your own, contact an independent informational broker listed in the Yellow Pages, or have a patent attorney perform the search. If you conduct the novelty search, go to a library that has a patent depository. But remember, patents and the patent law are complicated, and a patent professional may be in the best position to interpret your search.

Acquiring a patent is not an inexpensive project. Using a patent attorney to file a simple mechanical patent by completing the application process, preparing the necessary written documents, and submitting one sheet of drawings will cost you approximately $2000 at the low end, depending on the attorney's hourly rate, experience, and competence. The cost could increase significantly depending on the technology of your invention and whether the Patent and Trademark Office immediately allows a patent pending after your initial application. More than likely, the process will involve arguments and/or corrections and could take from 6 months to 2 years, with 18 months being average.

Because of the intricacies and detailed regulations, I advise researching the patenting process first. Remember to obtain referrals for competent patent attorneys or agents.

> ➪ **Courtney's Smart Tip**
> **Perform as much of the groundwork as possible yourself and then consult a professional patent attorney or agent.**

How to Find a Corporate Partner

QUESTION

I have what I think is a practical invention that a company like Reynolds or Alcoa Aluminum might be interested in. I've got the usual problems: no funds, no business experience, no attorney, and so on. Can you tell me how I can get one of these large companies interested in my invention?

ANSWER

First, you must decide what type of protection you need for your invention. Avoid using a loose-leaf notebook for your log book. Start a log book as soon as possible. Record in ink your ideas, notes, sketches, calculations, tests, contacts, telephone numbers, and so on. Use pages in the log book consecutively. Don't leave blank pages in between or blank spaces above your signature.

> ➪ **Courtney's Smart Tip**
> **Creating a paper trail is one of the easiest and cheapest ways to begin protecting your invention. Use a log book that has bound (not looseleaf) pages.**

Describe your invention in detail. Then date and sign the appropriate pages. Find at least one witness who will sign and date each page, stating that he or she has read and understood the contents of that page. An inventor's log book, properly maintained, can be used as documentation in the event of any legal disputes as to who made the invention first, and sometimes to predate *contemporaneous prior art.* This is a term that refers to earlier drawings or like documentation for the same subject matter.

In addition to your log book, you could file a disclosure document with a check for $10 payable to the Commissioner of Patents and Trademarks, Washington, DC 20231. Include two copies of the document and a stamped, self-addressed return envelope. This document should include a detailed description of your invention, including text and drawings. The disclosure document program maintains the record of your invention for a period of 2 years, during which time you can decide whether to apply for a patent and subsequently reference the disclosure. This program establishes only the date of conception of your invention; it is not a patent application, and provides no protection.

Next, perform a patent search to determine if your invention is novel, patentable, or already covered by another patent. You can conduct the patent search at a library that has a patent depository or hire an information broker or patent attorney. Be sure to work with local professionals.

If you are interested in patenting your invention, consult *Patent It Yourself.*[2] Perform as much of the groundwork as you can. Because of the intricacies and detailed regulations in obtaining a patent, hire a local patent attorney to assist you with the rest of the process.

If your idea is not patentable, consider continuing to maintain it as a trade secret, which can be licensed like a patent. Patents last 17 years and require disclosure of the formulas and technologies involved.

Trade secrets last as long as you can keep them a secret. They are not easy to duplicate, since the information concerning your invention has not been disclosed.

Patent rights have several advantages over trade secret rights. Patent rights may be enforced in the federal courts without the need to meet other federal court jurisdictional criteria. Patent rights protect against loss of rights to a later inventor. A patented product can be marketed without fear of loss of enforceable rights, as defined by the claims, through reverse engineering.

After you have decided how to protect your invention, begin your search for a potential manufacturing company. Go to the library and consult the *Thomas Register of American Manufacturing,*[3] which lists the name and addresses of industry manufacturers.

Also, ask for related trade journals and magazine articles. Learn as much as you can about the industry. Find information about industry conferences and trade shows. Attend one that has the most potential prospects for your invention. Talk to as many representatives of these companies as possible and make them your "friends," in order to avoid being just another anonymous person with an idea.

The Time Required to Acquire a Patent

QUESTION

I mailed a patent application to the U.S. Patent Office about 6 weeks ago and have not received a response. How long does it take, and does this mean my chances for obtaining a patent are bleak?

ANSWER

You should be receiving a filing receipt from the U.S. Patent and Trademark Office soon. It takes approximately 6 to 7 weeks from the time a patent application is mailed until a filing receipt is received. If you do not receive a filing receipt within this time, call the Patent Office Status Branch at (703) 308-7704.

The filing receipt you receive will be a one-page blue document which contains the serial number assigned to the application, the filing date, the group to which it has been assigned for processing within the Patent Office, and the amount of money received for the application at the time of filing, plus additional filing information. In addition, it will indicate whether a foreign filing license has been granted, whether the applicant is a "small" or "large" entity, the title of the application, and its preliminary classification for searching.

The back of the receipt explains the foreign filing license, indicating that the applicant either may immediately file foreign counterpart applications or must wait for 6 months from the U.S. filing date. If you plan to sell your invention outside the United States or are concerned about it being manufactured and sold abroad, it would be wise to consider filing a foreign counterpart application. Your U.S. filing will give you a priority date if you seek a foreign patent. Be aware that the foreign filing grant only allows you to file; it does not provide foreign application or foreign rights in the invention.

About 3 to 12 months after the application is filed, a patent examiner reviews the application for form, sufficiency of disclosure, and other statutory and regulatory requirements. The examiner reviews the prior art submitted by the applicant and also searches for prior art. The examiner then makes a determination of whether the claims are allowable in view of their form, and in view of the prior art.

It is common to receive an "examiner's action" rejecting some or all of the claims because the invention lacks novelty, or is obvious in view of specific prior art, or because the application or claims do not comply with some formal requirement. The examiner's action usually includes a copy of the statute or rule used in making the rejection. If an idea is rejected, a response must be filed within a time limit set by the Patent Office, usually 3 months from the mailing date of the examiner's action. If a petition is filed, response time may be automatically extended by 1, 2, or 3 months for a fee of $55, $180, or $420 respectively. Often, the rejection may be defeated or avoided by amending the claim or specification, and/or by arguing its merits.

It takes up to another 3 months to receive a second "examiner's action." If the application is rejected again, it may be a "final rejection." Then your only recourse is to place the application into form for "allowance" by complying with all of the examiner's requirements, and to cancel all claims which have not been allowed. As a practical matter, if you respond promptly with additional amendments and arguments, the examiner has the discretion to consider them and to allow the amended application. If the final rejection is unwarranted, it may be appealed within the Patent Office or, if not successful, to the federal courts. There are strict time limits for each of these steps.

When the examiner allows an application, a patent will be granted upon payment of an issuance fee and will remain in effect as long as required maintenance fees are paid and as long as the patent is not later invalidated in litigation or reexamination in the Patent Office. As of October 1, 1992, for a small entity the patent issue fee is $585, and the first 3½-year maintenance fee is $465. Fees for large entities are double these rates. Patent Office fees have increased by a total of about 92 percent since 1989.

6-4 Trademark Protection

When to Consider Obtaining a Trademark

QUESTION

I have started an employment insurance consulting company and was wondering if I should trademark my company logo. Any advice?

ANSWER

It is a good idea to trademark your company logo at the federal level, especially if you operate in other states besides your own, and if you are planning to grow your venture. Obtaining a trademark is not a costly, complicated, or lengthy process. It protects your trademark or service mark and distinguishes it from those of your competitors. It not only indicates origin but also can serve as a guarantee of quality.

Your intent to establish a mark can be shown by affixing the letters TM to a trademark or SM to a service mark. These symbols are usually smaller than the actual trademark and most often follow the mark. These marks can be registered with state or federal trademark offices. Service marks are used in the sale or marketing of services rather than products. Since your business provides a service, you would file for a service mark.

A trademark automatically acquires "common law" legal rights within the geographic area on goods, and nationally if advertised. If it is a word, it should be used as an adjective. It serves as a symbol that a business uses to identify and distinguish its products or services from others. According to U.S. law, a "common law" trademark is obtained by first use, and it is kept by continuous, proper use. Registering a mark with the U.S. Patent and Trademark Office is optional, but it enhances the odds of avoiding infringement, and provides a stronger weapon for contesting infringement. Before a trademark user may file an application for federal registration, the user should place the mark on goods that are shipped or services that are sold in interstate commerce. However, it is now possible to file an "intent to use" application if there is a bona fide interest to use the mark in the near future.

Filing for a trademark is not the same as filing for a corporate or business name. Registering a federal trademark involves completing a written application form, including a drawing of the work, and providing three specimens showing the actual use of the mark in connection with the goods or services. The filing fee is $210. Trademarks have a 10-year life and are renewable for additional 10-year periods unless abandoned. Proof of continued use and a $100 fee must be filed between the fifth and sixth years, or the federal registration will be canceled. Issuance of a U.S. registration takes about 9 to 16 months.

When applying for a federal trademark, you should perform a search to determine if another person or organization is using the same or a confusingly similar mark in the same channels of trade. If so, you probably cannot qualify for the same trademark. Determine your status before using your mark, since your marketing efforts could be hurt if you must change your mark or logo after you have been using it for some time. Names in use can be found in the *Trade Names Dictionary*,[4] the *Thomas Register of American Manufacturers*,[3] and in the Yellow Pages. There are also database searches available through most libraries with federal depositories.

Once a trademark is federally registered, the R symbol, or the words "registered in the U.S. Patent and Trademark Office," may be used. Failure to do so may prevent you from recovering damages for trademark infringement. To register a state trademark, contact your secretary of state.

Trademarks are an important marketing tool in that they help distinguish your goods from those of your competitors. Your business reputation allows you to introduce a new product or service more successfully by simply using your trademark on it. Trademarks add value to your venture as intellectual property and assist in raising capital. For example, the formula for Coca-Cola or the golden arches logo identifying McDonald's is an extremely valuable asset. You can also license the use of your trademark to others. Once you have protected it, you have the exclusive right to use it and seek protection from the courts, if someone else infringes on it.

For further information get a copy of *General Information Concerning Trademarks*, from the Superintendent of Documents, U.S. Government Printing Office, Washington, DC 20402; telephone (202) 783-3238. Or call the Trademark Office's automated telephone service at (703) 557-4656 to obtain an application or ask questions. It is also advisable to have an experienced intellectual property attorney review your search and oversee the searching and registration process.

6-5 Copyright Protection

How to Obtain a Copyright

QUESTION

I have just invented a board game called "The ABCs of State Capitals" and have obtained a copyright. Now I am looking for funding and someone, perhaps a partner, to promote and sell the game. How do I proceed?

ANSWER

Obtaining a copyright is the first step to take in marketing a board game. However, what are you copyrighting? Make certain that your copyright covers the board, the rules, the cards, and the box. This can all be accomplished in one application. If you have forgotten to include any of these items, file a second application with another $20 application fee to the Registrar of Copyrights in the Library of Congress.

Once you have properly protected your idea, you have accomplished 5 percent of the work necessary to take a board game to the marketplace. You have only 95 percent of the additional work left and are entering the entrepreneurial stage. In order to secure funding and a possible partner, you must write a business plan to determine whether your idea is feasible. The business plan will reveal whether there is a market for "The ABCs of State Capitals." Investors will not give you capital if you cannot prove to them that there is a sufficient market for your game to yield a handsome profit.

Who are you going to target as your customers? What is your customer profile? How large is the market? Have you tested the game out with potential customers? Have you acquired any orders? What approach will you use for selling the game? What benefits does your game provide to customers? Is there any direct competition? How is your game board superior or unique to that of the competition? These and similar questions must be answered in order for you to prove your market and secure financing.

How much money will you need to undertake the venture and how much money will be generated? What are potential sales the first year and for the next 4 years? When will you reach the cash breakeven point? When will investors recoup their investment and what type of return will be generated? What is the risk versus potential return on investment?

Lastly, what type of management is in place to achieve the goals you have set? What is your expertise in bringing this game to market and managing the business? Who else do you have on your management team?

All these questions should be answered in your business plan. Few investors or potential partners will talk with you until you can show them your plan, prove your market, determine how much money you will need, and project when you will become profitable. If you have not yet written a business plan, consult a book such as *Program for Writing Winning Business Plans,*[5] or take a course specially designed to teach you how to write one.

What Copyrighting Protects

QUESTION

I recently found a game on the market called "The ABC's of State Capitals." I have a copyrighted game that I am selling named "The ABCs of States and Capitals." How can someone else copyright the name of my game when I have prior copyright? Is this fair?

ANSWER

Your copyright does not cover the name of your game. It covers the elements of the game itself such as the box, the rules, and the board. If you wanted to protect the name of your game, you should have trademarked it.

Copyrights protect authors of literary works such as art, books, music, motion pictures, videotapes, photographs, articles, software programs, games, and magazines. Registration is a low-cost procedure administered by the U.S. Copyright Office. According to copyright law, a literary work is automatically protected from the time of its creation, but it is best to include a copyright notice on the material.

Keep in mind that a copyright does not protect ideas. It simply gives you the right to prevent others from copying the particular way in which you express your ideas. If you want to protect your ideas, restrict access by making them trade secrets, to be disclosed only under the terms of a written confidential disclosure agreement.

To be protected by copyright, your work must satisfy three requirements. First, it must be original; second, it must be incorporated in something tangible; third, it must fall within one or more of the categories of works provided for in the Copyright Act. Use the copyright symbol, which can be ©, the word "copyright," or the abbreviation "copyr." Also include the year in which the material was first distributed publicly and the copyright owner's name or an abbreviation by which the owner's name can be recognized. You are not required to use a copyright notice on your materials, but it is desirable to do so for protection. Also include a warning statement like "All rights reserved" (which also provides protection in South America) or "No part of this material may be reproduced without permission." Place the notice on your material where it can be seen by an ordinary user under normal conditions (e.g., on the title page).

It is also advisable to officially register your copyright by filing the proper form, which can be obtained from the Registrar of Copyrights, Library of Congress, Washington, DC 20559. The cost is $20 and you can do it yourself quite easily.

It takes about 3 to 4 months to have your application processed before you receive a certification of registration. A copyright is good for 50 years after the death of the author. If you need additional information call the U.S. Copyright Office hotline at (202) 287-9100. Another excellent resource is *The Complete Copyright Protection Kit,*[6] which contains up-to-date information on how to register, transfer, and legally enforce a copyright and how to avoid violating rights if you use someone else's material. The kit costs $25 and also includes various copyright forms.

A trademark is different from a copyright or a patent. A copyright gives protection for an artistic or a literary work, while a patent gives protection for an invention. By contrast, a trademark is a word, name, phrase, device, or symbol used by a business to identify its products, services, or organization. To protect the name of an educational game, you must trademark it.

6-6 Licensing Inventions

How to License a Product to Raise Capital

QUESTION

I have an invention that I would like to sell to a manufacturing company. How do I protect my idea when contacting potential companies about my new invention? How can I obtain a licensing agreement?

ANSWER

Sometimes trying to protect your invention before you have applied for a patent can be tricky, and may be impossible. Many inventors send a confidential disclosure agreement to a potential licensee thinking that a signed form will protect their idea. A confidential disclosure agreement, in its simplest form, is merely a contract by which the recipient of the information agrees to keep an idea or invention a secret and not to use it.

However, companies will rarely sign these agreements unless you have already established a relationship with them. Instead, most send back another agreement for you to sign stating that the information which you have provided is not confidential. They are under no obligation to protect your idea, and can use it unless it has been protected by a valid patent, trademark, or copyright. Do not sign such an agreement, except as a very last resort, unless you have an allowed patent pending or issued patent. In the absence of a confidential agreement or a patent, you have no property rights to license. Once you have disclosed your idea or invention without a confidential agreement, anyone who has previously promised to keep it a secret may be released of that duty.

If you have an invention that is innovative and has valuable technology, try to negotiate a patent license agreement. Licensing is an excellent strategy for an inventor to generate revenues, without much risk, while avoiding costly start-up investments. Licensing gives rights to an entity to make, use, and sell the innovation in return for cash royalties.

Manufacturing companies may sign a licensing agreement with an inventor who has a proven track record and business experience. If you do not have these qualifications, refrain from sending a blind letter on your invention without first establishing a relationship or contact with a potential manufacturer. Once a relationship is established, send a confidential disclosure agreement. Send such letters simultaneously to a list of potentially interested manufacturers. This strategy saves you months of waiting for a possible disappointing response before writing to the next potential licensee.

Keep in mind that negotiating a licensing agreement is a complicated procedure. Seldom does the technology transfer take place in a lump-sum payment. Instead, you will probably have a continuing relationship with your licensee. Such an agreement must be carefully worded and should involve a patent or technology transfer attorney to ensure protection and fairness for both parties. Consult local experts or find a reputable licensing expert or broker who works only on a contingency basis and receives payment from a percentage of the deal. They may charge a finder's fee or take an on-going share of your royalties.

> ➪ **Courtney's Smart Tip**
> **Avoid invention marketing companies that charge large, up-front evaluation fees, prepare a report touting the invention, and then make minimal efforts to commercialize it.**

A good place to start looking for a licensee is within your industry. The *Thomas Register of American Manufacturers*[3] is an excellent source for names; your local chamber of commerce and business support centers can also provide leads. Sometimes local venture capitalists or bankers will know of potential licensees.

How to Negotiate a Licensing Agreement

QUESTION

Several years ago I started a company to develop sports-related products. I took different ideas, productionized the design, designed and built the prototype or production tooling. I am seeking companies or people to license my products. My problem is locating companies or people interested in entering into a license agreement. How can I find potential licensees?

ANSWER

You are right on track. The first step in licensing is finding a company or person interested in your product idea. The best place to begin is at your local library. Look through the *Thomas Register of American Manufacturers*[3] for potential names of companies in your industry.

This resource book lists industry manufacturer names, addresses and thousands of different businesses. Also look at Dun & Bradstreet's *Reference Book of Corporate Management*,[7] which gives detailed biographical descriptions of many leading companies and their principal officers. All communications with a potential licensee should be directed at top management.

Next, go to the store aisles where your competitors' products are displayed. Most packages give the name and location of a producer. Make a list of these competing companies. They may be interested in expanding their product lines and are a good source for a potential license.

Try to find out as much about licensing arrangements as possible. Organizations which deal with licensing issues include the Licensing Industry Merchandisers Association, the National Association of Small Business Investment Companies, and the National Venture Capital Association. Your local chamber of commerce, small business development centers, venture capitalists, and banks can also assist with licensing leads.

After you have located businesses in your industry that might be interested in a license agreement, you must determine what you want from such an agreement. Will you ask for any up-front money to pay for out-of-pocket expenses for developing, prototyping, patenting, or other associated costs? Success in negotiating for up-front money will depend largely upon how badly the company wants your idea.

How large a royalty percentage will you ask for? Five percent is generally a good starting point. A fair royalty should give you from about one-quarter to about one-third of the actual profits. What type of exclusivity will you be willing to negotiate for? Be cautious about giving away your exclusivity rights. Consider using exclusivity rights as a bargaining wedge. In most cases, if you can find one licensee, you will probably be able to find more.

How much do you want to be personally involved in marketing the product or overseeing its production? Should you consider hiring a lawyer to represent you during negotiations? If the potential licensing agreement is complicated, it is wise to have legal counsel represent you.

After you have answered these questions and researched licensing arrangements, begin writing query letters to potential licensees. Incorporate information on the demand for your product, including any marketing research and/or testing results. Identify potential purchasers. Describe the applications and alternatives for the product. List any proprietary rights such as potential or existing patents, trademarks, or copyrights. Explain your qualifications and business background.

Most important, demonstrate how the licensee will benefit from your product. Writing query letters can take considerable time and you will probably receive your share of "we're not interested" letters. Don't get too excited about receiving a letter of interest. Often, the first interested party will not be your last. Avoid making a hasty decision in signing a contract. A sound licensing agreement will benefit both you and the licensee.

6-7 Trade Secrets

How to Keep a Recipe a Trade Secret

QUESTION

I have created a new dog biscuit recipe which has a unique shape, name, ingredients, and appearance. I need to protect my idea before marketing the product and selling it to a major manufacturer in the pet food industry. I have read some books on patents, copyrights, and trademarks, but remain confused. Which one of these will protect the recipe, shape of the biscuit, and the name? I also understand that I cannot get a patent unless I have marketed my product for a time. How do I protect my idea until it gets registered?

ANSWER

Protecting an entrepreneur's intellectual property can be tricky and complicated. That is why many entrepreneurs seek legal counsel from a patent attorney. You can do much of the legwork yourself and save considerable money.

You could copyright your recipe by contacting the Registrar of Copyrights, U.S. Copyright Office, Library of Congress, Washington, DC 20559 and sending in an application with a $20 filing fee. However, copyrighting your recipe will not give you much protection, and will make it available to anyone who wants to research the archives. A competitor could change a few minor ingredients, and you probably would not have any recourse against this tactic.

A better approach would be to make your dog biscuit recipe a trade secret. You'll need to exercise a great deal of control to keep your recipe a trade secret and ensure that only a select few have access to it. Take every precaution to keep the recipe a secret. If possible, do not reveal the entire recipe to one person so that no one except you knows all the ingredients.

There are no filing fees or legal expenses for establishing a trade secret. The law recognizes your trade secret as your intellectual property and protects it as such. You must document that you have made the recipe a trade secret, and keep the formula in a safe place. If you allow the recipe to lie around unprotected, the court is apt to tell you that you must not consider the information to be of much value. You must be able to show the efforts you have made to protect your recipe. Use a confidential disclosure agreement which allows you to reveal your ideas in confidence without fear of losing your trade secret status. Then, place specific provisions in employees' agreements so that they will neither disclose to others nor use for their own purposes any trade secrets they acquire while working for you.

> ➪ **Courtney's Smart Tip**
> **Protect a trade secret by stamping all relevant information "confidential."**

If the shape of the dog biscuit is unique, you might be able to obtain a design patent on it from the U.S. Department of Commerce, Patent and Trademark Office, Washington, DC 20231. The Government Printing Office, Washington, DC 20402, publishes *General Information Concerning Patents* for $2. Or consult *Patent It Yourself,*[2] an excellent resource book.

It will be necessary to conduct a patent search. You can conduct the search yourself if your local library has a patent depository for the U.S. Patent and Trademark Office. Or you could contact a professional patent search firm or patent agent, or have a patent attorney perform the search. Lay as much of the groundwork as you can, and then work with a patent attorney to develop a specific business strategy. To protect your dog biscuit while marketing it, you can use the words "patent pending" on the box once your patent application is on file. This provides a warning until you receive a patent.

Lastly, if the name for your dog biscuit is truly distinctive, you can trademark it. Federal registration is not needed in order for a trademark to be protected. However, it is advisable to obtain one by contacting the U.S. Patent and Trademark Office cited above. Include the trademark symbol TM or SM (if the mark identifies a service) to indicate your claim of ownership, even if no federal trademark application is pending.

Remember, protecting your intellectual property is only 5 percent of the work necessary to take your dog biscuit to market. But it is an essential ingredient to launching a successful dog biscuit business.

Use Trade Secrets to Protect Your Invention

QUESTION

I have been operating a tax consulting firm for the past 3 years. Recently one of my employees started his own tax consulting business. I am afraid he will try to take many of my valuable customers with him. Is there anything I can do to stop this from happening?

ANSWER

Customers and customer lists can be treated and protected like trade secrets if they are of significant value to your business. Trade secrets include customer lists, techniques, designs, materials, processes, and formulas.

Employees come and go, and can become competitors as well as attract other employees to competing firms. Some businesses are plagued with the problem of sales "reps" or other marketing people who form new firms by taking favored customers with them.

In general, the law states that an entrepreneur has the right to employ his or her skills and knowledge to earn a living, but the proprietor also has the right to protect the venture's property. Former employees cannot violate the law to cheat the employer by starting a competing business. Misuse of a position of advantage includes divulging trade secrets, soliciting former employers' customer lists, pirating an invention, and breaking noncompete agreements.

Trade secrets last as long as you can keep them secret. The most famous example is the registered formula for Coca-Cola, which is locked away in a high-security vault. Trade secrets can be licensed the same way as patents. Three conditions must be met to have a trade secret: (1) the trade secret must have economic value, (2) it must be kept secret, and (3) the owner must attempt to protect it.

An exit interview is an excellent time to remind departing employees of their obligation of confidentiality. Give them a copy of the confidential information agreement which they signed to remind them of their duties and protect your customer lists.

The legal aspects of the employer-employee responsibilities regarding proprietary rights can be very intricate. Consider contacting a lawyer who specializes in these types of issues.

Treat Your Customer Lists as Trade Secrets

QUESTION

Two of my employees recently quit and went to work for one of my competitors. Now I have begun to lose old customers and find that this competitor has changed its pricing structure to pattern mine. What can I do to protect my pricing policies and customer lists?

ANSWER

It is very likely that your former employees have used pricing and customer information to compete with you. If you have never made this information a trade secret, advised them it was a secret, and had your employees sign a confidential information agreement, then you probably don't have much recourse. Employees who leave your company can easily use such information in their new jobs. Or they could venture out on their own and start a competing company. To avoid this problem in the future, consider designing a comprehensive trade secret protection program for your company.

Trade secrets are any proprietary information used in the course of business to gain an advantage in manufacture or commercialization of products or services. They can be formulas, devices, patterns, techniques, customer lists, sales forecasts, databases, manufacturing processes, or compiled information that has a specific business application. They must have economic value; they must be secret; and you must attempt to protect them. The most significant factors in determining whether your confidential information receives legal protection are (1) the degree to which you take steps to protect the information and (2) the ease of obtaining the information from other sources.

Trade secrets are not covered by any federal statute but are recognized under a governing body of federal and state common laws. To be classified as a trade secret, the information must not be generally known in the trade. Famous trade secrets include the recipe for Kentucky Fried Chicken and the formula for Coca-Cola.

In order to keep customer and price lists a trade secret, you must keep the information secret and take precautions to keep it secret. First, establish policies on identifying and maintaining trade secret information. Second, require employees to sign a confidential disclosure agreement that protects against their giving out trade secrets either while they are employed or after they leave the company. Lastly, mark these documents "confidential" or "secret." Then employees or others coming into contact with the information will immediately be put on notice of its confidential nature and the need to take precautions to avoid disclosure.

Confidential documents should be locked in a vault or other secure location. Trade secret information stored on or accessible by computer must be protected from disclosure to unauthorized parties. Build passwords into your computer system to prevent unauthorized access.

Dispose of trade secrets documents carefully. Don't just throw them in the trash with other nonsensitive material. Consider purchasing a shredding machine. Also, monitor and limit the duplication of these documents. Use the exit interview to remind departing employees of their confidentiality obligation.

Understanding the details and following these steps are the keys to effectively protecting confidential information. You must be able to demonstrate that you have taken every precaution to maintain such information as a secret or you could lose legal protection. Also, any visiting sales representatives, vendors, customers, inspectors or others needing access to such information must be informed of its secrecy and sign a confidential disclosure agreement. One overlooked way trade secrets are lost is through conventions, trades shows, seminars, casual conversations, or similar activities.

Consult *The Complete Guide to Business Agreements*,[8] the *Entrepreneur's Resource Handbook*,[1] or other business form books that contain confidential disclosure agreements. Revise the sample form to fit your situation and then have your attorney review it before implementation. The form should indicate that you consider this information a vital part of your business. These agreements may allow you to stop any signee from using the information. Laws vary from state to state, so check with an intellectual property attorney.

Lastly, trade secrets can be sold or licensed and used as a financial strategy for increasing revenues. In today's competitive environment, your continued success may well depend on your ability to protect your valuable trade secrets. Continuous, systematic, and diligent monitoring is essential.

6-8 Invention Marketing

Beware of Invention Marketing Companies

QUESTION

I came up with an invention that I submitted to a company back East. The company liked it and asked me whether I wanted additional research. I agreed for "X" amount of dollars. The research study, 26 pages long, contained only glowing reports. Now, the company wants to sell my invention and is asking for an additional $5000. However, I am unable to come up with the money. Securing a loan from any financial institution is doubtful. What do you suggest I do?

ANSWER

There are many out-of-state companies, most located in the Northeast, that work with inventors to help them introduce new products to the marketplace. Beware of such companies, and think twice before sending them any money. The problem is that most of these organizations are great on promises but short on delivery. Here's how they operate.

First, these companies advertise to inventors for researching new products to determine potential sales in the marketplace. These initial reports, like the one you received, always paint a rosy picture of potential success. For the most part, they contain demographic information about potential customers, size of the market, and examples of similar successful products, including yearly sales volume. The summary highlights the great potential of your invention and the hundreds of thousands of dollars you could earn.

The charge for a first report ranges from $500 to $800. Unfortunately, the lengthy report you just paid for contains information you could have obtained yourself. The "boilerplate" language in such studies allows companies to produce them quickly with little research. These types of reports are always attractively and professionally packaged.

The next step is to entice you to go for the big plunge and pay between $2000 and $8000 for an in-depth marketing and sales plan to bring your invention to the marketplace. The second report is filled with promises of potential success and forecasts of earning much money. However, few of these companies ever deliver on their promises. Instead, they sell you encouragement and potential that are seldom realized.

> ➪ **Courtney's Smart Tip**
> **To determine whether an invention marketing company is legitimate, ask one of its representatives for at least three references from other inventors in your state whom the company has represented. Contact those sources.**

Talk with other inventors who used a particular marketing company to ascertain what kinds of services were provided. Was the inventor satisfied? Was the invention brought successfully to the marketplace? How much money did it cost? Is the return on investment worthwhile?

Invention marketing companies often say they cannot give out names of past clients because of the confidentiality issues surrounding inventions. But ask yourself how such companies can successfully market a product if it is confidential. If the invention has been patented, confidentiality is not relevant. Any company that refuses to give you references in your state has a poor track record. Checking your local better business bureau is not likely to reveal any meaningful information. The majority of other customers are out of state and seldom send reports of dissatisfaction to the better business bureau. Consequently, the company probably shows a clean record.

There are a few legitimate companies that *do* deliver, but they operate very differently. They provide the up-front money to bring your invention to market. They negotiate with inventors and pay a royalty for products. Usually, they do not invest in unproven inventions or unproven inventors. They are very selective in investing in new inventions. Get references and investigate the company before you invest any more money.

Research Invention Marketing Companies

QUESTION

How can I find legitimate invention marketing companies for my new invention?

ANSWER

The invention business is rapidly expanding, with the number of patents alone increasing 40 percent between 1985 and 1990. The problem is that most inventors do not know how to market their products, so they turn to invention marketing companies to do the work for them.

Unfortunately, the invention industry is saturated with fraudulent invention marketing companies that charge high up-front fees for initial research reports and subsequent marketing and sales plans that forecast great potential for the invention and stress the hundreds of thousands dollars that the inventor could earn.

Many of these companies are being investigated by the Federal Trade Commission. According to *The Wall Street Journal,* less than 1 percent of customers ever get a penny from their inventions, despite the fees of up to $10,000 that inventors pay to invention marketing firms.

James Peters, chief deputy district attorney for Arapahoe County, Colorado, shares the following tips for considering whether to contract with an invention marketing company:

- Obtain a list of satisfied clients.

- Make a reference check to determine whether clients' ideas have been successfully marketed.
- Ask where successful products are being sold, and if possible visit the outlets.
- Try to estimate sales volume.

If you are looking for an invention marketing company that can take your invention from the idea stage to the marketing stage, you need to learn whether the firm has had this type of experience and its success rate. Many companies make grandiose claims, but in reality have marketed only finished products.

Therefore, ask for a list of products that the company has taken from the idea stage to the marketing stage. Obtain the names of the inventors. Contact them to determine whether the invention marketing company took their idea all the way to marketing or whether their product was already completed when the invention company took over. Try to ascertain if the marketing efforts of the invention marketing firm were successful. Inquire how much money the inventors earned from their ideas.

Request the names and locations of the manufacturers producing the inventions for the company both in the past and currently. Also ask for the names and locations of distributors involved in marketing the inventions the firm handles. Try to discover how successfully these inventions have been marketed and sold. Unfortunately, few inventions make it to the marketplace, and those that do experience limited success. Invention marketing companies usually make overly optimistic claims, forecasting that the inventor will get rich quick.

Look for a pattern with invention marketing companies of accepting practically all ideas and rejecting only those whose inventors did not come up with requested money to produce the research and marketing reports. Obtain a list of ideas and corresponding names and addresses of those inventors whose ideas were rejected. Ask why. Then verify this information with those who have been rejected.

Verify all claims that the invention marketing company has made to you. Perform as much "due diligence" as possible. It will cost you time and a few dollars, but the effort will be well worth it in the long run. Remember, few if any invention marketing firms ever carry out their claims. They make great promises, but are short on delivery.

Look Out for Empty Promises

QUESTION

Should I contract with an invention marketing company to market my new invention?

ANSWER

Be wary of invention marketing companies. Many invention marketing firms form subsidiary companies to supposedly manufacture and distribute inventions. Be sure to inquire whether the manufacturer and/or distributor that the company uses is an independent company or a subsidiary of the firm.

If the invention marketing company claims to be experienced in obtaining patents for inventions, determine the specific type of patent search that will be done. Try to ascertain whether the firm has obtained any patents. What is its past history? Request the names and addresses of clients, including the type of idea patented. Then verify this information with the inventors. Find out how satisfied they were with the patent work.

In addition, ask for the name, educational history (degree and school), and professional background of the person(s) performing various research and marketing studies for the company. You can then contact the school and/or professional society to verify this information. For example, if an engineer is involved, you can contact one of the engineering societies, since all engineers are registered. If a patent attorney is involved, you can contact the American Bar Association and the U.S. Patent Office. It is important to determine if the people working for the invention marketing firm are qualified to perform the work they claim will be performed.

Numerous invention marketing firms claim they attend and exhibit at trade shows to promote and market an invention. Obtain a list of the trade shows they have attended in the past. Then determine whether they have just attended or *exhibited* at these trade shows. Anyone can purchase a ticket and walk around a trade show. Exhibiting and marketing products is another matter involving considerable time, effort, and money. This information can be verified with the trade show association. You can secure a contact number for any trade show through the Trade Show Bureau, whose national headquarters is in Denver, Colorado, at (303) 860-7626.

Also, ask for a list of products and clients for which manufacturers or distributors were obtained at these trade shows. You want to ensure that the firm has had a successful history at marketing new inventions at trade shows. Again, verify this information with the manufacturers and distributors.

If the invention marketing company asks you to sign a contract, inquire as to whether the company provides a refund if you are dissatisfied with its services. Ask about the circumstances under which clients are eligible for refunds. Then request a list of clients who have obtained refunds in the past. Check to ensure that any referred clients are not employees of the company. You can then verify the circumstances and decide if this is a contract you would feel comfortable signing.

Look critically at what services the invention marketing company provides to determine if they are worth the fee being quoted to market your product. Evaluate the company's history of successfully marketing other inventions.

Lastly, check with the better business bureau in your area, the consumer fraud division of your local district attorney's office, the attorney general's office, and the consumer advocate in the local media for any complaints on these types of companies.

This sounds like a lot of research, but it's worth every minute you spend. Like many inventors, you may find that the invention marketing firm turns down your idea because you ask these questions. However, most of these firms have poor track records and cannot, or will not, provide answers to your questions. Don't accept the excuse that this is confidential information. A reputable company would have no problem answering your questions. After your investigation, you may find it is better to learn how to market your own invention.

6-9 Pitfalls to Avoid

1. Thinking that a U.S. patentability search can, by itself, be relied upon as an indication that the invention will not infringe another person's current patent.
2. Disclosing your invention to others without first having a signed confidential disclosure agreement or having filed for a patent.
3. Contracting with an invention marketing company that charges a large up-front fee, makes minimal efforts to commercialize an idea, and will not identify any "satisfied clients."
4. Hiring an inexperienced attorney to assist you with protecting your ideas, materials, inventions, and the like, instead of using an intellectual property attorney.
5. Not checking for the availability of your company mark or logo before using it, and not including it on all your marketing materials.
6. Sending a blind letter to an unknown person as a potential licensee, with a request to sign a confidential disclosure agreement.

The Good News. Protecting intellectual property is not difficult, but it does take time. It can become a great asset to your business if it is done properly. Always consult an expert intellectual property attorney to ensure that you are properly protected.

6-10 Entrepreneurial Resource Checklist

References

1. Courtney Price, Richard Buskirk, and Mack Davis, *Entrepreneur's Resource Handbook*, 2d ed., Premier Entrepreneur Programs, 1992.
2. David Pressman, *Patent It Yourself*, Nolo Press, Berkeley, Calif., 1988.
3. *Thomas Register of American Manufacturers.* Lists who manufactures what products and where manufacturer is located. Available in most libraries.
4. *Trade Names Dictionary* and *International Trade Names Dictionary*, Gale Research Inc., Detroit, Mich.
5. Richard Buskirk, Courtney Price, and Mack Davis, *Program for Writing Winning Business Plans*, 2d ed., Premier Entrepreneur Programs, 1992.
6. Intellaw, Inc., *The Complete Copyright Protection Kit: Information and Legal Forms You Need to Protect What You Create*, Denver, 1992.
7. Dun & Bradstreet, *Reference Book of Corporate Management: American Corporate Leaders*, Information Services Staff, New York, 1993.
8. Nicholas, *The Complete Guide to Business Agreements*, Enterprise/Dearborn, Chicago, 1992.

Further Reading

Books

Door, Robert D., and Christopher H. Munch. *Protecting Trade Secrets, Patents, Copyrights, and Trademarks*, Wiley, 1990.

Pamphlets

General Information Concerning Patents, U.S. Government Printing Office, Washington, DC 20402, (202) 783-3238.

Basic Facts About Trademarks, Patent and Copyright Office, Washington, DC 20231, (703) 557-3158.

Contacts

1. Better Business Bureau

   Contact your local better business bureau's consumer fraud division to determine if the invention marketing company has been involved in any cases of fraud.

2. Registrar of Copyrights
   Copyright Office
   Library of Congress
   Washington, DC 20559

Contact this agency to register copyrights. Or call the Copyright Office hotline at (202) 287-9100.

3. Patent and Trademark Office
   Washington, DC 20231

   Contact this agency to find out information about patents and trademarks and to register them, or call the Patent Office Status Branch hotline at (703) 308-7704 to check on the status of your patent application.

4. Licensing Industry Merchandisers' Association

   This organization provides information about licensing agreements and licensing issues.

5. Rocky Mountain Inventors and Entrepreneurs Congress
   P.O. Box 4365
   Denver, CO 80204
   (303) 433-6200

   This association of inventors, innovators, and entrepreneurs provides information and education to its members in the Rocky Mountain region on organizing, developing, protecting, and/or producing and commercializing their ideas.

6. National Association of Small Business Investment Companies (NASBIC)
   1156 15th St., NW, #1101
   Washington, DC 20005
   (202) 833-8230

   Firms licensed as small business investment companies (SBICs) under the Small Business Investment Act.

7. National Venture Capital Association
   1655 N. Fort Myer Dr., Suite 700
   Arlington, VA 22209
   (202) 528-4370

   The NVCA publishes an up-to-date directory of its members. It will send out a copy of its directory of 200 members when requested in writing to the above address.

8. National Technical Information Service Center
   Center for the Utilization of Federal Technology
   U.S. Department of Commerce
   P.O. Box 1423
   Springfield, VA 22151
   (707) 487-4838

   This agency provides support for negotiating licenses to commercialize inventions at various federal laboratories and government agencies.

9. NASA Tech Briefs
   Associated Business Publications, Inc.
   41 E. 42nd Street
   New York, NY 10017
   (212) 490-3999

   This organization publishes information about NASA's inventions available for licensing.

10. Wisconsin Innovation Service Center
    Program Manager
    402 McCutcham Hall
    University of Wisconsin
    Whitewater, WI 53190
    (414) 472-1365

    This organization will provide a comprehensive and confidential evaluation report of your idea for an invention that includes legality, safety, environmental impact, profitability, and competition for about $150.

7 Venture Marketing Strategies

7-1 Overview

Marketing is one of the most difficult tasks for entrepreneurs who must get it right the first time, since most are poor. Marketing mistakes are made because entrepreneurs do not thoroughly research their marketplace and customers to discover the best techniques to market their products or services. They do not appreciate the difficulties faced in penetrating target markets and gravely underestimate market penetration costs. If any market research data is collected, it is mostly demographic information which is a good start, but only one input. Smart marketing techniques require that you go beyond just knowing your potential customers to understanding common lifestyle characteristics that they share. Today, astute entrepreneurs recognize the importance of seeing the world through their customers' eyes.

Many marketing dollars are spent foolishly. Most new founders think that printing a business card and sending out brochures will bring in customers. Because entrepreneurs fall in love with their products and services, they think people will beat a path to their doorway—that having a better product or service will bring in the customers. It seldom happens. Instead, people are usually indifferent to the venture.

Smart marketing tools include obtaining free publicity, attending and working trade shows, using focus groups and mystery shoppers, expanding customer base with existing customers, asking for customer referrals, scheduling follow-up contacts after mailing out marketing materials, using business cards as mini-billboards, buying preemptible television time, developing telemarketing techniques, and using sales reps. Each of these smart marketing tools is described in this chapter.

In today's tough and ever-competitive marketplace, you must be more creative than your competition. You must be intimately familiar not only with your marketplace but also with your market area, current events, and consumer trends. You must use your talents, imagination, and energy to develop affordable but effective marketing techniques that increase your sales and maximize your profits.

7-2 Smart Marketing Strategies

1. Become familiar with computer databases to collect industry information about your market.
2. Learn as much as you can about your competitors including their strengths and weaknesses.
3. Turn to the Yellow Pages to identify your competitors.
4. Use focus groups to gain customer insight and develop innovative marketing techniques.
5. Use mystery shoppers in your store to evaluate your sales staff.
6. Develop an index-card profile on each of your customers, noting demographic information and purchasing habits.
7. Ask for referrals from your customers to develop new sales leads and then send a thank-you note for every referral.
8. Ask customers for testimonial letters to use in your marketing materials.
9. Build your own mailing list.
10. Use phantom sales to test the market with a new product or service.
11. Stay in close contact with your customers by utilizing memorandums, newsletters, and special sales postcards.
12. Quantify your marketing goals whenever possible.

13. Make your marketing goals specific, measurable, and time-bound.
14. Target your market segments and then develop different marketing strategies for penetrating each of them.
15. If you are a new start-up with limited marketing dollars, concentrate on obtaining free publicity through feature stories.
16. When purchasing TV advertising, consider buying preemptible time whenever possible.
17. Use your business cards as a marketing tool by making them memorable and highlighting the unique features of your business.
18. When purchasing a 900 number, shop around for legitimate telephone service bureaus and compare setup and equipment charges.
19. Consider buying an 800 number when 20 percent of your revenue comes from customers outside your local area.
20. If you are a retailer, consider accepting consignment merchandise that fits your inventory.
21. Try to avoid selling on consignment unless it is the only way to get your product or service to market.
22. Use experienced and reputable sales reps to market your product or service.

7-3 Marketing Research

Gathering Information About Competitors

QUESTION

A couple of years ago, I started a monogram shop in a shopping mall. I have found myself struggling to generate profits and expand my market. How can I investigate my competitors and learn more about competing more effectively with them?

ANSWER

Learning as much as you can about your competition is an excellent entrepreneurial strategy and a marketing must. Ideally, you should obtain this information before you open and while you are writing your business plan. Some entrepreneurs work for their competition before starting a new business. They try to learn all the "ins and outs" of the business ahead of time.

One of the best strategies to learn more about your competition is to locate a "competitor at a distance." Often, your direct competitors will not divulge much information about their operation. You will be more likely to obtain significant industry and competitive information from a business outside your geographic area. Try to find several competitors in other states who operate the same type of business in a similar demographic area.

For example, contact your industry trade association and inquire about the industry leaders with a comparable business in another part of the country. Call or go visit those entrepreneurs. Because they will not view you as a direct competitor, they are likely to share a wealth of information with you.

Go to your library and access an information database that contains an industry periodical and journal index. Work with the business librarian to properly search this datasource. Look through INFOTRAC, a database that lists published articles providing both industry and competitive information.

Work with the librarian to obtain financial information and statements from your competitors in Dun & Bradstreet's Corporate Reports and Standard & Poor's Profiles. Also look for the book *Contacts Influential*,[1] which lists company information by state.

Go to city hall to see if any financing statements have been filed pledging collateral. Or check with the secretary of state to see if any liens have been placed on collateral. Publicly held companies publish annual and interim reports with various government bodies. The New York Stock Exchange listing of applications and the Securities and Exchange Commission's 10K and 10Q forms include offering circulars for new security issues. Some include an annual statement of condition about the corporation.

For privately held companies, talk to potential suppliers. Try to determine what services they might provide by asking for examples of similar work. What volume can they handle? Ask for references to see how your competition operates. Talk to dealers, reps, and distributors. Find out what they think about competing firms. Sometimes these people enjoy talking about the problems and concerns they have. For example, what types of problems have they encountered with late deliveries?

Find former employees who have worked for your competitors. Ask them about problems at those businesses. Do comparison shopping. Analyze your competitors' way of doing business. The more information you obtain, the better prepared you will be to plan your marketing strategy and to launch your new business.

Another strategy is to seek out and contact your competitors' customers. Try to determine what they like about the business and what aspects they are dissatisfied with. If possible, conduct a telephone survey or attend a meeting where competitors' customers will be present. Attend a local or national trade association meeting or convention where you will find a variety of competitors and suppliers. Introduce yourself, ask questions, and listen. Finally, ask your banker, accountant, or attorney for information about your competition or your industry.

> ➪ **Courtney's Smart Tip**
> **Become a detective and learn as much as you can about your competition to differentiate your product and/or service.**

Once you launch your venture, continue accumulating competitive information. Projecting market trends and determining your competitors' strengths and weaknesses is an ongoing activity that can give you a significant edge in the marketplace.

Using Trade Associations

QUESTION

I am planning to open a gourmet chocolate store. I have started to write my business plan, and I am searching for marketing information about my competitors and demographic data on potential customers. What available sources of information are there? Where should I begin?

ANSWER

There are many different types of organizations and publications to contact to obtain market statistics and demographic information. The U.S. Department of Commerce covers all 50 states and has 47 offices throughout the country. It has tons of data at its disposal, both published and unpublished. Typically, it can provide information by industry, size, and geographic location. Specify whether you are looking for local, domestic, or international data so your call can be directed to the appropriate agency. There may be no charge, or they may charge a nominal fee, depending on the complexity of your request.

Trade associations are also an excellent source for obtaining industry-specific information for marketing statistics and financial data.

They provide information on gross industry sales, broken down further into major product categories. In addition, trade associations furnish industry guidelines that can assist you in tracking your business.

Much of the information is reported in percentages, which makes it even more helpful to compare your performance to similar businesses. The percentages are broken down by size of business, sales volume, and geographic area. For example, you can find data on average inventory turn for your type of business, typical gross and net margins for comparable ventures, and average sales and marketing expenditures.

The key is to find the appropriate association for your business. Go to your local library and examine Volume 1 of the *Encyclopedia of Associations.*[2] It contains detailed information on various trade associations, including their addresses, telephone number, membership information, and the like.

Write to or call the major trade association(s) relevant to your venture. Ask them what type of data they publish. Inquire as to whether there will be a charge. If you can befriend someone on the association staff, you may be able to obtain meaningful industry information they do not publish. Trade associations are membership based and usually get very excited about new businesses joining their industry. They will try hard to convince you to join up so they can collect a membership fee, which pays for their overhead and operating costs.

Joining appropriate trade associations is money well spent. They have membership lists of like businesses, and publish trade journals that contain excellent information on current trends, market surveys, and forecasts in your industry. Such trade journals are a good source to obtain free publicity for your business. Editors write feature stories about entrepreneurs, new products and/or services, and other human interest stories.

Try to get to know the trade magazine editors who might write about your venture or provide a wealth of additional internal information about the industry. Read the advertisements in trade journals for valuable information about competitors and their products.

Attend the national and regional meetings of trade associations to obtain other types of industry statistics. You can identify major competitors, discover leaders in the industry, meet suppliers and distributors, and learn about the future directions of your industry. You can also talk to experts in your field. Attending some technical sessions will reveal information about future products and new technology. All this information can be yours for the price of a ticket to the annual meeting. Many associations hold trade shows in conjunction with the annual meeting.

Using the Library to Locate Market Research

QUESTION

I am thinking about starting a dry cleaning business in a new shopping center close to my house. But I do not know if there are enough people living in my area to support this business. What kind of information do I need to determine if there is a big enough market for this business and where can I find it?

ANSWER

To begin with, you need specific information about the dry-cleaning market in your geographic area. How many people are living in your market area? Look at how many customers there are per dry-cleaning store in your geographic area and in your county. It is also important to know how much money dry-cleaning customers are spending in your area and how much they are spending in surrounding locations.

Next, you need to gather information about your direct competition. How many competitors are there in your area? What are their sales? How many people does each store employ? What is the average sales per employee?

You can start to collect this demographic information by visiting your local library. Work with a business librarian and find the latest U.S. census population data. You can determine the number of people in your market area, their age range, household income, and other demographic information. You will have to project what changes have occurred since the data was collected.

Helpful publications to consult include *Sales and Marketing Management* magazine. Its "Annual Survey of Buying Power" contains much useful information about retail sales and population statistics by metropolitan areas. Simmons Market Research Bureau (SMRB) and Mediamark Research Inc. (MRI) also list product categories and demographics characteristics for varying levels of consumption and sometimes report brand consumption within a product category. These sources don't describe specific markets or report on service industries, but they can be used as input in your data collection process.

While at the library, consult the *Encyclopedia of Associations*[2] and get the name of the dry-cleaning industry association. Contact the association and ask for market studies or other information on the dry-cleaning industry along with referral sources of additional information. Don't forget to ask your librarian for other data sources.

Turn to the dry-cleaning section of the Yellow Pages and count the number of competitors in your area. Visit some of these stores. Also contact owners outside your market area who run successful ventures. Talk to them about the industry, new trends, purchasing habits, and how their businesses are doing. Ask them about the problems they experience and market potential.

Some of this information may also be available through your local chamber of commerce, especially if it has a research division. Collecting data on your market and competition is the first step in determining if your venture idea is plausible. The next step is to write a business plan to determine if the idea is feasible and if you can earn a profit.

Expanding Your Business by Researching the Industry

QUESTION

For the past several years, I've been doing upholstery work. I need to update my skills and learn more about what is going on in this industry. I have been looking everywhere for any information on upholstering, but with no success. Can you give me any information? How can I expand my business?

ANSWER

There are several different sources that you can contact to obtain information on the upholstery industry and updated upholstery courses.

First, become more familiar with your industry. The Yellow Pages are an excellent source for obtaining industry information. Look under upholsterers, upholsterers' supplies, upholstery fabrics, and wholesale manufacturers. *Furniture and Design* magazine publishes a yearly directory of suppliers in the furniture, design, and manufacturing industry. To obtain a copy, call (312) 222-2000. *Designers* magazine, P.O. Box 48968, Los Angeles, CA 90048, also publishes an annual manufacturers directory. Obtain as much information as possible from your competitors and your suppliers.

It is important to establish strong relationships with various suppliers and interior designers. Suppliers will be anxious to sell you their fabrics and therefore should be able to refer you to potential clients. Interior designers are always interested in finding good, reliable, and reasonably priced upholsterers.

Get reference letters from your past clients. Put together a small notebook that contains pictures of the furniture you have covered and illustrates the quality of work you can provide. Visit local merchandising marts and design showrooms. Introduce yourself and your business to the various showrooms. Ask for referrals. Make the same contacts with used-furniture stores.

There are several upholstery publications. You can obtain a free subscription to *Upholstery Design and Manufacturing* (UDM) magazine, which features new technology, equipment, materials, and trends affecting the upholstery industry. Write to 1020 S. Wabash, Chicago, IL 60605. Also contact *Upholstery Manufacturing* magazine, P.O. Box 640, Collierville, TN 38027, to obtain a free monthly subscription. Check with your local business librarian for additional resources.

You might try advertising your upholstering services by placing a small marketing pamphlet in your local grocery stores or on various community bulletin boards. Better yet, develop new clients from your existing customer base.

> ➪ **Courtney's Smart Tip**
> **Ask your customers for referrals and offer them future discounts for any new customers you get from their referrals.**

Get your local newspapers to run a special-interest story about your business by offering to present them with a unique angle or story. Offer your services to a local charity event and try to get the media to cover the event and your contribution. Call the Trade Show Bureau in Denver at (303) 860-7626. Ask for help in identifying trade shows in your industry that you might want to attend. The bureau can also refer you to the national association that represents the upholstery industry. Attend one of its regional or national meetings.

You can also contact local community colleges or universities and inquire about adult education classes in upholstery. Check the Yellow Pages for independent upholstery trade schools in your area.

The upholstery industry is very competitive. Strengthening your reputation, building from your existing customer base, and obtaining referrals from suppliers and interior designers are the best ways to expand your business. In this industry, word-of-mouth advertising can make the difference between a successful and an unsuccessful business.

QUESTION

I have come up with several ideas for selling a new version of backpacks. I am not a designer, craftsperson, or seamstress. But I do want to try to sell these backpacks. I have temporarily named my versions "Brat Packs." What I need are feedback, constructive criticism, and a positive next-step direction. I have not been able to find information from my local better business bureau, chamber of commerce, or other resources. What direction should I pursue as a next step?

ANSWER

First, you need to nail down both a wholesale and a retail price. How much will it cost you to have these backpacks made? With whom can you subcontract to make the backpacks? How many can they produce? Will you need backup subcontractors?

Begin by finding a reliable and competent subcontractor to produce your backpacks. Ask for recommendations from other entrepreneurs selling similar products. Negotiate with the subcontractor to make several prototypes to take to market. Establish a relationship with the subcontractor to begin making the backpacks for you as soon as you have secured orders.

In the meantime, investigate your competition. Find out what similar-quality backpacks are selling for. Can you be competitive with other backpacks on the marketplace? Will you be able to make the profit margin you want? If you find you have a competitively priced product, you are now ready to go to prospective retailers.

Identify retailers who might be interested in selling your backpacks. Make appointments to see them. These retailers are probably the best source for providing direct feedback about your product. If there are problems or objections to your backpacks, determine whether these objections can be overcome. Go back to your subcontractor and revise your prototype. If you do not encounter any negative comments, ask these retailers to purchase your backpacks.

To obtain additional customer reactions to your backpacks, run a focus group. That is, invite a group of 10 or so potential customers to a conference room to discuss the features of your backpacks. Consider giving each participant a backpack and a $25 check or some other small gift for participating. The quality of responses and amount of participation tend to improve when participants are given some token for their time. Focus groups are valuable, low-cost sources of information on which to try out new ideas before making the financial commitment to sell your backpacks in the marketplace.

Once you have obtained orders from area retailers for your product, you are ready to begin. Before investing a lot of money in your business, determine the creditworthiness of the retailers. Ask for credit references or try to get them to make a deposit on their orders. If you are cash-poor, you might try to obtain an inventory line of credit to produce your product. Usually, lenders will not advance more than 50 percent of the value of your inventory.

Using Focus Groups

QUESTION

I have a small word-processing business. I'm doing OK but my business is not growing and I've lost a few customers. Could there be something wrong with my services? Maybe my customers have new needs that I don't know about. How can I learn more about their preferences?

ANSWER

Ask your customers. Keeping your customers means listening to them on a continual basis. Researching customer needs is often the missing ingredient in marketing efforts among business owners. Customers have strong views, undiscovered needs and preferences, good ideas, and a desire to have things improved. They are seldom asked.

Try using focus-group interviews to gain customer insight and help solve your declining sales problem. All business owners can benefit from using this marketing technique with current or potential customers, especially to increase market share. Focus groups help you gain fresh perspectives on customer outlooks as well as obtain new ideas to improve your market position and penetration methods.

In the more sophisticated version of a focus group, marketing experts use one-way mirrors, closed-circuit videotaping, and exhaustive analysis of the recorded sessions. But entrepreneurs are using focus-group interviews in a simpler version that provides a richness of data on a limited budget. Essentially, it is a get-together with 7 to 10 people who are typical of your customer base and who are unfamiliar with one another.

Most people enjoy participating in focus-group sessions and endeavor to give useful feedback. In fact, you will probably find that your customers appreciate being asked their views. They are flattered that you have chosen them and sincerely want to listen to their views. In addition, they realize that you are trying to improve your business. You should pay members a small amount of money or give them a gift for participating.

The moderator plays an important role in the focus group. Consider using a skilled outside moderator to protect against bias. The moderator leads the focus group through in-depth and "freewheeling" discussions. To find focus-group moderators, look under marketing consultants in the Yellow Pages or call the marketing department at your local college or university. You can also contact your local chamber of commerce for referrals.

A typical focus group takes 1½ to 2 hours. The atmosphere should be relaxed to ensure an informal discussion of participants' opinions and feelings. Serve some light refreshments at the beginning of the discussion. The discussion format and interview questions should be carefully prepared ahead of time. The moderator asks broad questions at the beginning and then focuses the group on the specific information you want to obtain.

The moderator skillfully probes the group, stressing that there are no right or wrong answers and that sharing different points of view is essential. The moderator can take notes during the discussion or have it taped. Findings are then analyzed to interpret feedback from participants and relate it to your business.

Focus groups are rapidly becoming a major entrepreneurial marketing tool for gaining insight into customers' thoughts and feelings. They are an inexpensive way to maintain quality in your business. They help to screen new concepts, generate ideas on how to increase sales, or provide other key information founders want to know. Get in the habit of continually researching your customers' needs and opinions.

Using Mystery Shoppers

QUESTION

I own a small women's dress store in a local mall. Lately, I have received several complaints from customers that my sales associates have been abrupt and discourteous. I have talked to my staff about these complaints. They agree to do a better job and seem to when I am around. Do you have any suggestions as to how I can motivate them to treat customers better?

ANSWER

Your concerns are well founded. Research shows that the average business never hears from 96 percent of its unhappy customers. But the average person tells about 10 people about it.

The good news is that about 60 percent of complaining customers will do business again with a store if their complaint is resolved. Talking with your sales staff and making them more aware of customer complaints is the first step. Karl Albrecht's *Service America*[3] and *The Only Thing That Matters*[4] emphasize the importance of providing excellent service to customers. Ask your staff to read one of these books and then discuss how your business could implement some of the suggested strategies.

> ➪ **Courtney's Smart Tip**
> **Contract with a "mystery shopper" to shop your store and evaluate your sales staff.**

Mystery shoppers are a relatively new technique in retailing. A mystery shopper pretends that he or she is a customer and evaluates and records how your sales staff interacts with shoppers. The mystery shopper will look for prompt recognition when entering the store. Your sales staff should acknowledge walk-in customers within a minute. Next, the shopper will observe what kind of greeting is given and the way your sales staff builds rapport with new customers:

- Do your salespeople demonstrate product knowledge of your merchandise? Do they discuss and stress merchandise features or benefits? Customers rarely buy product features; instead, they buy because of product benefits.
- Do your salespeople attempt to sell companion items to match the clothing the customer is interested in? How do they assist the customer to the dressing room? Do they attempt to finish the outfit with suggested accessories?
- How do they handle customer objections? What types of comments and suggestions do they offer? Are they honest in their assessment of how various clothing items go together? Do they ask for the sale?
- Do they offer to hold the merchandise or have it put in layaway? How is the customer greeted at the cash register? How is the transaction handled?

Mystery shoppers are an excellent resource to help you understand the type and level of customer service offered at your store. They are also an inexpensive way to evaluate your sales staff. On the average, most mystery shoppers charge about $30 to $50 for spending an hour in your shop and preparing a written report of the sales experience, offering suggestions for improvement.

Look in the Yellow Pages under market research, market analysis, sales training, marketing consultants, or shoppers to find mystery shoppers. Check with your local chamber of commerce or university marketing programs. Check references whenever people are recommended to you. Better yet, ask a friend or business associate to shop your business. Or contact your mall association and suggest that a mystery shopper be hired for all the shops in the mall. Always prepare a list of what you would like to have evaluated before using a mystery shopper.

Another approach to improving customer service is to hold a sales contest offering rewards for outstanding and consistent service. Involve your salespeople in designing both the contest and the evaluation program.

QUESTION

Several years ago I purchased a fast-food franchise which has made a small profit. But lately I have been receiving more customer complaints than usual. Although staff turnover is high in this industry, I continue to provide the same amount of training and supervision. What can I do differently?

ANSWER

Today service is king and execution is your most important product. Hire a mystery shopper to determine exactly what kind of service your staff provides. This is an excellent way to monitor employee performance and find innovative ways of improving customer service. Mystery shoppers measure your customers' views of performance, service, and salesmanship.

Mystery shoppers are trained to observe efficiency, honesty, and sales techniques while they pose as regular customers of restaurants, retail stores, or other types of businesses. The normal routine is for mystery shoppers to enter your restaurant and observe staff behavior and the service provided. After gathering enough information, they record and evaluate your restaurant. They will report how long it took before they were waited on, whether the employees came across as being friendly and sincere, and whether employees tried to interest them in other products. They observe whether sales are rung up properly and rate the quality of the food as well as the interior of the restaurant.

Mystery shoppers' reports are observational, not judgmental. They quantify customer perceptions and measure individual improvements. The reports can then be used as part of your training and incentive program. It is a way to get your staff focused on the customers, because any one of them might be the "mystery guest."

Employees receiving high ratings or perfect scores from mystery shoppers are usually rewarded with some type of special bonus, such as a gift certificate, a parking space, time off, or a small cash award. Sometimes mystery shoppers write notes about deserving employees and give them to the owner. Then you can include $10 or $20 in the note to recognize outstanding performance.

When you recognize excellent performers, other staff members can learn to improve customer service by following their examples. Some owners post shopper reports by the time clock as a way to foster team spirit. The reports can also be used to train new employees, stressing how to become customer-focused and to begin thinking like your customers.

Before hiring mystery shoppers, identify exactly what you want measured. Typical areas for evaluation include the quality of the food; the initial appearance of your store from the parking lot to table; the friendliness, knowledge, ability, and helpfulness of the service and management staff; employee efforts at suggestive selling; and point-of-sale devices.

Never rely on just one rating from a mystery shopper. Instead, have your restaurant shopped several times. Then look for trends and make changes where appropriate. Consult one of the best-selling customer service books, such as *Service Within*[5] or *Delivering Knock Your Socks Off Service,*[6] to get new ideas about improving customer service.

Lastly, look for other ways to obtain continual customer feedback. Consider giving your customers a short survey card to complete. Offer recognition and rewards to employees who consistently provide exceptional customer service.

7-4 Developing Your Marketing Strategy and Plan

Why a Market Plan Is Important

QUESTION

Last year I opened a fast-service copy business in a small shopette. Although I was the first store offering this service in the area, many competing shops have recently opened, causing my sales to drop. How can I win back customers?

ANSWER

Successfully marketing a product or service is one of the most complex problems all entrepreneurs face. Every type of entrepreneurial enterprise requires marketing to compete and survive. How does an entrepreneur begin? Before you can decide on which marketing techniques to implement, you must develop a marketing plan.

A marketing plan consists of two primary elements: goals and strategies. Goals are what you want to achieve and strategies are how you expect to achieve them. Goals will determine the scope of your ambition in a particular time frame and allow you to allocate your resources appropriately. Quantify your goals whenever possible—for example, "increasing market share by 10 percent." Strategies should be specific, measurable, and timebound.

There are many items to take into consideration before developing your marketing plan. Study the growth trends of your industry, evaluate your competition, analyze your key customers, and appraise the realities of the current marketplace. Market planning begins by clearly identifying all the market segments to which you intend to sell. The next step is to arrange the identified markets in order of priority. Target marketing is the fundamental strategy used by successful businesses.

Next, examine the market segments that seem most attractive and target them for penetration. Develop special marketing tactics for each target market—a strategy known as market segmentation. Target your markets and then develop a marketing program for penetrating each one. Your business plan should explicitly identify all markets and then provide the basis for your selection of target markets.

If you have not yet written a business plan, go back to square one and develop it. Each of your identified target markets should be considered almost as a separate marketing program. Unfortunately, many entrepreneurs start their ventures without proper research and without writing a business plan or marketing plan. Then, when sales stagnate or decrease they begin to look for solutions. A marketing and business plan can help you devise a strategy to increase sales.

The foundation of your marketing plan will be the marketing mix, which includes such elements as promotion, advertising, publicity, direct mail, sales training, pricing, positioning, and customer service. Many entrepreneurs feel that placing a few ads or using coupon mailers constitutes a marketing plan; then they wonder why they do not achieve better results. When someone mentions marketing, people automatically think of advertising. Instead, new start-up ventures with limited marketing dollars should concentrate on publicity and promotion. There are many inexpensive ways to market products and services.

Deciding how to penetrate each target market is truly an art and takes much planning and experimentation. The difficulties in attempting to penetrate just one market can be overbearing, especially when there is limited money to spend on marketing products and services. When putting together your marketing plan, consider potential pitfalls and how you will deal with them. If you know ahead of time what to expect, you'll be better able to surmount obstacles as they arise.

> ⇨ **Courtney's Smart Tip**
> **Start with a modest marketing plan that is short and simple. Allow for flexibility. Reexamine your marketing plan yearly.**

Strive to achieve the goals set forth in your marketing plan. A marketing plan is like a fancy and attractive car without gas. The fuel that powers your car is the marketing techniques you use to achieve the goals in your plan. To maximize your dollars, ensure that all your marketing efforts reinforce each other. You should be striving to establish a well-connected, forceful image. Use marketing to strengthen your identity.

How to Inform Potential Customers About a Product

QUESTION

On camping and fishing trips with my family, I found that I spent most of my time baiting fish hooks for my wife and three daughters. Consequently, I invented a plastic gadget that automatically baits fish hooks. I am a cement finisher and do not have sufficient funds for financing and marketing this product. How can I sell my patent or find someone willing to finance and market an apparatus for baiting fish hooks? I am convinced that the market is out there.

ANSWER

Developing and patenting a new product for which you strongly believe there is a market is the first step to launching a successful business venture. Figuring out how to sell it is the hard part. Begin by conducting some preliminary research on the number of fishermen and the number of fishing licenses sold annually. Then conduct a beta test with potential customers which will verify and document that your invention truly works and customers would use and recommend it. Try to obtain testimonials from selected experts. You also need to identify what types of fish potential customers could catch with your apparatus and in what types of waters. Contact local fishing stores to find fishermen to test your product.

Next, stop listening to your friends and neighbors who applaud your new invention. Instead, determine if there is a sufficiently large market to justify manufacturing and marketing your product. Take the mystery out of who will purchase your great invention. Check out your competition. If there is none, try to find people who are making a similar product. What has been their track record? Is their product successful? How has it been marketed?

You have two main strategies to pursue for financing and marketing your invention. The first is to bootstrap your venture by producing a small number of baiting gadgets and trying to get one of the local sporting goods stores to carry them. You can then determine if there is a market and more accurately forecast potential sales volume. In addition, you could ask these stores for a list of their suppliers. Look for suppliers that have accompanying product lines with nationwide distribution. Ask if they would be interested in handling your product.

Try to attend one of the local sporting goods trade shows. Bring along your baiting apparatus to see if anyone is interested in purchasing it. Or sign up for a booth at the trade show and try to sell the product yourself. Watch some of the fishing shows on television and look for the names and addresses of the producers at the end of the programs. Contact these individuals and ask them about ideas for marketing your product.

Locate some of the primary fishing catalogs, such as *Bass Pro Shops* and *Cabela's.* Contact the catalog companies and ask if they would carry your product. If one of them gives you a large order, you could take the purchase invoice to a lender for additional money to manufacture and ship the product. Catalog companies purchase products at wholesale prices and make their profit by charging the suggested retail price.

Another strategy is to contact a manufacturer involved in producing similar fishing products. The manufacturer might purchase your patent and pay you a royalty on every fish-hook baiter sold. Or it might agree to manufacture the product for a percentage of the sales price. Frequently manufacturers have established distribution systems that could carry your product.

Unfortunately, many manufacturers will not do business with you unless you have a proven track record. Likewise, some suppliers or department stores might also require that you have an established customer base. Follow up on these leads by further researching your potential market. Eventually, a fishing manufacturer, supplier, department store, or catalog company should bite your bait.

> ⇨ **Courtney's Smart Tip**
> **Marketing is getting someone to start carrying your product.**

How to Prepare a Sales Forecast

QUESTION

I'm getting ready to start a new business selling children's toys. I need to make some sales forecasts to determine the size of my market so I can ascertain if my idea is feasible. Can you tell me how to best prepare sales forecasts?

ANSWER

Forecasting sales volume and testing your market are essential steps to take before deciding whether to launch a new venture.

> ➪ **Courtney's Smart Tip**
> **Use phantom sales to test your toy market by advertising your proposed products, asking for a response, and then gauging the response of your target market to determine if the response is sufficient to justify the venture.**

Try selling your proposed products first, and then decide whether to proceed. Your only costs are promotional expenses.

Entrepreneurs may fall into a number of traps when assessing their markets and forecasting sales volume. First, most assume that there is a market and that others are as interested in their product or service as they are. Do not convince yourself that a potential market exists for your idea. Instead, try to prove your market. There are many toy stores around. Why will customers come to yours? What will motivate them to purchase toys from you? You need to obtain some solid evidence that your target market needs your proposed toy store and is willing to purchase from you.

Second, most entrepreneurs tend to underestimate the difficulty of penetrating their intended market. It takes far more time and money to penetrate a target market than most people imagine. Do not assume that everyone who purchases toys will buy from you. Such gross overoptimism not only destroys the credibility of your forecast but can also distort the rest of your projections. Don't overexaggerate your potential market. Most entrepreneurs fall short of their original sales expectations and predictions. Sales forecasts begin with an estimation of the venture's market potential. Then some market penetration factor is applied to it to arrive at the venture's sales potential. The common trap is to grossly overestimate how much of the market the new business will be able to capture.

Third, entrepreneurs regularly pull sales figures out of the air largely on the basis of what they hope for rather than on solid market information. The best way to overcome this trap is to consult with potential suppliers in your industry. They are excellent sources for estimating sales volume. Sometimes they have developed sophisticated statistical models for forecasting your sales.

Also study your competitors' sales experience. What were their first sales? What does your competition now sell? What do new firms in the toy industry usually sell? You can gain valuable insights into sales forecasts by evaluating what others sell now and what they have sold when they first started. Try to find the sales records of some store similar to yours. What were its start-up figures? Remember that sales are the result of marketing and selling efforts. Compare and contrast your selling efforts with those of your competition.

Develop multiple forecasts that will yield different results. Use all of them to gain a better understanding of the range of sales forecasts. You must develop a "must do" or breakeven forecast—that is, the sales volume you must achieve first to break even and then make a profit. Your sales goals must be directly related to your "must do" forecast.

Even the greatest minds in the world cannot accurately forecast economic activity and global events. Astute entrepreneurs set up their ventures in such a way that they can respond quickly to resultant sales volume when market changes occur.

How to Market a Service Business

QUESTION

I have developed a consulting care-giving service for the elderly. I would like to market my services to corporations to help employees on their staffs who are coping with the responsibilities of caring for their elderly relatives. I have been stymied by not really knowing how to market to corporations without personal contact. How can I go about marketing and selling my services? Are there any books you would recommend?

ANSWER

Marketing services is quite different from marketing products. Our economy is shifting to the service sector. Ninety percent of all new jobs and 67 percent of the gross national product are generated annually by the service sector. What complicates your problem is that there are many consultants selling similar services.

It is hard to figure out where you are going if you have not given serious thought to and developed a strategy on how to get there. Take the first step by developing a business plan that will help you focus your energies and build a strategy for launching your venture. I suggest that you get a copy of *Program for Writing Winning Business Plans*,[7] for a step-by-step method of producing a business plan.

Unfortunately, just having a good idea that you think will sell in the marketplace is not enough. Although you have already developed several brochures for your venture, a detailed marketing plan is needed. *Big Marketing Ideas for Small Service Businesses*[8] covers how to advertise and publicize a service business successfully. It offers practical and innovative suggestions on everything from how to cultivate the right business image to designing and producing effective brochures and ads, to the secrets of generating free publicity. Or pick up a copy of Ken Dychtwald's *Age Wave,*[9] one of the leading books on aging America.

While preparing these plans and researching your industry, contact both for-profit and nonprofit agencies that are involved in serving the elderly. For instance, contact an association that provides information about elder care services in nursing homes, assisted living facilities, and churches. Be mindful that virtually any service can be duplicated. Therefore, understanding your marketplace, staying on the leading edge, and growing your venture will depend on the soundness of your business plan and marketing tactics.

7-5 Expanding Your Customer Base

How to Attract New Customers

QUESTION

I rent video equipment to the home or professional videographer and offer an editing suite and production services. What is the most effective and least expensive way to inform the public about my services? I have tried telephone soliciting, coupon mailers, flyers, and newspaper classified ads. Only Yellow Pages advertising has been effective. My finances are limited and I have not yet been able to take a paycheck for myself from the business. How can I attract the public and increase my customer base?

ANSWER

Try focusing on marketing to your current customers. Too many times entrepreneurs pay too little attention to their current customer base. Instead, they spend all their efforts looking for new markets—an approach that can take significant dollars yet produce few returns. Focusing on current customers will yield higher returns for your marketing dollar. Have you discussed in detail the full array of your services with every customer? Have you fully developed every dimension of what you could be offering to meet the needs of your current customers?

➪ Courtney's Smart Tip
Use the effective and cost-saving entrepreneurial marketing technique of cultivating your current customer list.

Have you asked your current customers for testimonial letters that you could use to attract new customers? Have you asked your customers for new business referrals? Consider asking each of your customers for the names of three other people who might be interested in your services. Contact these referrals to expand your market and attract new customers.

Do you keep in close contact with your customers on a routine basis? What do you do to show that you care about their needs? Do you solicit new ideas from customers about how you could improve and/or expand your current services? Have you considered writing an informal newsletter, mailing out a "for your information" memo, or sending a fax about a special you will be offering?

Today, with desktop publishing capabilities, producing a newsletter to disseminate information to a customer base can be a fast and simple task. Since you are in the video business, it might be appropriate to develop a video newsletter about new equipment or write a feature on how one of your customers has utilized your services. Always consider different informational items that might interest your customers while reminding them of your business and services.

A good entrepreneurial rule is to constantly stay in close contact with your customers. Too many entrepreneurs neglect their current customer base. They look toward advertising as being the best avenue for improving their market share. It is quicker and much easier to place an ad than to develop a sound customer base. The cost of placing advertising in the media is often prohibitive, especially for a new business with a limited marketing budget.

Likewise, using brochures is a lazy replacement for direct marketing, making personal calls, and following up on customer referrals. Direct-marketing techniques are usually more successful and less costly for entrepreneurs. Brochures are helpful, but should be combined with other marketing strategies.

Try establishing your own customer database. Every entrepreneur needs accessible records containing valuable, but often overlooked, customer histories and data. Such information should include each customer's name; current address and telephone number; number of years in business; personal background such as family, lifestyle, and special interests; information about how the customer found your business and the customer's particular needs; and what the customer is looking for in establishing a successful business relationship. The "Mackay Envelope Corporation 66-Question Customer Profile" in *Swim with the Sharks*[10] contains invaluable ideas about what type of customer information will best fit your needs.

A good customer database can provide vital statistics for you to develop and grow your business. It can be the launching pad to expand your market economically. Analyze your current customer base and have fun with it. Develop creative ways to stay close to your customers.

How to Develop New Sales Leads

QUESTION

I have owned a flower shop for the past several years. I am doing all right, but not making the amount of money the store is capable of producing. Can you help me develop new sales leads to increase my market and my profits?

ANSWER

Increasing market share and profits is a constant struggle for most entrepreneurs. To begin with, focus on your current customers. Many entrepreneurs neglect this important resource and instead look for new markets to expand into. One of the best sources of sales leads is people you have done business with in the past.

Develop an accurate customer profile on each buyer, including specific demographic information. Such information includes age, sex, education, occupation, head of household, nationality, income, and geographic location. Each of these characteristics will help define the customer profile for your flower shop.

Next, determine why and when these customers purchase flowers. Almost everyone in your geographic area probably sends flowers at some time. But when do your customers tend to buy flowers? What are the special occasions or times of year when your sales are the highest? After you obtain this information, you can begin to look for common customer characteristics and purchasing trends. Avoid trying to be all things to all people.

> ➪ **Courtney's Smart Tip**
> **Follow the 80-20 rule: 80 percent of your business comes from 20 percent of your customers. Concentrate your efforts on that 20 percent.**

Build your own mailing and calling list. On the basis of previous orders, contact customers when they are most likely to be thinking about purchasing flowers. You can develop an attractive one-page flyer describing a special you are offering. For example, if you discover that many of your customers order flowers for Valentine's Day, you could advertise a variety of special arrangements for this occasion.

Timing is key. You will experience a great response rate and higher sales when you send promotional material to your best customers on occasions when they purchase flowers. Your customers have different needs. Preparing a blanket mailing that is not directly tied to your particular customer base will probably not generate much increased business.

Another way to increase your sales leads is to call on your best customers in person or contact them by telephone. Personal calls are one of the more effective marketing methods and one of the least expensive, especially when tied to promotional materials. You could make out an index card on each of your customers, indicating when they would like to be called and reminded about sending flowers. Many of them may want to be notified when Secretary's Day or Mother's Day comes around. Your customers may sincerely appreciate a call at these special times of the year.

Don't forget to ask for referrals from satisfied customers to develop new sales leads. When you receive a sales lead, give a small token of appreciation: a discount on the customer's next purchase, a thank-you note, perhaps a free plant. Remember to always cultivate new sales leads from your existing customer base.

After you have developed a customer profile, you can increase your customer base by looking for new clients who fit the profile of your current customers. You may discover that many of your patrons work for the same company or belong to the same service club. These would be excellent groups of people to market your services to. Your current customer base will indicate the areas of expansion that will help you better target your best markets.

Lastly, experiment with using coupons in newspaper ads or flyers. Ask people to bring in the coupons for some kind of redemption. Each of these coupon redeemers is a new sales lead. Be sure to obtain the customer's name and address to expand your mailing list.

7-6 Advertising and Promotion

Using Feature Stories

QUESTION

I recently started a new business which does national computer searches for higher-education funding from the private sector. How do I get an article written about my new company in a major newspaper?

ANSWER

There are many different ways to attract media attention, gain visibility, and establish credibility. As all entrepreneurs realize, promoting a business can be extremely costly. Considering the skyrocketing costs of advertising and traditional promotional tools, such as direct mail, trade shows, and selling, new ventures are usually hard-pressed to maximize the results realized from a limited promotional budget.

One feature article in a newspaper or an appearance on a television or radio talk show can generate hundreds of inquiries and a substantial amount of new business. In fact, many say that feature coverage is at least twice as credible as advertising. This is an excellent way to obtain free publicity and promote your services.

The first step is to target specific media that reach the audience with whom you would like to communicate. Single out the media most advantageous for you. Next, observe the various stories covered by your target media so you understand what they are looking for. In your case, it may be more appropriate to contact several trade magazines rather than your local newspaper. Editors of newspapers and magazines, as well as producers of radio and television programs, are constantly under pressure to deliver news and feature stories that appeal to their audiences.

Research what your target media need. Then, develop an angle that creates interest.

> ➪ **Courtney's Smart Tip**
> **The best way to increase the chances of getting publicity is to develop an angle or a newsworthy hook.**

Convince the media that you have a good story or a feature item of interest to their specific audience. What is different or unique about your service? Is there a special benefit or community activity involved with your service? Have you received a recent award or sponsored a seminar or contest? Do you have any trend forecasts or industry overviews of interest? Can you write a how-to article? Are you a colorful entrepreneur with a fascinating background or unique personality profile? Be interesting, timely, and factual in the angles you present.

Have your story written before contacting the media. You might consider writing both a shorter piece and a longer one, since space availability varies. Then decide on the media editor who is responsible for the type of story you are pitching. Secure a referral if possible.

Start by establishing a working relationship with these sources. Call to schedule an appointment. Take people out to breakfast or lunch, or for a cup of coffee. Because media people are exceptionally busy, they may just ask you to send the story. Do it. Don't wait for someone to interview you. You never know when media people need to fill space and will use your story because it is convenient. After sending your story and giving people an opportunity to review it, follow up. When you call, make sure the person you speak to is not under a deadline.

> ➪ **Courtney's Smart Tip**
> **Establish a relationship with the media instead of blindly sending out press releases. After sending your story for press release, follow up and ask if and when the story will be used.**

Send a well-prepared feature story that highlights an area of interest to the media. If people say they are not interested, ask what types of stories they are looking for. You might be able to reconstruct your angle to suit their needs. Leave the door open for another try.

Remember the differences between advertising and publicity. With advertising, you pay to have a specific message conveyed to the public. You control the message and the manner in which it is presented. You tell potential customers what you want them to know about your service. With publicity, you have no such control. You provide media people with information that you believe is worth telling. They decide whether to cover your story and what to write about your service. You have no control over what is written. It's a tricky business. Your ability to approach the media with a solid, newsworthy story could well give you the publicity break that you are looking for.

How to Buy Cut-Rate Local Network TV Spots

QUESTION

I have a small tire business and I'm interested in advertising on television. A business associate told me that 30-second local network spots are available at bargain rates. How should I go about purchasing TV time inexpensively?

ANSWER

First, have you written a marketing plan that specifies that advertising on television is one of the best ways to reach your target market? It is important to find the best and most cost-effective ways to reach your audience. If you have determined that TV advertising will be effective, you probably can purchase small blocks of local television time at a reduced rate. It depends on the supply and demand for TV advertising time in your area.

Contact a television sales rep, a media buying service, or an advertising agency that works with entrepreneurs. Media buying services usually charge 5 percent of your total bill and provide expertise in various types of media. Advertising agencies may charge on a fee or project basis or may take a commission on the media rate. Some larger agencies may refund part of the agency discount to the client. Remember that agency advertising rates are usually negotiable.

To keep costs down, do as much of the work as possible yourself and establish a solid working relationship with a sales rep. Look for a rep who is building clientele and hungry for more sales. Find someone who is genuinely interested in your business and has flexibility in scheduling inventory. Sales reps have detailed demographic information that helps to match your target customers with various audiences, viewing times, and programs. A good sales rep can be worth his or her weight in gold in helping you plan your television campaign, assisting with programming, and designing packages with the most effective schedules.

> ➪ **Courtney's Smart Tip**
> **Whenever possible, purchase preemptible time, which costs less but can be bumped.**

Most stations will try their hardest not to lose revenue and will try to schedule your commercials at a later, and possibly better time. If timing is important and you are running a tire sale, don't buy preemptible time. If your commercials are part of an image campaign, preemptible time will satisfy your needs.

Entrepreneurs frequently contract for rotation spots—commercials that rotate on more than one program and during certain time blocks. The more flexibility you have in scheduling your commercial, the lower the rate. Usually the second and fourth quarters of the year are more heavily sold than the first and third quarters.

If your message is simple and involves using slides and voice-overs, you can probably develop the spot yourself. Use the in-house commercial production studio at your local television station. If you are purchasing time from the station, it will probably just charge you at cost to produce your commercial. If your message is more complicated, you may want to use an advertising agency to produce a professional, customized commercial.

Also, if you have a short billboard message that is promoting a special sale, consider buying a 10-second spot, which is usually easier to schedule at a discounted price. A 10-second commercial costs about 60 percent less than a 30-second spot, although there are fewer 10-second spots available.

Options for advertising in the media are enormous. Read *Advertising Age* and other journals to learn more about the industry. Contact your local advertising association and ask for a media start-up kit.

Using Business Cards as Marketing Brochures

QUESTION

I am starting a new pet store in an area shopping center. I am in the process of designing a logo to use on my stationery and business cards. My printer advised me to keep the card simple; a friend advised me to include more information about my business. What do you suggest?

ANSWER

This is a difficult question to answer, since the design of your card depends on your industry and target market. Most entrepreneurs regard their stationery and business cards as just props needed when launching a new venture. Your business card, letterhead, and stationery should reflect the image you are trying to portray.

Most often business cards are simple, plain, and unimaginative printed paper rectangles that are handed out without much thought. Business owners fail to realize that they can use their business cards as effective and inexpensive marketing tools. Business card designs are becoming more creative. Why not design your card to sell your particular product or service rather than just to provide information about contacting you? Distinctive business cards range from those made with unusual materials and imprinting methods to those that convey a solid message and establish their own identity.

To determine how effective your business card is, observe what others do when you hand them your card. Do they look at it and comment or put it directly into a pocket? If it goes into a pocket, you have failed to catch people's attention and may want to redesign your card. Next, look at other business cards and notice what catches your eye. To attract attention and create an impact, vary the size of type and the spacing.

Then design a card that is memorable and highlights the uniqueness of your venture. Your business card should have the same typeface as your letterhead and stationery. Present a consistent image. Make sure that your business card directly communicates to your target market. It may be necessary to design several different business cards that appeal to different segments of your market.

Think of your card as a mini-billboard. Some experts suggest including the services and benefits you offer. Most business cards give only the basics—name, address, and phone number. They fail to indicate the kind of business and what special services and products it offers. When glancing through cards, people frequently forget where they received the card and what business the company is in. Don't let this happen to you.

Be creative and use design alternatives. Instead of using an average-size business card, consider a card that fits into a rolodex or one that folds in half. A folding card can feature your services and become a brochure, a wallet-size advertisement for your business. The outside of the card contains standard business information, while the inside contains a headline followed by a list of features and benefits.

Add color to your card if possible. Use it as background or to make type stand out. Adding color may raise your printing bill about $20 but is well worth it. Also, a texture such as high gloss, matte, or rag content might enhance your card.

Make the most of your business card to help with your referral business. Never be without one. A good business card can be as effective as a TV commercial. Ask for business cards from other contacts you meet. Mail out your card with letters and other brochures.

> ➪ **Courtney's Smart Tip**
> **Revise your business cards every 4 to 5 years to keep up with new trends and changing tastes.**

For more information, contact Avery N. Pitzak, president of the American Business Card Club, at (303) 690-6496. This association is a worldwide network for exchanging business card designs and ideas. It costs $10 to join the club and to receive newsletters and other mailings.

7-7 Telemarketing

Using 800 Telephone Numbers to Expand Market Share

QUESTION

I have just self-published a book and plan to sell it from my office at home by advertising in trade magazines and appearing on both radio and television talk shows. Would it be a good idea to set up an 800 telephone number for orders, or would an 800 number be cost-prohibitive?

ANSWER

If over 20 percent of your projected revenue will come from clients outside of your local calling area, installing a toll-free 800 number is an excellent marketing strategy. Many marketing surveys reveal that customers first call businesses that advertise a toll-free 800 number. And for every long-distance customer who would normally call you, you can expect to gain two more customers if you have an 800 number. Your average revenue per transaction should indicate whether the cost of installing an 800 line is cost-effective for your business.

Today, telephone and communications systems provide many timesaving and cost-effective features to entrepreneurs. Obtaining an 800 number is not as complicated and expensive as it used to be. It is as easy as setting up a business telephone line. You do not need a separate telephone line installed for your 800 number, as was required in the past. Many of these new 800 features are offered as a result of the growth of entrepreneurship and small businesses.

One variety of toll-free telephone service allows callers within the United States to place orders or make inquires by calling 800 lines that are answered by commercial communications organizations. These companies provide a complete range of services, from telemarketing fulfillment to database development.

The costs of 800 services vary widely. Start your research by contacting the major telephone companies and comparing their prices and services. Ask if there is an installation charge and, if so, how much it costs. Look for special promotions. Sometimes the companies will offer installation or a month's service for free.

Monthly fees for an 800 line vary from $6 to $20, plus per-minute use charges. Ask if the company offers a volume discount. If you average a certain dollar amount per month, you may be eligible for such a discount. The cost for inbound toll-free telephone reception and order-taking services is usually a monthly minimum fee for a certain amount of orders.

Check to see if the company offers any special discounts for heavy usage from certain areas. For example, if your business receives many calls from a particular city, the company may reduce the charges on a "favorite city discount." Such discounts are available both nationally and internationally. Also ask if the company gives credit for wrong numbers. In order to avoid potential problems with wrong numbers, request an 800 number that has not been assigned for some time.

Telephone billing policies are critical to business owners. Look for a company that bills in 6-second increments rather than by the minute.

Then, if a customer calls and you talk for 1 minute and 10 seconds, you will not be charged for the full 2 minutes. This will save you some money.

An 800 number adds credibility and is cost-effective for home-based businesses. It will give your customers the impression that you have a solid and reputable company even if you work out of your garage or basement. It adds credibility and prestige to your image regardless of whether you operate a small or large venture.

Using 900 Telephone Numbers to Sell Products and Services

QUESTION

I have a small financial management consulting company and recently read an article about 900 numbers. How can I go about setting up one of these numbers for my business?

ANSWER

It's the immediacy that entices callers to initially dial 900 numbers for either information or service. What keeps them calling is the currency, professionalism, and uniqueness of the information being offered. If you can provide quick, convenient, and accurate information, a 900 line may be a good supplement to your business. However, it is important for you to thoroughly research 900 lines to see if you can be successful using them. Your credibility and reputation in the industry will determine whether potential customers call your line.

Essentially, customers pay a per-minute fee to receive the information the business is selling on the 900 line. This pay-per-call service has experienced tremendous growth over the years and currently generates nearly $1 billion a year in sales. Telephone companies act as carriers of the lines, and handle all the billing of 900 calls on the consumer's regular phone bill. Calls are charged at a predetermined rate, and the carrier is paid a percentage of each call, or sale. The balance is sent to the information provider within 30 to 90 days of billing.

Three phone companies that provide 900 numbers are Sprint, MCI, and AT&T. They offer similar services but charge and bill somewhat differently, and each has different policies on processing collectibles. All three companies offer discounts for volume usage. At this writing, standard charges for businesses using a 900 number are about $3 for the first minute and $1.50 for each additional minute. The average 900 call lasts 10 minutes. Of course, the length of calls varies with the type of service or product being sold.

Start-up costs vary tremendously, depending on the type of information being provided. For many entrepreneurs, these costs may seem extremely high. That's why it is important to contact a telephone service bureau that has a good reputation and reliable references from both the carrier and customers. Typically, a service bureau has a fully equipped and staffed facility that services a number of different information providers.

There are several reputable service companies that help owners start and operate 900 lines. Call-Interactive (402) 498-7000 works out of Omaha, Nebraska, and WTS (214) 920-1900 is in Dallas, Texas. Look for other service bureaus that do business in your industry. Ask your industry association for referrals. *Always get referrals.*

The Information Industry Association, 555 New Jersey Avenue NW, Suite 800, Washington, DC, is involved with the creation and distribution of information services. In exchange for a stamped self-addressed envelope, you will receive a free two-page brochure titled "Customer Service Guide for 900 Programs." The booklet explains how 900 lines work and provides a mini-directory of 900 numbers along with other valuable information. You might also look into *Entrepreneur* magazine's business guide "Operating a 900 Number for Profit." Or consult Robert Mestin's book *How to Succeed with Your Own 900 Business.*[11]

Remember, there are ongoing marketing costs associated with a 900 line. Experts suggest that entrepreneurs allocate enough dollars to market their 900 numbers for at least 6 months without relying on incoming revenues. Like any other marketing technique, 900 numbers do not automatically make customers beat a path to your doorway. How you market and advertise a 900 line will significantly affect your sales.

7-8 Expanding Your Market Through Consignment

Placing Merchandise in Stores on Consignment

QUESTION

I operate a small appliance store. Recently, one of my suppliers asked me whether he could place some merchandise in my store on consignment. I don't know if this is more advisable than if I just purchased it as my own inventory. I will not be making as much profit on this consignment merchandise. What do you think I should do?

ANSWER

Consignment merchandise, like every other element of business, has both positive and negative aspects. Consignment merchandise means that you do not take title to the inventory, but try to sell it for another person. As a result, your profit margin is much lower but your inventory cost is zero. As a rule, you will receive 40 to 50 percent of the sales price for consigned merchandise.

> ➪ **Courtney's Smart Tip**
> **Consignment offers more advantages to the retailer carrying consigned merchandise than to the entrepreneur placing goods in a retail location.**

Consider these advantages. First, and most important, there is no financial investment for you as a retail seller. However, you should carry only high-quality products or product lines that are fully insured and adequately promoted. These types of products may be hard to find. Determine beforehand whether there is a market and whether your customers will purchase the items. Consigned goods may tie up inventory space that you do not have.

Second, consignment merchandise offers you the opportunity to carry goods that you might not otherwise be able to stock. Because of cash flow restraints, your inventory may be limited. Consignment goods may allow you to carry a complete line of merchandise without typing up your operating capital. You can expand your product lines and carry top-quality merchandise without making any additional investment or owning the goods.

Third, consigned goods allow retailers to carry the latest and most popular models of a product line without risking obsolete inventory problems. For example, if the manufacturer introduces a new or improved product, the retailer will not be left with old inventory or out-of-date merchandise that is hard to move.

Overall, for many retailers, consigned merchandise means that they can offer more products, both in the quantity of items offered and in the variety of product types. In some industries, of course, consignment merchandise is the norm. For instance, if you own an art gallery, the majority of the artwork will be sold on consignment. In some cases, the manufacturer placing the consigned goods in your store will be involved in promotion. Most manufacturers are interested in selling their products as rapidly as possible so they can earn a profit.

But consignment is not without its problems. On the negative side, the goods may not move but will instead take up valuable shelf and inventory space. Another disadvantage is that buyers may return the consigned merchandise for full credit after you have paid the manufacturer. Negotiate an agreement up front on how you will handle returned goods.

Accepting Consignment Goods to Expand Inventory

QUESTION

I am trying to market wood-laminated canoe and kayak paddles but I am having trouble getting my product in sporting goods stores. Several managers of these stores have offered to take my products on consignment. Should I accept their offers?

ANSWER

Generally, consignment is not a recommended route for an entrepreneur, unless the product is new, untested in the market, and it's one of the only ways you can get your product into retail stores. One of the key problems is that middlemen or distributors may not give your consigned merchandise as much attention as the goods in which they have their own money invested. The profit margin for retailers is less on consigned merchandise, so their motivation to sell your product may be less. They are usually more concerned with selling products that cost them money if not sold. If you choose consignment, you might consider offering incentives to retailers to motivate them to sell your goods quicker.

Another major problem with consignment is that you cannot count any delivered merchandise as a sale. Consignments should not be recorded in your ledgers. You do not know whether the transaction is a sale until it is either paid for or returned. All that has occurred is that some of your goods are being stored on someone else's shelf or in a warehouse. For these reasons, consignment merchandise causes numerous accounting problems. Since consigned goods are not sold, they cannot be counted as income. If the goods are shown as accounts receivable, you are falsely inflating your income statements, and your financial statement becomes distorted. Consigned merchandise should be tracked separately to avoid such problems.

Further, once the goods are sold, it may be difficult to receive payment for them. Record keeping and sales reporting must be kept current and verified regularly, and periodic inventory counts must be made to ascertain sales in order to receive payment for goods sold. How will returns be handled? Auditing consigned merchandise is an administrative headache.

Other obstacles abound. What happens to your merchandise when the retailer is cash-poor and is unable to pay for sold merchandise or declares bankruptcy? Damaged merchandise can also be an ordeal. Some employees are not as careful with consigned stock. If any of your merchandise is damaged, you must take it back and absorb the damage costs.

> ➪ **Courtney's Smart Tip**
> **If you decide to put your merchandise on consignment, buy insurance coverage.**

Consigned goods remain your merchandise and not the property of the retailer. What would happen if your merchandise were damaged by flood, hurricane, or fire? Insurance is essential and can represent a significant added expense, depending on the value of your goods and the conditions under which they are sold and warehoused.

Bankers, venture capitalists, and other lenders will look at consignment merchandise with a jaundiced eye. They much prefer to see solid sales in which money comes back, not your goods. You may be painting a weak image of your company if many of your goods are on consignment.

On the positive side, placing your goods on consignment may allow you to gain wider distribution. Distributors do not have to pay to carry your goods and might be willing to add it to their product lines at no cost. This could be an avenue of additional sales. Also, you can control the pricing of consigned merchandise and thus avoid price cutting in the marketplace. If your goods sell, you should be able to convince the retailer to purchase them outright on a regular basis. This might enable you to establish a solid market position.

In certain situations, you may have no choice but to place your goods on consignment. If your merchandise is going to sell at the retail level, a consignment deal must be accepted. This is especially true if you have new, untested products or if you want retailers to stock a large inventory in anticipation of forthcoming demand. Astute entrepreneurs should carefully consider all the pros and cons before placing their goods on consignment. Consignment is great for the retailer but could be a disaster for you.

> ➪ **Courtney's Smart Tip**
> **Instead of consignment, consider giving the retailer delayed-payment terms with generous return privileges.**

7-9 Using Sales Representatives

Using Sales Reps to Market Products and Services

QUESTION

I have just developed a new software product, and I am considering using sales representatives to market my software. Is it a good idea to use reps, and how do I go about finding good ones?

ANSWER

Contracting with independent sales representatives can be an excellent way for you to market your product, especially if your venture is underfinanced. Many entrepreneurs use outside reps as their initial sales staff and marketing department.

Sales representatives are granted the exclusive right to sell your product in a certain territory. Sometimes, they participate in setting the price, terms of sale, and/or other marketing decisions. An important advantage is that you do not add sales reps to your payroll. Reps get paid only when the customer pays for the goods sold. No sales, no collection, no pay. Commission checks are not written until you receive payment for the goods. This approach enhances your cash flow and minimizes the capital requirements for your business.

Good sales reps have knowledge of a specific territory and prospective customers. Generally, they carry several products in the same line. Thus, their frequency of contact per customer may be higher than with a hired sales force. Their customer lists are extremely valuable and can give your product or service instant credibility. Lastly, you can build a rep team much quicker than a direct sales force of your own.

On the other side, reps may have more productive lines than yours and therefore devote much of their energies to promoting their bread-and-butter lines with the highest sales. Commissions may be high. Depending on the industry, reps may want between 5 and 25 percent as commission. Also, reps may need a great amount of time and support from others in your company to close a sale. They are sometimes difficult to monitor, train, and motivate. Reps may lack the time to successfully promote a new line and build up your markets. Overall, you lose some control over your market and customers by using reps.

One good method of finding competent reps is to search in the trade directories. These directories identify what reps are in a given area, what types of lines they handle, and what types of customers they service. Or find out what reps your competition uses. Look up a manufacturer of complementary products and call the sales manager to inquire about what reps are used.

You can also contact various local or national associations of reps and dealers. Some organizations employ a variety of sales reps who cover large territories. Search them out at your industry trade shows along with independent reps. Chambers of commerce often maintain lists of reps and agents as well.

After identifying several reputable reps, ask for references from current clients. Make a thorough check. Many reps have convincing sales pitches but mediocre performance. Ask the rep to schedule a few sales calls to some of his or her prospective customers. Observe the rep's sales techniques and ability to close the sale. Clarify the sales volume you expect from the rep's territory. Draw up a performance contract based on a guaranteed amount of sales. If the rep does not perform, then you can cancel the contract. Be careful of escape clauses that allow reps to bail out when it seems advantageous.

If the sales rep is your only means of penetrating the marketplace, any rift in your relationship can place you at risk. Use several reps or rep organizations to market your product or service.

Building Successful Relationships with Sales Reps

QUESTION

I have decided to use sales reps to market my unique silver jewelry. What should I do to make the relationship as successful as possible?

ANSWER

First, you need to be in constant contact with your sales reps by phone or in person. Ask what is happening, and keep track of performance goals and accomplishments. Offer to help reps in their marketing efforts. Continue to supply your reps with qualified sales leads. Provide your reps with a detailed sales manual that includes competitive comparisons, photos, journal articles, and any other type of product information that can be helpful. You will also need to furnish your reps with demonstration kits, point-of-sale displays, training sessions, and other support materials. Often, the entrepreneur will sell the demonstration kit to the rep at cost, because of the dollars invested in it. Reps can later sell your merchandise and make a profit.

Rehearse the sales pitch with the reps you decide to hire. List possible customer objections and counter with good arguments for purchasing your jewelry. Give reps a list of happy users for customer references. Furnish them with all the ammunition they might need to make selling easier. Keep your reps motivated by sending out a newsletter describing new company developments, territory sales volume, or spinoff products. This is an inexpensive way to keep the communication lines open.

Send your reps a copy of all press releases and marketing packages you prepare. Try using sales contests, prizes, incentives, monthly discounts, or double commissions. Remember, you are competing for their time with the other product lines they carry. Have someone in your company go out in the field with your reps. Be ready to jump on a plane when they call for help. Support your reps all the time, especially when they ask for assistance.

Follow up on your sales leads. Determine how the sales rep interacted with the customer. Let the rep know you are interested in both successful and unsuccessful sales leads. Continually develop new customer lists.

> ➪ **Courtney's Smart Tip**
> **Pay your commissions on time.**

Nothing distresses a rep more than waiting for commission checks. Some entrepreneurs defer paying their reps when cash flow problems arise. Don't fall into this pattern. Loss of a key rep could cripple your sales volume for many quarters. Pay your reps on time.

Hold quarterly or annual sales meetings. Pay for the hotel, meals, and other rep expenses. Let the reps cover their transportation costs. Hold sales sessions and ask for their input. Let them become a part of your management team. Recognize outstanding rep performance. Always deliver on your product promises. Avoid late delivery and unresponsive warranty servicing. Reps need the long-term good will of their customers more than they need you. Reps can usually find another source for the products they want to handle.

Try to avoid house accounts. These are accounts you have personally established and sometimes sell to at a lower profit margin. Reps are leery of lucrative accounts that you keep for yourself. They do not like to see large shipments of product going into their territories without commissions being paid to them. An option is to offer the rep the house account as soon as his or her total sales volume from other customers in the territory reaches a certain amount. Then the rep has a good incentive, and you are not risking paying a commission check to a mediocre seller.

Whether you use reps or hire your own sales force depends on the product, rep quality, market characteristics, and your financial condition.

7-10 Attending Trade Shows

Exhibiting at Trade Shows

QUESTION

I have a new product I want to market and am thinking about either attending or exhibiting at a trade show. Is this a good strategy and would it be worth the costs?

ANSWER

Trade shows are one of the more popular—and more economical—ways for entrepreneurs to market new products or services. Their main advantage is the ease of meeting and talking with qualified buyers. Studies show that about half the people attending a trade show are there to buy. Picking the right trade show is the tricky part—there are more than 8000 annually in the United States. Overall, the numbers indicate that trade shows are more cost-effective than sales reps. The average sales rep contacts five customers a day. That same rep contacts approximately five qualified leads per hour during a trade show.

Studies show that most sales leads require 4.3 calls to close a sale. About half of sales leads generated from a trade show can be closed with just one field call. The cost of obtaining a qualified trade show lead is about half that of making a field sales call.

There are potential disadvantages to consider. The costs of exhibiting at a trade show can easily run in the thousands of dollars for a small space. Entrepreneurs cannot risk picking the wrong show. Also, sales from a trade show may not materialize until months after the initial contact is made.

Outline your marketing goals and consider whether you want to focus on penetrating a national, regional, or local market. Decide which trade shows are best for you. At a "vertical" trade show, most of the goods are similar and have a specific theme. At a "horizontal" show, a wide variety of products are featured. It is also important that you estimate how many contacts, sales leads, and actual sales you need to make the trade show cost-effective.

Now you are ready to research the best trade show for your new product. Consult the *Trade Show Week Data Book*, which cross-lists thousands of shows geographically, chronologically, alphabetically, and by industry classification. Ask your librarian for other references. Trade show industry associations can also provide helpful information. Call or write the Trade Show Bureau in Denver, Colorado; the National Association of Exposition Managers in Aurora, Ohio; the International Exhibitors Association in Springfield, Virginia; or the

Exhibit Designers and Producers Association in Milwaukee, Wisconsin. Ask lots of questions and obtain as much information as possible from these associations.

Contact other entrepreneurs in the same industry who have exhibited at various trade shows. Ask which shows they found to be most profitable. Talk with sales representatives, dealers, and competitors.

Once you have selected an appropriate trade show, obtain an EVC report from the show manager. The report, published by the Trade Show Bureau's Exposition Council, lists detailed information about the show, including expected attendance and audience demographics. Use this list to send out invitations or call attendees. Plan your preshow promotions and encourage all good prospects to stop by and visit your booth. Consider holding a special event or get-together during the show to further discuss the features of your product. Offer special discounts and packages good only during the trade show. Finally, evaluate your performance during the trade show to determine if you should continue marketing your product this way.

> ➪ **Courtney's Smart Tip**
> **Follow up on all leads and contacts made during the show as soon as you return to the office.**

How to Introduce a New Product at a Trade Show

QUESTION

What are the advantages of marketing at trade shows to introduce a new product or service or to expand existing markets?

ANSWER

For a relatively low cost, you can reach a large number of high-quality prospects by spending a few days attending or exhibiting at the right trade show. Thousands of trade shows are held all over the world, but finding the *right* one can be tricky. The question to consider is: What trade shows should you attend to intercept your target customers?

Studies indicate that 50 percent of the people attending trade shows do so for the purpose of seeing new products and services. Thus, they are ideal marketing opportunities for entrepreneurs. Many founders claim that the success of their ventures is largely attributable to the effectiveness of using trade shows.

What are the benefits of attending trade shows? First, the prospects, many whom you probably do not know, come directly to you. It is an excellent chance to encounter people in the industry whom you would otherwise never have an opportunity to meet. Second, you can display and demonstrate product quality or superiority. You can answer any questions from prospects about your product or service. In addition, you can use this meeting to establish a successful business relationship by inviting them to a follow-up breakfast, lunch, or dinner meeting.

Here are some entrepreneurial dos and don'ts when it comes to attending trade shows:

- Do select a trade show at which the right prospects will be attending and visit as many exhibits as possible. Preplan your marketing strategy and set some specific objectives to achieve while attending the show.
- Develop some quick screening questions to ask, so you can quickly identify solid prospects. Follow up on all leads and contacts as soon as you return to the office.
- Don't wait until the last minute to sign up for booth space. Instead, try to secure prime exhibit space. Don't run out of product to sell and/or samples to give away. Don't use giveaways that have nothing to do with your product or service. Don't run out of business cards.
- Don't allow anyone representing you to wear inappropriate clothing. Ensure that people are properly trained to answer all questions from prospects.
- If you plan to exhibit, promote your product or service in advance by sending out invitations to visit your booth. Talk to exhibitors before the show to determine possible tie-ins.
- Hold a meeting with everyone on your team who will be covering the booth. Assign specific responsibilities to those involved in your exhibit. Reward the high achievers who get the most orders.
- Have news releases to give to reporters and editors who visit. Some seasoned entrepreneurs prepare press kits to disseminate at the show.
- Evaluate your performance while the experience of participating in the trade show is fresh. Determine what worked best and continue using the most productive approaches.

Successful entrepreneurs learn to work trade shows for all they're worth. Nowhere will you have a better chance to meet the key players in your industry and learn what is happening. The contacts you make can ultimately provide you with significantly increased business that will firmly establish and increase your market share.

Marketing Through Trade Shows

QUESTION

My partner and I are trying to put together a wholesale lamp business. What information can you give us on trade shows that exhibit this type of product?

ANSWER

Before you begin trade show marketing, you need to develop a detailed plan that outlines both the markets you are going to target and how you plan to penetrate each target. Once you have written a marketing plan for your lamp business, you are ready to research the trade shows in your industry.

There are three major information sources on trade shows: *Trade Show Week Data Book,* (800) 521-8110; *Trade Show and Exhibit Schedules,* (800) 253-6708; and *Trade Shows Worldwide,* (800) 877-4253. You should be able to find these publications in your local library.

Also, contact one of the lamp trade associations, such as the American Lighting Association at (312) 644-0828, and ask for appropriate trade shows to exhibit at. Query others in your industry about the best shows to attend. Ask how well the shows were promoted by the organizers. Find out if the organizers provide a profile of attendees.

With a start-up business, it is wise at first to attend one of the trade shows you are considering displaying at. Observe what goes on. Talk to your competitors. Notice how potential customers are treated. Ask those attending what they like and dislike about the show.

Since your marketing dollars are most likely limited, it is important to choose the trade show that attracts the right audience for your business. The High Point International Home Furnishings Market is a leading trade show in your industry. Once you have selected the right show, plan your preshow promotional material. Do not neglect this essential task. You must give attendees a reason to stop by your booth. Send out an attractive postcard or letter before the show giving potential customers a reason to visit you. You might feature a new model or offer a trade show special. Make the mailer attractive and eye-catching.

Follow up with at least one additional mailer. Around 80 percent of exhibitors neglect to do preshow promotions. Yet this is key to successful marketing at a trade show. Over 75 percent of attendees arrive with an agenda of what they want to accomplish. You need to intercept them ahead of time to ensure they stop and shop at your booth.

Now you can begin developing a lead system of new clients. Contact the U.S. Trade Show Bureau at (303) 860-7626. This is the industry's resource center for information about the latest trends, successful practices, and hot topics of interest. The bureau has a catalog of publications to assist entrepreneurs with exhibiting at trade shows. The charge for these publications averages $3 for members and $5 for nonmembers.

You might also consider joining the Trade Show Bureau, which provides a myriad of services to members, such as locating appropriate trade shows, suggesting pertinent marketing publications, and sending out its own monthly publication. The October issue is a video and pamphlet on preshow promotion. The bureau also publishes a membership directory and has an abundant number of contacts. Newcomers and veterans of trade shows are supplied with the latest research on "boothmanship," sales training for trade shows, and other tips. For example, did you know that the most important selling times are usually the first and last hours of a trade show?

The lamp business is an extremely competitive industry in which new products are instantaneously copied and brought to market in a short period of time. Learn the industry well before proceeding. Subscribe to the monthly journal *Home Lighting and Accessories*, which is the "bible" for the industry.

7-11 Pitfalls to Avoid

1. Assuming that there is a market for your product or service just because you think it is a wonderful idea.
2. Overexaggerating the size of the market and the number of potential customers who might purchase your product or service.
3. Underestimating people's inertia and the difficulty of penetrating your target market.
4. Miscalculating the amount of time and money it takes to successfully penetrate your market.
5. Inflating sales volume.
6. Failing to continually research customer needs.
7. Paying too little attention to developing a current customer base to expand sales.
8. Purchasing untested mailing lists and sending marketing materials without an immediate follow-up call or additional mailings.
9. Sending out brochures and thinking that many people will respond.

10. Putting your goods on consignment without purchasing insurance to cover loss or damage.
11. Failing to use performance contracts when hiring sales representatives.
12. Failing to pay earned commissions to your sales reps in a timely manner.
13. Designing and using standard, unimaginative, white business cards.
14. Attending a trade show without researching who will be attending and identifying your target customers.
15. Sending out press releases without first contacting the media, determining their interest, and then following up about possible publication.
16. Failing to give away samples or gifts while exhibiting at a trade show.
17. Failing to develop and follow a marketing plan with realistic goals and budgets.
18. Forgetting to ask your customers for referrals for new business.

The Good News. You can improve your marketing success by listening to your customers, observing which marketing strategies your competitors use, and developing innovative low-cost marketing techniques for your venture.

7-12 Entrepreneurial Resource Checklist

References

1. *Contacts Influential* (check your local library).
2. *Encyclopedia of Associations,* Vol. 1, Gale Research Inc., Detroit, Mich. This reference lists national organizations, including trade, business, and commercial.
3. Karl Albrecht and Ron Zemke, *Service America: Doing Business in the New Economy,* Dow Jones-Irwin, New York, 1985.
4. Karl Albrecht, *The Only Thing That Matters,* Harper Business, New York, 1992.
5. Karl Albrecht, *Service Within,* Business One Irwin, New York, 1990.

6. Kristin Anderson and Ron Zemke, *Delivering Knock Your Socks Off Service,* AMACOM, New York, 1991.
7. Courtney Price, Richard Buskirk, and Mack Davis, *Program for Writing Winning Business Plans,* PEP, Denver, Colo., 1991.
8. Marilyn and Tom Ross, *Big Marketing Ideas for Small Service Businesses,* Dow Jones-Irwin, New York, 1990.
9. Ken Dychtwald, *Age Wave: Choices and Challenges for Our New Future,* J. P. Tarcher, Los Angeles, 1988.
10. Harvey Mackay, *Swim with the Sharks,* Morrow, New York, 1988.
11. Robert Mestin, *How to Succeed with Your Own 900 Business,* Aegis Publishers, 1993.

Further Reading

Books

Blankenship, A. B., and George Breen. *Do-It-Yourself Market Research,* McGraw-Hill, New York, 1989.

Cohen, William A. *Developing a Winning Marketing Plan,* Wiley, New York, 1987.

Cohen, William A. *The Entrepreneur and Small Business Marketing,* Wiley, New York, 1991.

Cook, Kenneth. *AMA Complete Guide to Small Business Marketing,* New York, 1991.

Gross, T. Scott. *Positively Outrageous Service,* Mastermedia, 1991.

Phillips, Michael, and Salli Raspberry. *Marketing Without Advertising,* Nolo Press, 1990.

Putnam, Anthony O. *Marketing Your Services,* Wiley, New York, 1990.

Computer Databases

Dow Jones News Retrieval Services

Compact Disclosures

INFOTRAC

Magazines

Sales and Marketing Management,
Bill Communications Inc., New York.

Advertising Age

Contacts

1. American Business Card Club
   (303) 690-6496

This association is a worldwide network for exchanging business card designs and ideas. Contact Avery N. Pitzak, president.

2. Simmons Market Research Bureau

   The bureau lists product categories and demographic characteristics for varying levels of consumption.

3. Mediamark Research, Inc.

   This research group lists product categories and demographic characteristics for varying levels of consumption.

4. Information Industry Association
   555 New Jersey Avenue NW
   Suite 800
   Washington, DC

   This association is involved with the creation and distribution of information services and publishes a free two-page brochure, "Customer Service Guide for 900 Programs."

5. Trade Show Information

   There are three major publication sources for trade shows: *Trade Show Week Data Book,* (800) 521-8110; *Trade Show and Exhibit Schedules,* (800) 253-6708; and *Trade Shows Worldwide,* (800) 877-4253. You should be able to find these publications in your local library.

6. Trade Show Bureau
   Denver, CO
   (303) 860-7626

   This national bureau is the industry's resource center, providing information about the latest industry trends, successful practices, and hot topics of interest. An extensive catalog of publications assists entrepreneurs with exhibiting at trade shows.

7. U.S. Department of Commerce

   The department publishes extensive data and demographics on various industries.

8 Financing Your Venture

8-1 Overview

Looking for start-up and expansion capital is an ongoing and increasingly difficult task as financial funds for entrepreneurs dry up during the 1990s. Most entrepreneurs fail to realize that start-up ventures are financed by personal savings and/or friendly money.

Your success depends on the type of business, its age, your industry, financial contacts, referrals, how much money you have already invested in the venture, how much money you are looking for, and matching the outside money source to your business.

Choosing the right source to contact is key to your future growth and development. A few money sources are interested in initial market research and development, but most look to later stages of growth when the venture has an operating history. Some finance only small amounts of money, while others have no maximum limit. Some finance only debt, some prefer equity, and some look for a combination of the two. Some investors want to be a part of the management team, while others don't want to be involved.

There are a wide range of financing sources, terms, and conditions which make raising capital even more difficult. For example, banks have tightened their loan policies from the aggressive lending of the 1980s. Today, bankers are structuring loans with less leverage, requiring heavy collateralization by homes and other personal assets.

The notion that commercial banks are interested in making loans to start-up ventures is a myth. If a bank turns you down, ask if the institution is an SBA lender. A growing number of financial institutions are learning the ins and outs of SBA lending to offset their risk on loans to young companies. If the bank still turns you down, ask an investor to guarantee your loan.

Some entrepreneurs turn to venture capital firms for seed money to launch their businesses. Here too, the young, start-up business can hit a wall. Most venture capitalists prefer to invest in older, more developed companies that offer opportunities for high growth—up to 60 or 70 percent annually.

The result is that most entrepreneurs fund their ventures with personal savings or money from friends and family. The most common funding sources at the early start-up stage involve M&Ds (moms and dads). Other sources of financing include family and friends, professional acquaintances, past employees, potential customers and suppliers, government programs, other entrepreneurs, private investors (commonly called angels), corporate strategic alliances. One of my venture capitalist friends labels many of these sources as DDFFs (doctors, dentists, friends, and other fools).

One of the more contemporary financing approaches involves credit cards. Some entrepreneurs who cannot secure a bank loan or a line of credit are financing their ventures by getting cash from different credit card companies. Sometimes, founders select members of their management team on the basis of how many credit cards they possess and the lending limits on each card.

Another contemporary source of funding involves factors, or finance companies. A factoring company purchases your accounts receivable and then advances you cash. Instead of looking to the borrower's credit, factors look at the credit of the borrower's customers and usually do their own collecting. Finance companies are secured lenders that provide funds backed by the borrower's assets. This collateral includes accounts receivable, inventories, plant, and equipment.

You can't know too many people or funding sources in the money market. The name of the game is contacts and referrals—made *before* you need money. Network with all money sources, because many of the old deal makers are out of the picture or financing with different criteria. The rules are constantly changing in the money-raising game.

8-2 Smart Strategies for Financing New and Existing Ventures

1. Learn as much as possible about the money market and how to raise capital from different funding sources.

2. If you are raising money from friends and family, structure the deal professionally by signing a note or other type of agreement concerning the terms of the loan.
3. If your friends or family do not have any cash to lend you, consider asking them to guarantee the loan.
4. Contact the economic development agency in your city or state to find out about government seed capital funds.
5. Avoid looking to a "banker" for a financing relationship. Instead, look to a lender that is interested in you and your venture.
6. Get referrals to money sources you are considering contacting for capital.
7. Always have an updated business plan and current financial statements when meeting with potential lenders or investors.
8. Use lines of credit to accommodate cash flow crunches and seasonal credit demands of your business.
9. To create your own line of credit, submit credit card applications simultaneously to obtain several cards with cash advance privileges.
10. Consider using factoring to solve short-term cash flow problems when you experience long delays between making and selling your product or service.
11. Consider establishing a strategic alliance with a corporation to secure funds to develop and/or expand your product or services.

8-3 Developing a Financial Strategy

The Best Sources of Capital for New Ventures

QUESTION

I am in the process of establishing a round-the-clock day-care center for children from 2 to 10 years old. Where can I find a venture capitalist to fund my business?

ANSWER

Many entrepreneurs think that the premier source of funding for their ventures is a venture capitalist. However, the amount of money available for venture capital has fallen dramatically since 1987. Most of this capital is lent to older, more developed companies that offer opportunities for strong returns. Many venture capital firms quote a funding rate of around 1 percent of all applicants.

The truth is that most start-up firms are financed almost entirely by the owners' personal savings—approximately 90 percent. There are many advantages to financing a new venture with your own money. First, you save a lot of time. It can take months and almost a full-time effort to secure money from outside sources. That may be time you sacrifice at the expense of other critical activities. The time you spend chasing money would be better spent chasing the market.

Second, money is expensive. Private investors and venture capitalists seek very high interest rates, since they typically demand upward of 50 percent return per year for their funds. Many enterprises are not sufficiently profitable to afford outside funding. Third, control over your venture may be severely jeopardized by outside financing. Venture capitalists may demand voting control of your business. After several rounds of financing, your portion of the venture may dwindle to a tiny percent. Many entrepreneurs feel that one of the main reasons they start a business is to control their own destiny. Using outside money, especially from a venture capitalist, may alter that desire. Your investors may want to control your destiny.

There are other sources of financing for early start-ups. These include family and friends (the most common source) as well as professional acquaintances, past employees, potential customers and suppliers of the new venture, government programs, wealthy businesspeople, and private investors. At the early stages of development, founders provide much of the seed capital for the venture. This may be in the form of forgone salary during the early stages rather than in outlays of hard cash.

Seed Capital for New Ventures

QUESTION

Where can I find money for my new lawn care and sprinkler business?

ANSWER

Finding capital is a standard problem for most entrepreneurs. Raising money is an art. Fortunately, it is one you can learn. It is critical to gain knowledge of the money market, the people in it, and how to interact with them. The fact is that "alternative" (nonbanking) sources provide the best avenue for aspiring entrepreneurs. Each of these sources is discussed below.

Self-Financing. There are many virtues to financing your new venture yourself. These range from being able to maintain total control of your business to being able to use the cheapest source of money. You can furnish your own capital through savings, income from a second job, or internal financing of an existing business. If you start your business on a shoestring, you can expand when you have generated enough capital. For entrepreneurs who love freedom and independence, this is one of the easiest and best approaches to take.

Relatives and Friends. Parents can also be a good, quick, and excellent source of financing. Even if they do not have large savings in the bank, they may have other assets that can be converted into cash. They may own a house free and clear of any mortgage payments, and could possibly obtain a second mortgage. Alternatively, mom and dad could cosign a loan for your business. Uncle Clyde, Aunt Tillie, or your old school buddy could also loan you money for your new business. There are times when this is the wisest action to take; however, there may be problems later on. Be careful with money from extended family or friends. First, approach the deal professionally, as you would with an outside or traditional money source. Cut your deal, commit the terms to writing, and honor it as you would a deal with outside investors.

Verbal agreements can be disastrous and people's memory will fail over time. Family and friends can nag you to death and be tougher than outside creditors. If you lose this money, you'll pay for the rest of your life both in respect and in relationships.

Professional Advisers and Business Associates. Outside investors such as lawyers, business advisers, board members, successful entrepreneurs, and other professionals may invest seed capital in your venture. Informal investors often have noneconomic reasons as well as capital gains in mind when they invest. Sometimes members of the infrastructure will contribute their professional fees in exchange for stock in your company. To find such investors, ask for referrals.

Credit Cards. One of the more novel approaches to financing new ventures is obtaining cash through plastic (i.e., credit cards). Some entrepreneurs have recruited members of their management team on the basis of the number of credit cards they held and their credit limit on these cards. When additional capital was needed, the management team just applied for additional credit cards. This is a costly way to finance a business, but when people are desperate, they become very creative.

Customers in Hand. Look to your potential or current customers as plausible sources of financing. There may be instances when customers want your product or service so badly that they will either put a deposit up front with their order or supply the money you need to process and deliver the order. Existing customers can be an extremely cheap source of money. Ask for an installment or prepayment when they place an order. Even if you give customers a discount for paying COD, you may be money ahead.

QUESTION

I would really like to start a new business and be my own boss. How can I get seed money to start such a business? Any information you have would be helpful.

ANSWER

There are no easy answers for locating money to start a new business. Seed money, sometimes called venture capital, is the money that goes into a business before it starts operating. Don't confuse seed money with "seed capital" from venture capitalists.

Sources of financing and penetrating a market are the two major problems most start-up businesses face. It is easier to attract financing if you have a track record and a proven market. But most start-ups do not have either.

The most common source of financing a start-up business is yourself. The second most common source is "friendly money" obtained by contacting people you know and asking them to invest. There are many advantages to using your money to start the venture. You maintain control of the business while utilizing the cheapest form of financing available.

Once you have exhausted your own financial resources, think about contacting relatives, friends, business associates, and other private sources. If they do not have much money in savings, they may have other assets that can be converted into cash. They may own a home on which they could obtain a second mortgage. Or they may have stocks, bonds, or other assets that could be pledged.

Unfortunately, most entrepreneurs think of the bank as the most likely place to find financing. Although banks are often the quickest and cheapest source of money, they are probably the worst place to go unless you have sufficient collateral to guarantee the loan. Banks require assets that can be used as collateral along with a visible means of paying off the loan at a reasonable time in the future. Businesses usually need several years of operating history before they are considered creditworthy; most cannot get financing unless someone agrees to guarantee the loan.

Typically, a bank will ask for historical as well as pro forma balance sheets, income statements, cash flow projections, year-end financial statements, tax returns, and a business plan. The bank will also request a current personal financial statement and your personal tax returns for the past 3 years. Founders of new ventures do not have this type of information. Banks seldom furnish start-up money. Any money you are able to borrow from banks at the beginning of your venture will probably be loaned to you personally or on some basis other than your business.

> ➪ **Courtney's Smart Tip**
> **Pursue friendly money sources. Network with everyone you know. Ask people if they can refer you to others who may be interested in investing in your type of venture. Keep widening your circle of funding contacts with successive referrals.**

Studies over the past 25 years indicate that most seed money for start-ups comes directly from the entrepreneur, partners associated with the business, and wealthy individuals. You can locate potential investors through the SBA, your banker, lawyer, realtor, or other professionals. A limited amount of seed money may be available in your local community from regional development agencies. Contact the economic development office in your area to find out about such programs. Other sources of seed money are mortgage brokers (using your house equity as security) and credit unions.

Your ability to raise money depends on the soundness of your venture, your sales skills, how exciting you make the deal, your sources of friendly money, and the prospect's appetite. Use the following checklist as a guide to developing a financial strategy and securing funds for growth.

Smart Money Sources at a Glance

1. *Friendly money.* Friendly money sources include yourself, mom and dad, relatives, and friends. This is one of the quickest, cheapest, and easiest financing methods, especially for new start-ups.
2. *Commercial banks.* If your venture has no collateral, few assets, and/or little operating history, banks may not be a good source of funding. You must be willing to pledge your personal assets to secure a bank loan. Banks look for both primary and secondary sources of repayment.
3. *Finance companies.* Finance companies are primarily asset-based lenders, extending financing against receivables, inventory, equipment, and other "hard" forms of collateral.

4. *The SBA.* The SBA grants two types of loans. The most common type is a bank loan for which the SBA guarantees a large portion, typically 70 to 90 percent. The SBA in turn will require that the loan be collateralized with personal commitments from the principals.
5. *Leasing companies.* Leasing companies loan to businesses for the purchase of automobiles, trucks, computers, office furniture, and other equipment to help offset the initial outlay of cash for major purchases. Entrepreneurs usually are required to provide a personal guarantee to secure the lease.
6. *SBICs.* State financial aid is provided through SBICs (small business investment centers) licensed by the SBA. Typically an SBIC makes loans for equipment purchases, facility improvements, new buildings, and sometimes working capital.
7. *Venture capitalists.* Venture capital firms specialize in investing money in return for an equity position. They look for ventures that offer extremely high growth potential in a short period of time—for example, ones in which they can quintuple their investment in 5 years. Venture capitalists fund only about 1 percent of the deals that come across their desks.
8. *Investment bankers.* Investment banking firms specialize in taking companies public through an initial public offering (IPO). They look for businesses that will achieve maximum growth with the right infusion of capital.
9. *Private placement.* A private placement is an investor-based securities issue that is exempt from the registration requirements of public offerings. Private placements involve offering stock, subordinated debt, convertible debt, or some other option to friendly sources, wealthy individuals, or venture capital firms via a private placement document. Private placements come under Regulation D, adopted by the Securities and Exchange Commission (SEC), which facilitates the raising of capital by small businesses.

8-4 Borrowing from a Bank

Choosing the Right Bank

QUESTION

I have been operating a small landscape business for 8 years. It does well in the summer but dries up during the winter months, forcing me to deplete my savings. I have tried snow plowing as a second business, but it rarely brings in enough additional income. I would like to open a sandwich shop and have been seeking a small business loan for $25,000. I have not been able to find a bank that is willing to loan the funds. Where can I go?

ANSWER

Before approaching a bank for a commercial loan, you must write a business plan that proves to the loan officer that you have thoroughly investigated your venture idea and can demonstrate that the business will earn a profit, that it has growth potential, and, most important, that you will be able to repay the loan. Even then, the bank may decide not to make the loan.

Why? Many banks prefer not to fund new ventures. They like to see a track record of a couple of years. "But," you say, "I have run another small business for 8 years. Isn't that enough?" Because you have operated a landscape business does not mean that you can manage a sandwich shop. Management skills are not necessarily transferable from one industry to another. Besides, you have chosen a high-risk industry—the restaurant business.

Do you have any experience in the restaurant business? If not, does anyone on your proposed management team have such experience? You must be able to show that you or someone associated with your new venture has related industry experience. A well-written business plan will confirm that there is need for a sandwich shop in the location you have chosen, that there are enough potential customers in the surrounding area to support your business, and that you can generate a profit.

If you are able to prove all these facts, seek out banks that specialize in working with entrepreneurs and making loans for start-ups. Try to find banks that loan to restaurateurs. Talk with friends, accountants, attorneys, insurance agents, and other business consultants. Try to secure referrals to loan officers representing at least three different banks.

> ➪ **Courtney's Smart Tip**
> **Avoid "cold calling" on a banker. Have someone call the banker and extend a personal recommendation before your first meeting.**

Developing and writing a business plan, establishing a banking relationship, and securing a loan could be a lengthy process. Start early. If possible, establish a banking relationship with a potential lender long before you need a loan. The willingness to fund a start-up venture depends on a bank's policies, current loan requests, and the bank's existing loan portfolio. If you do not have enough collateral to borrow against, or do not have enough assets in the business, you probably won't get a bank loan.

Try to secure a government-backed loan through the Small Business Administration or through state and local government revolving-loan funds. The SBA loan program provides a guarantee to banks of up to 90 percent of loans to small businesses, with maximal exposure of up to $750,000, or in special situations up to $1,000,000. Since not all banks are SBA lenders, ask the loan officer which government-backed loan programs the bank participates in. You might also contact your state's office of economic development to find out about local and state loan programs.

QUESTION

I am getting ready to start a small data-processing business and need to find a bank that will work with me, set up my accounts, and perhaps loan my business funds to expand at some future date. Do you have any suggestions on how to establish a satisfying banking relationship?

ANSWER

Finding the right bank and loan officer is an art—difficult at best, since bankers usually have a different perspective on businesses than do entrepreneurs. Discovering the right loan officer who understands your business and supports your strategic plans takes time and effort.

Successful banking relationships are built on the personal ties you develop with your banker. Search for several different banks that target businesses like yours for clients. Begin by contacting the bank at which you have your personal accounts, if the bank can meet your business needs.

Smart Guidelines for Establishing a Banking Relationship

1. *Get referrals.* Speak to colleagues, accountants, lawyers, insurance agents, or other business consultants. Knowing the right person to talk to through an introduction from a business associate is a good start in building a banking relationship.
   - Always act professionally. Set up an appointment. Don't just walk into a bank and introduce yourself. Dress for success. First impressions are critical. Demonstrate that you run a professional business.

2. *Be prepared.* Always bring in an updated business plan and current financials, such as cash flows, income statements, and balance sheets. Bankers need to know that you have thoroughly investigated the venture, proved that the business can earn a profit, and shown that the venture has growth potential. Offer to drop off the business plan before the meeting so the banker can have an opportunity to review your venture.
3. *Look for compatibility.* Determine how accessible the banker will be to meet with you regularly, return phone calls, and discuss your business problems. If possible, find a banker who has lending experience in your industry. A banker can be one of the most important professionals on your team.
4. *Ask about lending limits.* Determine if your financial requests can be accommodated. Make sure you give your banker a specific loan amount. Bankers become frustrated when discussing loans with entrepreneurs who are not sure of how much money they want or need.
5. *Shop around for services and rates.* Know what you want from the banking relationship and determine whether a bank can provide all the services your require. Banks have different objectives, charge different fees, and set varying interest rates. Refrain from negotiating the terms and rates of your loan until after the bank has approved your request.

➪ **Courtney's Smart Tip**
Establish a banking relationship with a potential lender *before* you need a loan.

Developing a banking relationship and securing a loan take time. Start early. A bank's ability to lend to a start-up business varies and depends on the number of current loan requests and the bank's existing loan portfolio. If you do not have enough collateral or do not have enough assets in the business, obtaining a business loan will be difficult.

How to Obtain a Line of Credit

QUESTION

I periodically need temporary injections of money to help me with my cash flow peaks and valleys. Is establishing a line of credit a possible solution to this problem? How do entrepreneurs access and use bank lines of credit? Are they difficult to obtain, or are banks fairly willing to grant them?

ANSWER

As a result of seasonal credit demands, entrepreneurs frequently encounter difficulties managing their cash flow. This is especially true of business start-ups during their early stages of development when they have not diversified enough to generate a constant positive cash flow. Once inventory has been purchased, it is necessary to ride out the cycle until accounts receivable have been collected. Without sufficient working capital, a serious cash flow problem could develop. These types of cash flow problems have forced many entrepreneurs to close down businesses that were making money on paper, but just ran out of cash.

Lines of credit accommodate the seasonal credit demands of your business along with ups and downs in your cash flow. They also enable you to purchase inventory in anticipation of future sales. Discuss establishing a line of credit with your bank at the beginning of your relationship. If you are just starting your business, the bank will probably not grant a credit line immediately.

A line of credit is a standard service provided by many banks that serve small businesses. Getting the loan approved depends on the business's ability to repay and/or the personal assets of the owner—for example, a second mortgage on a home, assignment of stocks and bonds, or assignment of the cash value of life insurance policies.

Banks extend a secured line of credit to most start-up ventures. The line may be unsecured if the business can demonstrate consistent earnings, an excellent capital position, and multiple sources of repayment. Traditionally, banks will commit a specified maximum amount of funds from which you are permitted to draw on as needed. You have the right to repay and reborrow during the agreed-upon time, which usually will not exceed a year. You pay interest only on the outstanding principal.

In addition, the bank needs to know how you will repay the line when your first source of repayment does not come through. Bankers look for enough elasticity in your operations to accommodate temporary reversals in adverse situations. What happens when you discover that your inventory is not selling as projected? What secondary sources of repayment are available?

Banks may also require you to pay down your line of credit when you have not followed your payment schedule, even though the total amount of money that you borrowed is not due for several more months. Banks do not like to approve lines of credit for use in managing cash flow. Instead, lines of credit are intended for cyclical borrowing needs at identified paydown intervals. A failure to pay back the money on schedule indicates a potential problem in your ability to manage cash.

Smart Tips for Establishing a Line of Credit

1. Most likely a bank will not issue a line of credit to a new venture without the owner's personal guarantee of repayment.
2. If your business is relatively new and the bank is not satisfied with the primary and secondary sources of repayment, it may ask for personal collateral from you to secure the loan.
3. If the venture is a partnership or corporation with more than one principal, the bank will most likely collateralize the loan from all the principals involved to obtain a line of credit.
4. You must present reasonable financial documents that follow standard accounting practices to obtain a line of credit.
5. Unless you are a well-established business, you must provide pro forma cash flow documents that demonstrate your ability to pay back the money. Pro forma balance sheets and income statements will also be required.

How to Secure Merchant's Credit Card Status

QUESTION

I am contemplating a small direct-mail business. I am considering setting up a merchant's credit with VISA/MasterCard as a convenience for those ordering merchandise from me. How can a new mail-order enterprise obtain merchant's credit card status? I found one book on the subject that costs $135. Do you have any suggestions?

ANSWER

It is difficult for a new business owner to establish credit and receive immediate approval from a bank for a merchant's credit card status. But it can be done. It hinges on the relationship you have established with your banker. Developing a good, sound relationship and proving your creditworthiness can ensure that you receive approval to use VISA, MasterCard, or other types of credit cards in your business.

Bankers are reluctant to approve credit card usage for a new mail-order business because of numerous credit card scams—especially when there are no signatures accompanying customer orders. An owner could set up a bogus mail-order business, advertise nationally, receive thousands of dollars in orders, close up the business, and skip town with a big wad of cash before customers even expected to receive their orders. A few bad apples have spoiled it for many new mail-order business owners.

Who is liable when such a scam occurs? The bank. Therefore, bankers view mail-order businesses as being extremely risky, unless the business owner is well known in the community, has a proven product or service, and has an established business and operating history of charge-backs. Most bankers also realize that new products and/or services could be defective. There may be a high rate of customer dissatisfaction and, consequently, charge-backs. What type of warranty do you offer? What are your return policies? How quickly do you deliver new orders? If the chance to dispute charges in your business is great, bankers will shy away from approving credit cards for your business.

Some industries are riskier than others for credit card charges and typically have higher rates of charge-backs. For example, selling services by telephone and offering mail-order vitamins and water purifiers have poor credit card histories. Also, telemarketing companies and businesses that use fulfillment houses to fill orders have higher-than-average charge-backs.

If the bank is skeptical about approving credit cards for your business, suggest that it hold a certain amount of funds for 90 days or so before you can collect your credit card charges. Such an arrangement could be written into the merchant agreement you sign with the bank. Or propose that the bank set up a reserve account or certificate of deposit that will guarantee a certain amount of funds if your charge-backs are higher than anticipated.

> ➪ **Courtney's Smart Tip**
> **Shop around for the best credit card rates available. These rates are always negotiable.**

Individual banks have varying rates, depending on how much they mark up credit card services, how good a customer you are, how many accounts you have with the bank, and the volume of business you do. These rates are always negotiable. The longer you have been in business, the more negotiating power you have. Regardless of the terms, bankers will perform "due diligence" to ensure that you are a reputable business owner, have a reliable product, and are creditworthy.

Credit card processors will also monitor your charge-back status. Once charge-backs have reached 5 percent or greater, they will start to worry. If your charge-backs reach 7 or 8 percent, they will most likely cancel your credit. Instead, they like to see 1 to 2 percent charge-backs. Their customer service area regularly observes how many complaints are received on your products or services. Either the bank or the processor can cancel your credit at any time. Once you receive approval, guard your credit.

How to Calculate Goodwill on a Balance Sheet

QUESTION

I am a sole proprietor and have been in business for over 3 years, operating from my home in retail sales. I am pursuing an SBA-backed loan through a local bank. The loan officer advised me to include goodwill on my balance sheet. I don't know how to calculate this figure. I called many different sources but none could help. Can you tell me how to compute goodwill for my balance sheet?

ANSWER

Determining a reasonable goodwill figure for your balance sheet is most difficult. There is no universal rule on how to figure goodwill, which adds value to your venture. Essentially goodwill is based upon future earning expectations. However, the difficulty lies in deciding the best way to measure and value future earnings. Goodwill is essentially the amount of the asking price for a company over and above the company's tangible net worth. In other words, if your asking price is higher than the venture's tangible net worth, you are selling goodwill. Sellers try to build in as much goodwill as possible, whereas buyers hope to minimize it. Sellers attempt to convince buyers that purchasing their company's name, reputation, and contacts is worth the higher price.

In most instances, goodwill is considered only when a company is being sold. Even though a strategic location, an impeccable reputation, or a superior product may create goodwill, it is usually not recorded by a company on its financial statements. Complicating the issue, lenders view goodwill very differently and focus on separate issues. Some look at it in terms of what presence the venture currently has in the marketplace, considering such factors as prestige and renown of the venture, record of successful operations over a long period, favorable customer relations, and ownership of a trade or brand name.

Other lenders look at goodwill as an amount which indicates the venture's future profitability.

Overall, most bankers consider goodwill "blue sky"—that is, only the owner's assumption of what the venture is worth over and above its tangible net worth. It is possible to add goodwill to your balance sheet as a noncurrent asset in the intangible column, which includes such items as leasehold interests, patents, trade names, trademarks, and organizational expenses (i.e., fees).

However, be prepared for lenders to discount this entry or eliminate it completely. Goodwill is not looked at as being a major cash driver of the business. Instead, the strengths of the owner and the management team are evaluated, as well as the strengths of your industry and the community you serve. On the balance sheet, lenders evaluate the net profits of the business and calculate the percentage of net profit in relation to total sales. They look for how much of your earned net profit is put back into the business in the form of retained earnings.

It is almost impossible to value the goodwill of your sole proprietorship, since you and the business are one and the same. If you sell your venture for more than its tangible net worth, then goodwill becomes an asset on your balance sheet. If you feel that a concrete valuation is important, you might contact a valuation expert or professional appraiser for assistance. Establish detailed and creative documentation to support the valuation you use.

If you are purchasing a business, remember that goodwill is not everlasting. A business with goodwill at the time of acquisition may lose some or all of its goodwill a short time later.

8-5 Venture Capitalists

Attracting Capital for New Ventures

QUESTION

I want to attract a venture capitalist to invest in my new business. How can I find one?

ANSWER

Numerous aspiring entrepreneurs make the common mistake of trying to access the venture capital world when very few start-ups qualify for venture capital funds. In fact, extremely few new businesses will ever receive funding from venture capital firms.

Why? To begin with, only a smattering of venture capital firms are interested in raw start-ups. The majority look for an established track record before considering investing in a project. Venture capitalists fund only a tiny percentage of all the business plans submitted to them—about 1 percent. Of that figure, less than 14 percent are start-up ventures.

Most professional venture capital groups have stringent criteria for their investments. They search for ventures with extremely high growth potential that will enable them to quintuple their investment in 5 years. Some of the smaller funds prefer to invest upward of $250,000. Some of the megafunds do not invest less than $1 million. However, all this depends heavily on the size of the venture, its growth potential, and its stage of development.

In addition, some venture capital funds invest only in certain types of industries—for example, high tech, software, bio tech, and health care. Entrepreneurs should seek advice and referrals from the infrastructure (accountants, lawyers, and investment and commercial bankers) when trying to decide which venture capital firm to contact.

Finding the Right Venture Capital Company

QUESTION

I am considering the possibility of starting a bus/shuttle service to transport bar and restaurant patrons. How can I attract and contact venture capital firms?

ANSWER

Venture capital is probably one of the least understood areas of financing. Many entrepreneurs think that these investors do the early-stage financing of relatively small, rapid growing enterprises. Today, venture capital is better defined as a professionally managed pool of participation through stocks, warrants, or convertible securities. If you think you have a venture that might qualify for venture capital financing, here is how you go about locating and contacting venture capital firms.

The first step is identifying venture capital firms that might be interested in your company. You can consult *Pratt's Guide to Venture Capital Sources,*[1] which lists more than 700 venture capital companies and the types of companies they invest in. *Raising Venture Capital and the Entrepreneur*[2] is a comprehensive guide to discovering money sources available through venture capitalists. You could also contact the National Venture Capital Association, which publishes an up-to-date list of its members and will send out free copies when requested, or the Western Association of Venture Capitalists, which publishes a directory of its members in 11 western states. (See the "Contacts" section in the resource checklist at the end of this chapter.)

> ➪ **Courtney's Smart Tip**
> **Always secure an introduction before contacting a venture capital firm.**

The more you can network with the infrastructure and other entrepreneurs to obtain referrals to venture capitalists, the better chance you have of securing financing from these investors. The referral may involve only a telephone call alerting the venture capitalists that your business is deserving of their consideration. Be sure to expose your deal to more than one potential venture capitalist.

Avoid mailing your business plan arbitrarily to many different venture capitalists. "Safety is in numbers" is not the case when obtaining venture capital financing. The best way to proceed is to contact 5 to 10 venture capital firms which, according to your referrals, have a reasonable probability of being interested in your company.

During the first contact, describe the venture, its products, the experience of your management team, the amount of capital sought, and the expected performance of the venture 2 to 3 years down the road. At this point, you must persuade the investor to find out more about your venture.

After this initial call, the venture capitalist will quickly evaluate whether the venture is worth having you submit a business plan, or perhaps make a presentation. Experts estimate that 60 to 80 percent of all ventures presented to venture capitalists are rejected during the first contact. Venture capitalists will agree to review your business plan only if they believe that your idea has significant growth potential in an expanding market, that your management team is well qualified to operate the venture, and that their investment will earn an appropriate return in terms of capital appreciation.

Studies suggest that venture capitalists focus on five areas in their investment screening: (1) the caliber of your management team, including a successful track record and relevant experience; (2) the industry and technology of the venture; (3) the distinctive characteristics and uniqueness of the venture; (4) your financial data, including pro formas of cash flow documents, balance sheets, and profit-and-loss statements; and (5) the overall terms of the deal. The management team is of key importance. Most venture capitalists would rather invest in a first-rate management team and a second-rate product than the reverse.

If the venture capitalist discovers no major flaws in the above areas, you will be asked to make an oral presentation to the investment group. At this stage, only 10 to 20 percent of all entrepreneurs who originally contacted the venture capitalist are still being considered. Don't be discouraged about being turned down at this point. Your venture must fit the investment objectives and philosophy of the firm. The firm must decide on the number and portfolio mix of businesses, buyout opportunities, types of industries, and geographic regions. The intuition or gut feeling of the venture capitalist to your deal also plays a significant role.

How and When to Approach a Venture Capitalist

QUESTION

I feel that my business would qualify for venture capital funds but do not know where to find them. Could you give me some sources to contact?

ANSWER

Start at your local library. There are over 2300 venture capital firms in the United States and more overseas. There are even more foreign investors coming to the United States looking for deals. Many are aggressively initiating projects in markets and technologies in which they have a special interest. Beware of advertisements that ask you to send \$150 to \$200 for lists of venture capitalists. The lists you receive from many of these mail-order companies are the same ones you can obtain *free* from the library.

Refer to one or all of the following books: *Venture's Guide to International Venture Capital*,[3] *Pratt's Guide to Venture Capital Sources*,[1] *Who's Who in Venture Capital*,[4] and *Handbook of Business Finance and Capital Sources*.[5] These books list the amount of money each venture capitalist wants to invest (minimum and/or maximum) and the types of business ventures preferred. Another excellent resource about the world of venture capital is *Venture Capital at the Crossroads*.[6]

In addition, contact the National Venture Capital Association at (703) 528-4370 for a free list of its members. The economic development centers and small business development centers (SBDCs) in your area should also have lists of venture capitalists. Local colleges and universities with outreach business development programs are another source.

Most firms specialize in one or two technologies, or markets, because they are familiar with the industry and/or have experienced past success. Some firms exist solely to invest in a specific area, such as computer software or robotics. Other firms specialize in stages of investment: seed-only, leveraged-buyout-only, mezzanine-financing-only, and so on. Some firms specialize by region. Others like to be the lead negotiator of all the terms and structuring of the deal before bringing in follower investors. A few firms become actively involved financially and managerially in the seed stage of new ventures. They decide on a product or technology they want to commercialize.

Research the venture capital firm before making contact. If at all possible, have someone refer and introduce you to the principals. Cold calling is not recommended, but networking can produce valuable contacts. Financing from professional venture capitalists can be very attractive to entrepreneurs. Venture capitalists bring more than money to the deal. Many have had the experience of doing it successfully before and have "deep pockets" and contacts with others who can raise additional capital as the venture grows.

Keep in mind that all firms have stringent criteria for their investments and look for ventures that have extremely high growth potential. As a rule, firms fund less than 5 percent of the deals they review. More important, entrepreneurs usually give up between 35 to 60 percent of their equity to attract this type of capital.

8-6 Private Placements

When to Pursue Private Funding

QUESTION

I am the owner of a franchise for gourmet pizza restaurants. I hired an internationally known franchise consulting company to draw up all the necessary franchise agreements, ensuring that they conformed with all legal regulations. Since the franchise was founded in 1981, it has sold three restaurants, all of which are operating successfully. The flagship restaurant is owned by a limited partnership that is not part of the franchise corporation.

I need to expand my operations and sell more franchises. The franchise corporation does not own any hard assets and has limited capital and no money available to expand and attract potential franchisees. Essentially, the corporation is a shell established to market pizza franchises. What suggestions do you have to obtain sufficient capital to expand the business regionally and then nationally?

ANSWER

Since the corporation does not own any hard assets and has limited capital available to expand and attract new franchisees, seeking money from a bank or the Small Business Administration (SBA) is not a good strategy. At the same time, it is premature to go to a venture capitalist firm or an investment banker, because the company has not quite proven its business concept and currently presents too much risk for these types of funding sources. At this stage of the company's development, pursuing a private placement is the best available financing strategy.

Qualifying for Private Placement

QUESTION

How does private placement work and what steps does the entrepreneur have to follow to raise capital in this manner?

ANSWER

A private placement is a means of bypassing the strict and costly registration requirements of an initial public offering (IPO), which is closely regulated by the Securities and Exchange Commission (SEC). A private placement is quicker, easier, and cheaper than taking a company public, and is encumbered with fewer legal requirements. Private placements may be made for either debt or equity financing or a combination of both.

Most private placements are governed by Regulation D of the Securities and Exchange Act, adopted in March 1982. Essentially, under Regulation D there are no specific disclosure/information requirements and no limits on the kinds or types of investors the entrepreneur may seek when raising under $500,000. The entrepreneur considering a private placement should obtain a copy of Regulation D and become familiar with its restrictions. Copies can be obtained from most law offices, the library, or the SEC.

Even though Regulation D provides a safe harbor from SEC registration requirements, the entrepreneur remains subject to state and federal fraud provisions. Therefore, the entrepreneur must take great care to disclose all information as accurately as possible. If any violation of security law occurs, not only is the corporation liable but management as well as the company's principal equity holders can be held liable individually.

Because of the legal complications, it is strongly recommended that you seek the advice of a business attorney who specializes in private placements. Most business and legal consultants will advise that a disclosure document, sometimes called an offering memorandum, be prepared for all potential investors. How the offering memorandum is structured varies significantly. The length and detail contained in the document will depend heavily on your business structure, the type of investor you hope to attract, the investor's level of sophistication, and how much money the investor will contribute.

Any entrepreneur considering a private placement to raise capital must give considerable thought to who might be a probable investor. Networking with professional people in the infrastructure and with potential money sources is key. Your lawyer or accountant may know of some private investors or have contacts with underwriters who are looking for this type of investment opportunity. Remember, how the private placement is structured depends on the nature of the money source.

Another consideration is whether you will go out of state to raise funds. Although a private placement is exempt from full registration requirements under federal law, a registration statement must be filed with each state in which stock is to be sold. These so-called blue-sky laws must be satisfied regardless of the size of the issue. Blue-sky laws are designed to eliminate possible fraud. The majority of states have agreed that if the issue is qualified under the SEC's Regulation D, it fulfills the provisions of state law. But the entrepreneur is still liable for any inaccurate disclosure information about the corporation. Again, the advice of a skilled securities attorney should be obtained to ensure that you comply with all state regulations.

There are two main advantages to raising money through a private placement. First, it is a means of raising significant capital without having many assets and/or pledging personal collateral. Second, it allows investors an opportunity to cash out and sell their stock when the business is successful, providing them with an excellent exit strategy.

8-7 Taking a Company Public

Pros and Cons of Going Public

QUESTION

I own a medical supply company and have a great opportunity to triple the size of my business during the next year. To do so, however, I need capital—about $6 million. I have met with several venture capitalists but have no deal as yet. I am thinking about taking my company public. Should I pursue this strategy?

ANSWER

Taking a company public (called an IPO if it is an initial public offering) raises capital through federally registered and underwritten sales of the company's shares. It may take you more time and cost you more money than it is worth. Another consideration is that required disclosures to stockholders and others about company products, performance, and financial condition may be better kept secret, especially from your competitors.

The legal, accounting, and administrative costs of a public offering are higher and riskier than other ways of raising money. Legal fees alone can easily cost $75,000 or more. Filing fees with the SEC and in the state in which the company does business can add another $50,000 to $100,000. Audited financial statements, pro forma statements, and summary financial statistics could range from $20,000 to $150,000, depending on the size of the company and the complexities of the audit. Financial printing fees for the prospectus, SEC registration statement, and official notices could run $40,000 to $100,000. It is not uncommon for a small IPO of $6 million to cost up to $500,000 before any proceeds are realized—assuming the offering is successful. There is always the risk that the public will not purchase the entire issue or even a major portion of it. However, the company must still pay for these expenses.

Numerous federal and state securities laws and regulations govern these offerings. Taking a company public requires not only significant up-front expenses but the ongoing expense of complying with SEC regulations and reporting requirements. The time required to maintain the status of a public company can often be better devoted to operating the company, and the diversion of management attention could adversely affect performance and future growth opportunities. Management time has a real cost to the company and must be considered along with other standard expenses.

Once the company goes public, the management team may focus more on maintaining the stock price and computing capital gains than on effectively operating the company. Short-term goals of trying to maintain or increase a current year's earnings could be counterproductive and take precedence over longer-term goals of slowly strengthening the business. Trying to consistently increase earnings when the best strategy is to temporarily retrench can seriously damage the company in the long run.

Lastly, the value of the company's stock achieved through the public offering may be sketchy. If there is no real market for the stock, there will be no active trading and the value of the shares could decline to practically nothing. This is an inherent risk when taking a company public.

Only a small number of new or young ventures go public on one of the stock exchanges. New ventures suffer from lower stock evaluations and usually have to give up more equity. Because your stock is listed does not mean that you will realize a liquid gain. The SEC has strong restrictions on the timing and the amount of stock that officers, directors, and insiders can sell in the public market. It may take a number of years after the initial public offering before you realize a liquid gain.

Going public might be a terrific way to raise substantial sums of capital, but it is also a costly gamble. This strategy could backfire and your company could be worse off financially. The stage of your growth, the goals of the underwriter, and economic conditions must be right for the issue to be successful.

How to Find an Investment Banker for an IPO

QUESTION

I need to raise about $10 million to expand my software company and I am considering taking my company public. Is this a good idea and how do I go about finding an investment banker?

ANSWER

Taking a company public may be one of the best and most lucrative ways to raise major amounts of capital, assuming the company has approximately $5 million in sales. It is possible to raise long-term capital to initiate major expansions, acquisitions, and recapitalizations or to increase the value of management-held shares. As a rule of thumb, money raised from selling equity shares is considered long-term capital and should be used only to acquire or develop long-term assets.

One of the advantages of going public is that the company can obtain a higher stock price from an initial public offering (IPO) than from venture capitalization, debt financing, or private placement. An IPO also establishes a public price for the stock and gives a company a sense of wealth. Going public adds financial stability and increased borrowing capability. It also gives the owners an exit. No interest payments are required and the company can decide what, if any, dividends to pay.

Assuming the cost and SEC compliance procedures can be managed, there are other considerations about whether to go public. First, the company must be incorporated and large enough to hire a complete management team. The composition, expertise, and strength of the management team are key factors, as is the ability of the owner to promote the quality of team members. The products or services offered by the company should have high growth potential over the next 5 years. The more glamorous the products or services, the better the chances of selling the company's stock. It is also recommended that the company have one or two new products or services on the drawingboard, ready to be introduced over the next 2 years.

Investor appeal and public imaging are of key importance in taking a company public. Trade show participation, advertising campaigns, and other market promotion strategies are all good ways to bring attention to the company's products or services. The potential market and industry trade statistics should be growing. The company should have 2 to 3 years of progressively improving profitability, and pro forma projections should show continued profitability.

It will also be necessary to clear up any lawsuits, insurance claims, IRS discrepancies, bank disagreements, or other potential problems that could tarnish the company's reputation.

Once you have decided to proceed with an IPO, find a competent underwriter to handle and sell the issue. An underwriter will probably charge an initial fee of 1 to 2 percent of the issue's value, plus commissions of 7 to 10 percent of the value of the actual stock issued. The best way to locate a qualified underwriter is to get references from a national accounting firm or from legal counsel. Usually accountants and lawyers with experience in SEC regulations provide the best referrals for underwriters. Most underwriters are located in major cities, particularly in New York.

It is paramount that the underwriter be interested in your industry, your company, and in you. Some underwriters focus only on firms that are looking for over $10 million in going public. Some specialize in new ventures, while others prefer to deal with firms that have several years of "seasoning."

The decision of whether to take your company public requires serious consideration, careful planning, and the right economic and market conditions. Most entrepreneurs who are successful with IPOs spend several years planning their strategy and revamping their companies. Overall, IPOs are not a good financial strategy for most entrepreneurs, since investment bankers focus on financial deals of over $5 million—a figure that leaves out about 95 percent of new business ventures.

8-8 Tapping Alternative Money Sources

Financing a New Venture Without Personal Assets or Collateral

QUESTION

I would like to start a computer consulting and word-processing business, but need some start-up capital. I do not have any personal assets or collateral. Where can I find alternative sources of financing?

ANSWER

Nontraditional sources of financing include suppliers, sales of distribution rights, hard-assets lenders, and commercial finance companies.

Suppliers. When you are able to delay paying for the materials you receive, your vendors can help finance your venture. The more you can delay paying them, the longer you can use their money and save your own to cover operating expenses. Sometimes you may be able to receive payment from your customers before having to pay your suppliers. This tactic is called extended-term financing, or trade credit. There may be times when you are able to take 30, 60, or 90 days to pay for supplies. This means you have obtained a loan of 30 to 90 days. Suppliers offer such trade credit as a way of getting new customers and will often build the "bad debt" risk into their prices.

However, the cost of money may be expensive. You may have to forgo attractive discounts for paying early. Missing a "2/10, net 30 days" discount costs you 36 percent on an annual rate. You lose 2 percent for using the money an extra 20 days. But this may be the only alternative you have to exercise.

Other forms of trade credit include special or seasonal datings (a supplier ships goods in advance of the purchaser's peak selling season and accepts payment 90 to 120 days later) or consignment (a supplier ships inventory on consignment and does not require payment until an item has been sold).

Sale of Distribution Rights. There is money to be made in distributing the output of your new venture. Often people will pay money to obtain the distribution rights for goods. Franchises do just that in franchising systems. To get a lot of money from a distributor, you must be prepared to give a lot in return. The person may ask for the distribution rights for a large area, such as everything west of the Mississippi. Before selling any rights, put the distributor on a performance-guarantee contract.

Hard-Asset Lenders. Certain firms are in business to lend money against "hard assets," such as equipment and machinery or tangible assets with a recognizable liquidating value. Most firms that use hard-asset lenders have exhausted other avenues of borrowing, largely because of poor credit ratings. Prime plus 10 is a good interest rate in this segment of the money market. While hard-asset firms are best known for their activities in consumer credit, they still do a large business with commercial institutions.

Commercial Finance Companies. Frequently, commercial finance firms lend money to businesses that do not have a positive cash flow. They tend to be more aggressive than commercial banks in lending.

Essentially, they are asset-based lenders, extending credit against receivables, inventory, or equipment that they are familiar with.

Using Fund Raisers to Obtain Seed Capital

QUESTION

I would like to own a business but don't have a lot of money in savings. I don't own a house, and my car is several years old, which means I can't borrow much money on it. I need about $350,000 for a down payment on a new business. I am thinking about using a fund raiser to obtain the capital I need. I understand that the fund raiser will charge a fee. Do you recommend this approach? What are the pitfalls? Is the fee negotiable?

ANSWER

Fund raisers can be an excellent financing source if they are reputable and if your venture fits that type of funding. Investors want to see evidence of the planning you have done to launch and operate your new venture.

> ➪ **Courtney's Smart Tip**
> **Have a well-written, attractive, and professional business plan to bring to any source of capital.**

To develop a list of contacts and fund raisers, look in the Yellow Pages under business brokers or financial consultants. Talk to your banker, attorney, accountant, or other entrepreneurs for leads and referrals for fundraisers who are known in the community and work in your industry. Once you have received the names of potential fund raisers, check the types of deals they have recently completed. Are the deals similar to yours? Is the amount of money raised in the same range as what you need?

Some fund raisers work only with business owners who need $1 million or more. Others specialize in deals over $5 million. Most fund raisers will not handle deals of less than $500,000. It takes too much time and effort to try to raise money for smaller ventures. Some will not work with start-up businesses at all. Like lenders, fund raisers prefer to see that the entrepreneur has invested money in the venture. Make sure the money source fits your business. Then carefully check credentials.

Realize that fund raisers do not raise money for nothing. All charge some type of fee. Fees charged depend on individual rates and the amount of money raised. Some fund raisers require up-front money to cover expenses incurred researching the information contained in the business plan. Often, they will charge up to 3 percent of the amount of money you want just to conduct a "due diligence" check on your business. On top of that, most charge 10 percent up to $1 million and a sliding scale over that amount.

Fees may be somewhat negotiable, depending on the deal and its terms. Some fund raisers will not negotiate on fees. Their policy is "take it or leave it." Essentially you are paying for their contacts and expertise. Also, it takes time to research your business plan and to negotiate and structure the deal.

An alternative approach is to contact local financial consultants or registered brokerage firms that work with private placements—investor-based securities offerings that are exempt from SEC registration and are limited in distribution. Although most of these firms specialize in selling stocks and bonds, some of the smaller ones also handle private placements.

You might also identify local opportunities for joint venturing with manufacturers and other companies that have been successful with similar types of ventures. Many local newspapers print an annual list of the top 100 companies in their area. Scan this list for corporate partners that might be interested in your product or service.

Most of these sources will be interested in deals of more than $500,000. For amounts less than this, you will need to find private investors or use "friendly money."

Private individuals are often the most willing to invest seed money in a start-up venture. They may have differing motives for venture investment that lead them to accept higher risks than institutional sources. Sometimes these investors act independently, having strong confidence in their ability to evaluate deals and business owners. Your friends and contacts may play a key role in locating private investors. Create a circle of acquaintances who can act as money sources for your venture.

Finding Business Angels to Fund and Grow Ventures

QUESTION

Last year I quit my job and started a small cable assembly and supply business, which I operate from my home. It has really grown and now I must move into larger quarters. Unfortunately, I don't have any money for expansion, and my banker won't lend me any more funds. Where can I go to find money to expand my business?

ANSWER

Private investors, known as business angels, are a good place to start after you have tapped yourself, friends, and relatives. These wealthy individuals (or groups of individuals) willing to put money into local ventures are often the only source of risk capital for entrepreneurs. Studies show that each year approximately 1 million angels in the United States invest equity capital into ventures.

These people are not millionaires. In fact, the average annual income of an angel is $90,000. Many are business owners, managers, or professionals who are generally about 20 years older than the entrepreneurs they finance. Angels invest their own money, in small amounts. The majority of their investments are under $50,000, and few exceed $100,000. The average angel invests $35,000 in any one company and usually selects ventures within a 50-mile radius of home. Angels like to be familiar with the business or industry they are investing in.

The good news is that they love start-ups, so they are a much easier money source to tap than venture capitalists. Also, they generally offer better interest rates than banks and have fewer strings than venture capitalists. Over 85 percent don't want voting rights in the company. They may want to take on an advisory role. But they do expect returns of three to five times their investment after 2 to 5 years.

The bad news is that angels are hard to find. Start by looking in your industry and contacting your trade association or professional groups. Local economic development agencies should also have lists of potential investors.

> ⇨ **Courtney's Smart Tip**
> **To find angels, use intermediaries who are advisers to angels, such as merchant bankers, boutique bankers, financial consultants, and planners.**

Intermediaries who specialize in raising small amounts of capital develop a small network of angels who invest in the deals they find and recommend. Look in the Yellow Pages under investment management, financing consultants, or financial planners. One boutique investment banking firm is the Capital Institute, at (800) 748-6887. It has offices throughout the United States. Financial consultants and planners usually work through a brokerage firm and are involved in managing the investments of angels.

Contact the venture capital clubs in your area. They can be a good place to learn about the local angel community. The Association of Venture Clubs in Salt Lake City, at (801) 364-1100, can provide a list of clubs. Another source is the Venture Capital Network in Durham, New Hampshire, at (603) 862-3558. This organization, with offices in several cities, introduces entrepreneurs and angels through a computerized matching system. It has a limited number of members, but is worth contacting. There are also angel networks in Massachusetts, Texas, and Missouri.

When working with intermediaries, be cautious. Check out their references and their track records. Try to get referrals from lawyers, bankers, accountants, and insurance brokers. For more information about private investors, refer to *Finding Private Venture Capital for Your Firm*[7] by Robert J. Gaston and *Guerrilla Financing*[8] by Bruce Blechman and Jay Conrad Levinson. Both are excellent resources on financing tactics for entrepreneurs.

Establishing Corporate Strategic Alliances

QUESTION

I have been looking for money to finance the growth of my 2-year-old computer company. I have approached many different sources, but none has been willing to loan me money. Where can I look for funding beyond banks and venture capitalists?

ANSWER

Many new ventures make ideal candidates for corporate joint ventures. Today, as traditional lenders continue to tighten up their borrowing practices to entrepreneurs, corporate partners are becoming a major new avenue for financing. A joint venture or partnership agreement with a major domestic or foreign corporation can provide badly needed funds for research and development, as well as growth opportunities. There has been a significant increase in the number of direct investments by large corporations in new ventures during the past 10 years.

A corporate strategic alliance offers several advantages to entrepreneurs. First, corporate partners are usually willing to wait longer to receive a return on their investments than are bankers or venture capitalists. Often corporate partners are interested in taking an equity position in a business and do not seek as high a percentage of ownership as do venture capitalists.

Second, they can contribute more than just money to the new business. They may be able to offer good business advice, extend moral support, and provide state-of-the-art technology. Finally, a corporate strategic alliance can furnish valuable contacts in the business and financial community.

The chief disadvantage of a corporate strategic alliance is the loss of control. A corporate partner might demand that certain things be done when the entrepreneur is opposed to taking such action. Changing the corporate mission and goals could cause the corporate partnership to sour.

Elements in structuring a strategic alliance with a large corporation include finding a well-capitalized partner who has or is considering financing new venture proposals. Look for corporations that are interested in early-stage ventures like yours and have already invested in your industry. Work with your local business librarian to find various listings of potential corporate investors. The key is finding corporations with the resources, but not the time, commitment, or creativity to get involved themselves.

> ➪ **Courtney's Smart Tip**
> **Ensure that corporate allies have a strategic fit with your company. Try to ascertain whether they are familiar with your market, product, technology, and service area.**

Another option is to contact a corporation that might be interested in the right to license your product in certain areas. Go to the store aisles where your competitors' products are displayed. Nearly every package gives the name and location of its producer. Many corporations are eager to expand their product lines into new areas, or to sell improved versions of currently available products. With a licensing arrangement, you receive royalties and a ready-made marketing system without giving up equity.

Several good books are available for investigating licensing and finding corporate partners. *Dun & Bradstreet's Reference Book of Corporation Management*[9] gives a detailed biographical description of more than 75,000 principal officers of more than 12,000 leading companies. *Standard & Poor's Register of Corporations, Directors, and Executives*[10] lists 45,000 corporations and detailed information on some 450,000 potential licensee contacts. The *Million Dollar Directory*[11] and the *Middle Market Directory*,[12] both from Dun & Bradstreet, list thousands of companies with assets exceeding $500,000. Another excellent book, *Winning Combinations*[13] by James W. Botkin and Jana B.

Mathews, focuses on the coming wave of entrepreneurial partnerships between large and small companies.

Using Credit Cards to Finance a Venture

QUESTION

I have been trying to find additional financing for my new venture but have not been successful. I have gone to several banks for a line of credit, but have been turned down. A friend suggested that I use my credit cards for the cash I need. What do you think?

ANSWER

A number of struggling entrepreneurs—especially those who are not yet considered "creditworthy" by traditional lenders—have used credit cards in the early start-up phases of their ventures for working or expansion capital. Used judiciously, credit card financing can act as a bridge to get new ventures over initial financial cash binds.

However, consider this source *only* when there is no other way to secure operating capital. When you run into a cash crunch, credit cards may be the only available option. You should be able to acquire an unsecured line of credit of $1000 to $5000 from each credit card source. This type of cash advance is very similar to obtaining a line of credit from a bank. You can get cash when you need it by taking your credit card to your bank to receive cash or have it deposited in your account.

The major pitfall is that most credit card bills require payment in 30 days and carry high interest rates. You must consider whether paying higher interest rates is worth having the extra money immediately. In addition, you are personally liable for the debt. Keep in mind, too, that many credit card companies charge an additional fee or a higher-than-normal interest rate for cash advances.

The best way to use this method of financing is to submit credit card applications simultaneously so you can obtain several cards with a cash advance privilege. By applying for credit to a number of different sources at once, you can truthfully disclose that you have no other outstanding loans. Shop for the lowest rates possible. Credit card interest rates are extremely competitive, and newer companies may offer lower interest rates and more services.

Avoid using credit card financing to start a new venture or to pay for fixed expenses, such as equipment. Entrepreneurs should have enough cash from their own resources to launch their businesses. But, if you are not yet bankable, credit cards can provide needed capital very quickly.

> ➪ **Courtney's Smart Tip**
> **Use credit cards only as the last resort as a cushion for cash crunches. Replace credit card financing with conventional loans as soon as possible.**

From a tax standpoint, the same tax deductions are available with a credit card loan as with any other business loan. The right to deduct interest rates is determined by the purpose for which the money is used. Regardless of how high the interest rate is, interest is deductible at the time it is incurred, not when it is paid.

If you have other ways of financing your working capital, use them. If not, credit cards are a costly option for short-term or seasonal cash needs. Truly creative entrepreneurs using credit cards for operating capital have given a new meaning to our credit card economy.

8-9 The Small Business Administration

Obtaining an SBA-Backed Loan

QUESTION

I have come up with an idea for a new business, but I am at the starting point and desperately need to know how to obtain financing. I am interested in securing funding from the Small Business Administration, but I do not know how to contact this agency or how to proceed. Can you help?

ANSWER

The SBA is a significant source of financing for small businesses. Typically, SBA loans are used to finance plant construction or expansion, to purchase equipment, and to provide working capital. Under the SBA's Guaranty Loan Program, loans to entrepreneurs from private lenders, usually banks, are guaranteed up to 90 percent by the SBA. The maximal guarantee percentage of loans exceeding $155,000 is 85 percent. Working-capital loans generally have maturities of 5 to 7 years. Longer maturities are used to finance fixed assets, such as land and buildings. Lenders apply directly for SBA loans for their customers. Essentially, you are a customer of the bank, and the bank is a customer of the SBA. You will not deal directly with the SBA but will work through your lending officer.

Smart Tips for Obtaining an SBA-Backed Loan

1. Develop a business plan that contains proper financial projections, including cash flow, profit-and-loss statements, and balance sheets. Make your projections month by month for the first year of operation and then annually for the next 3 to 4 years.
2. Prepare a current, personal financial statement for any principals involved in the venture.
3. List the collateral to be offered as security, including an estimate of the present market value of each item.
4. State the amount of the loan request and the purpose for which the funds will be used.
5. Establish a business relationship with a full-service bank which participates in government lending programs.
6. Make an appointment with your loan officer and ask him or her to finance your loan.
7. If the loan is turned down, ask about the possibility of using the SBA's Guaranty Loan Program.

If the bank feels that you are a creditworthy customer and is willing to apply for the SBA loan, which greatly minimizes its risk, it will prepare a loan package to submit to the SBA. This loan package will contain the bank's credit analysis of your venture and the loan request.

The SBA will perform an independent review of the loan package. It will determine whether the business is eligible under its guidelines and whether the entrepreneur meets its credit requirements. The agency closely evaluates whether your sales and financial projections are realistic. In addition, it scrutinizes your repayment ability.

Many banks have signed participation agreements with the SBA. However, only 50 percent of these banks are active lenders and send in applications for SBA loans. Further, only about 25 percent of these lenders aggressively pursue SBA loans. Therefore, it is important to determine whether a potential lender regularly participates in the SBA's loan programs.

The interest rate the bank charges you will vary. A bank can charge up to 2.25 percent above the New York prime rate for loans with maturity dates of less than 7 years. On maturities over 7 years, the bank may charge up to 2.75 percent. An interest rate can be fixed or variable, depending upon your negotiation and relationship with the lender.

The SBA does offer a direct loan program, but currently the funds are available only to Vietnam era veterans and other disabled veterans who have a 30 percent or more compensable disability. To obtain additional information about the SBA's business loan programs, call its business development division. Ask for the brochure "Business Loans from the SBA."

You could also contact a local small business investment company (SBIC) or a minority enterprise small business investment company (MESBIC). These privately owned companies, licensed by the SBA, provide equity capital and long-term loans to entrepreneurs. Your local SBA office can provide you with a list of SBICs and MESBICs.

Financing Production Through the SBA Contract Finance Program

QUESTION

I own a growing manufacturing company that is running out of equity capital just as business is expanding and sales are increasing. My banker said he could not loan me any more money. How can I finance my production needs and fill my incoming orders?

ANSWER

Go back to your banker and ask him if it would be possible to obtain a loan through the SBA Contract Finance Program. This is a special financing program designed to lend a business money on the basis of a specific contract or purchase order from a customer. If your bank does not work with the SBA, or if you have already borrowed the maximum amount of SBA-supported financing that your business can qualify for, you may have to look to other sources.

Consider contacting one of the 400 or so certified development companies (CDCs) throughout the United States. These are public–private investment groups composed of local lenders, banks, and the SBA. Local CDCs are interested in fostering business in their communities. The major criterion for obtaining a CDC loan is that for each $15,000 lent, the business must create one new job or prove the retention of an existing job that might otherwise have been eliminated. Minimum loans are $50,000, but the average loan is between $1 and $2 million. Borrowers usually pay 10 percent of the loan value collateralized by property, machinery, equipment, or fixtures.

Creative loan packages may also be available through your state's department of commerce. Remember, these types of loans are made for specific transactions to existing companies, not for market development.

Commercializing New Technology Through SBIR Programs

QUESTION

I am the founder and president of a small electronics firm that needs capital for research and development. My banker told me that some of my new products may closely coincide with some research currently being conducted under a federal grant at our local university. Can I obtain research funding as well?

ANSWER

There is a good possibility that you can obtain funding through the SBA's small business innovation research (SBIR) programs. SBIRs allow small businesses to commercialize technology which they own or wish to develop through federally funded R&D grants. This program provides first-round grants (feasibility studies) of up to $50,000 and second-round grants (commercialization of technology) of up to $500,000 for R&D projects of interest to various government agencies. Ask the SBA to place you on its SBIR mailing list. You will receive periodic listings of areas of research that the government is interested in pursuing.

Next, ask the SBA about the Cooperative Research and Development Agreement (CRADA) Program, established to help businesses acquire technology from the federal government for the purposes of developing a technology of interest to both parties. A substantial portion of the R&D funding and/or facilities can be provided by the government for this purpose.

In addition to these programs, there are opportunities for acquiring licenses for federally developed technology through the National Technical Information Services (NITS) and the Federal Laboratory Consortium (FLC). (See the "Contacts" listing in the resources section at the end of this chapter.) In addition, most universities have set up licensing organizations or foundations to implement the transfer of their technology to qualified licensees.

The SBA or any university that sponsors technical research, research parks, or incubators can assist you in identifying the many opportunities that you might be interested in for your electronics firm. Even though you may have to cut through some red tape, the outcome can be rewarding. Once your technology has been acquired, you will have to pay royalties to the government or university. However, such royalties are usually far less costly than conducting your own R&D.

8-10 Factoring

Using a Commercial Factoring Company to Finance a Business

QUESTION

How can I use a commercial factoring company to finance my small business?

ANSWER

Factoring is designed to increase cash flow when funds are limited and accounts receivable are high. It is short-term financing to solve short-term cash flow bottlenecks. The cash-poor company sells its accounts receivable at a discount to a commercial finance company known as a factor. Cash is made available to the entrepreneur as soon as proof of shipment is provided or on the average due date of the invoice. Most factoring arrangements are made for 1 year.

Factors make their money by acquiring a company's invoices and collecting on them, charging the business a fee. Unlike banks, factors buy, pay for, and own the receivables outright. If your creditors don't pay, the factor may incur a loss. Some factors require that the entrepreneur establish a reserve for bad debt of approximately 5 percent of the account. If the account is not collected within 120 days, the factor will draw against the reserve. If the receivables eventually are collected, the factor's return on investment exceeds that of conventional lenders.

Many business owners use factoring when their banker turns down a loan request that they had tried to guarantee with their accounts receivable as collateral. Under factoring, accounts receivable are not used as collateral against a loan but instead are sold directly, at a discounted value, to a factoring company. For example, if the factoring company uses a one-time charge and discounts 6 percent, then for every $1000 in receivables, the seller receives $940.

Some factors discount according to a schedule, paying a smaller percentage up front and then paying an additional percentage depending on whether the receivables are collected within 30, 60, or 90 days. The factor takes over the entire collection procedure, including mailing the invoices and doing the bookkeeping. Each of your customers is notified that the account is owned by and payable to the factor.

If you are a new business and your accounts receivable are evaluated as marginal credit risks, you may not be able to find a factor that will accept your accounts receivable. Let's face it: although they take greater risks and are more liberal lenders than commercial banks, factors need to be assured that your customers will pay their bills. They will execute substantial credit checks on each debtor and carefully analyze the quality and value of the invoice before buying it; they look to the strength of the receivables and creditworthiness of the invoices that you are selling them. Factors will also establish credit limits for each customer.

Factoring is not the cheapest way to obtain money, but it does quickly turn receivables into cash. The advantages of factoring are receiving a cash injection quickly, paying bills in a more timely manner, obtaining more credit, and fostering better growth than traditional borrowing. Also, the fee is an expense and offsets taxable income. Essentially, the entrepreneur is buying insurance against bad debt.

The chief disadvantage of factoring is the high cost of money relative to traditional borrowing. Also, to many entrepreneurs, factors receive outrageously high returns. A business concerned with cash flow but not with collection might want to pursue the less costly route of using accounts receivable as collateral for a commercial bank loan.

Overall, factoring can be compared with using a credit card for your business. Factors work best with businesses that have cash flow problems because of long delays between making and selling goods and then collecting cash. Start-up ventures, emerging businesses, and service companies are prime candidates for factoring. For recommendations and references about which factoring companies to use, talk to your trade associations, to members of the infrastructure, and to other entrepreneurs in your industry.

How to Use a Factoring Company to Fund Growth

QUESTION

About a year ago I started a small advertising and public relations firm that is doing well but at times experiences cash shortages, especially when the payroll must be met. A friend suggested that I look into factoring companies as a source of financing. Do you recommend using them?

ANSWER

In the past, factoring was used as a last resort and was concentrated in the manufacturing and clothing industries. Today, all types of ventures—temporary office services, janitorial services, computer companies, pet shop suppliers, and many others—readily use this type of financing. Factoring has become the fashionable way for cash-poor start-up ventures to acquire working capital.

Typically, entrepreneurs use factoring as short-term financing to solve their short-term cash flow problems, especially when they are unable to borrow funds from traditional lenders. Many banks steer away from such asset-based lending because of the unpredictable nature of the underlying collateral and the difficulties in liquidating it.

In factoring, you sell your designated accounts receivable to the factor and draw against this line of credit as cash is needed. Typically, factoring companies secure their interest with your accounts receivable. As a rule, factoring companies accept the loss if your customer goes broke and cannot pay the bill that has been factored.

Factoring companies are accounts receivable managers that give business owners more time to concentrate on marketing and growing their ventures. Factoring enables a business to take advantage of discounts for large orders or advance payments for raw materials. It allows the entrepreneur to use the venture's tangible assets for securing other types of financing. Factoring can also finance growth by providing quick funds to take advantage of business opportunities.

In factoring, you deposit your accounts receivable with the factoring firm. These accounts are processed and reside there until cash is needed. If you run short of cash on payday, you can call the factoring company and cash out a portion of your accounts receivable immediately—provided that proof of shipment has been secured or the average due date on the invoice has been reached.

The services provided by factoring companies range from evaluating customer credit to mailing invoices, to pursuing collections. Regardless of how long you have been in business, factoring companies will evaluate the creditworthiness of your clients. They carefully analyze the quality and value of your invoices and look closely at each customer's credit to determine risk, since they need to be assured of receiving payment. Their collection services are designed to try to preserve your relationship with your customers. By contrast, a collection agency may use techniques that result in a loss of goodwill between you and your customers.

For more information, call National Factoring Services, Inc. at (303) 592-1919 or (800) 253-6700.

8-11 Funding for Nonprofit Organizations

QUESTION

I began a nonprofit organization, the Colorado Horse Rescue, to help horses that were impounded by the state and counties of Colorado. We are the only approved horse shelter in the state. We adopt horses out for a fee, match children and horses for 4H programs, and hold horses for owners until they are able to "bail them out." We are desperately in need of additional funding, management assistance (since we are growing so rapidly), and a sound growth plan. Where should we turn for help?

ANSWER

Nonprofit companies face particularly severe challenges, both as start-up ventures and as ongoing-businesses. There never seems to be enough funding; and raising capital through revenue generation is difficult at best. The situation worsens in tight economic times when corporate, foundation, and individual donations tend to shrink.

To address the need for additional funding, the Colorado Horse Rescue group should research foundations that have a specific interest in funding animal-oriented nonprofits and then submit a grant proposal to them. There are thousands of private foundations that promote specialized projects, regions, minorities, and special-interest groups. Some offer technical assistance or counseling to nonprofits and small businesses. All offer grants or low-cost loans. The challenge is to find the foundation that fits your organization.

For information about foundations, contact the Foundation Center in New York at (212) 620-4230 or the Council on Foundations in Washington, DC at (202) 466-6512. *The Chronicle of Philanthropy* is a newspaper directed to issues in the nonprofit sector, including fund raising and grant distribution. For information, call (800) 347-6969. A comprehensive resource, including names and addresses of large and small foundations, is *Free Money for Small Businesses and Entrepreneurs.*[14] In addition, many states publish foundation directories that contain local grant sources.

Another avenue open to your group is fund raising. Consider developing diverse funding sources from special fund-raising events, membership dues, individual donations, earned incomes, and so on. A key player in such fund-raising efforts is your board of directors, which you must have if your business is incorporated. One of the major responsibilities of a nonprofit board is to generate the funds necessary to support the programs of the agency. An excellent resource book on building nonprofit boards is James Hardy's *Developing Dynamic Boards.*[15]

To get the board involved and to generate a financial development strategy, you might hold a strategic planning session facilitated by an outside nonprofit expert. During the session, the consultant will provide information on board roles and responsibilities, including the skills and expertise needed to direct an effective nonprofit organization. Then the consultant will facilitate a discussion of mission, goals, objectives, and strategies. The result will be a strategic plan that outlines where the nonprofit wants to go in the next 3 to 5 years and how it plans to get there.

Another excellent source is the National Executive Service Corps (NESC), headquartered in New York at (212) 529-6660. This nationwide network of organizations provides management assistance and coaching to nonprofits through retired executives who have extensive experience in marketing, finance, and other functional areas.

8-12 Pitfalls to Avoid

1. Calling on a lender or investor cold. Always try to get a referral.
2. Calling on a lender or investor without bringing along a complete business plan to review and evaluate.
3. Mass-mailing your business plan to potential investors.
4. Contacting the SBA directly about obtaining a bank loan. The SBA is not a lender. Instead, find out if your bank is an approved SBA lender and will consider doing an SBA-backed loan.
5. Putting a monetary value on business goodwill. Most lenders consider goodwill "blue sky" and will discount or delete any balance sheet amount in excess of the venture's tangible net worth.
6. Responding to advertisements that ask you to send upward of $100 for lists of venture capitalists. You can obtain these same lists free from your local library.
7. Using credit card financing to start a new venture or to pay for fixed expenses such as equipment.
8. Contacting venture capitalists for start-up funding. Very few ventures, start-up or otherwise, qualify for or ever receive venture capital funding.

The Good News. Entrepreneurs who carefully plan their financial strategy and correctly forecast their cash needs at the onset, will be more successful at raising capital. Being able to match the right money source to your venture considering its stage of development and growth potential will most likely produce the funds you need when you need them.

8-13 Entrepreneurial Resource Checklist

References

1. *Pratt's Guide to Venture Capital Sources,* Venture Economics, Wellesley, Mass., 1993.
2. *Raising Venture Capital and the Entrepreneur* (check your local library).
3. *Venture's Guide to International Venture Capital,* Venture Magazines, S. and S. Trade, 1985.

4. *Who's Who in Venture Capital,* Wiley, New York, 1990.
5. *Handbook of Business Finance and Capital Sources,* Interfinance Corp., Minneapolis, Minn., 1985.
6. *Venture Capital at the Crossroads,* Harvard Business School Press, Boston, 1992.
7. Robert J. Gaston, *Finding Private Venture Capital for Your Firm,* Wiley, New York, 1989.
8. Bruce Blechman and Jay Conrad Levinson, *Guerrilla Financing,* Houghton Mifflin, Boston, Mass., 1991.
9. *Dun & Bradstreet's Reference Book of Corporate Management,* Dun & Bradstreet, New York, 1993.
10. *Standard & Poor's Register of Corporations, Directors, and Executives* (check your local library).
11. *Million Dollar Directory,* Dun & Bradstreet, Parsippany, N.J., 1993.
12. *Middle Market Directory,* Dun & Bradstreet, Parsippany, N.J., 1993.
13. James W. Botkin and Jana B. Mathews, *Winning Combinations,* Wiley, New York, 1992.
14. Laurie Blum, *Free Money for Small Businesses and Entrepreneurs,* Wiley, 1992.
15. James M. Hardy, *Developing Dynamic Boards,* Essex Press, 1990.

Further Reading

Books

Alaird, William. *Money Sources for Small Business,* Puma Publications Co., Santa Maria, Calif., 1991.

Dawson, George M. *Borrowing for Your Business,* Upstart Publishing, Portsmouth, N.H., 1991.

Lindsey, Jennifer. *Start-Up Money,* Wiley, New York, 1989.

Nicholas, Ted. *43 Proven Ways to Raise Capital for Your Small Business,* Enterprise Publishing, Wilmington, Del., 1991.

Directory of Venture Capital Clubs, P.O. Box 1333, Stanford, Conn., 06904.

Sieglin, Jeffrey. *Financing Your Small Business,* McGraw-Hill, New York, 1990.

Tuller, Lawrence A. *When the Bank Says No!* Liberty Hall Press, Blue Ridge Summit, Pa., 1991.

Magazines

The Chronicle of Philanthropy
1255 Twenty-Third St. NW
Washington, DC 20037
(800) 347-6969

Venture Capital Journal
Venture Economics
75 Second Ave.
Needham, MA 02194

Contacts

1. National Venture Capital Association (NVCA)
   Arlington, VA
   (703) 528-4370

   Ask for a copy of the NVCA's 200-member directory.

2. Western Association of Venture Capitalists
   3000 Sand Hill Rd., #1-90
   Menlo Park, CA 94025
   (415) 854-1322

3. Association of Venture Capital Clubs
   P.O. Box 3358
   Salt Lake City, UT 84110
   (801) 364-1100

   Ask for the institute's list of venture clubs.

4. Venture Capital Network
   Box 882
   Durham, NH
   (603) 862-3558

   This "dating service" for angels and entrepreneurs uses a computerized matching system.

5. National Association of Small Business Investment Corporations
   618 Washington Building
   Washington, DC 20005

   The association provides information about securing financing from SBICs.

6. National Technical Information Services (NTIS)
   5285 Port Royal Rd.
   Springfield, VA 22161
   (703) 487-4838

   You can locate government inventions with specific commercial value and then negotiate a license with the agency.

7. Federal Laboratory Consortium (FLC)
   (301) 975-03086

8. National Executive Service Corps (NESC)
   (212) 529-6660

   This network of national organizations provides management assistance and coaching to nonprofits through retired executives.

9. Small Business Administration

   Local SBA offices will provide information about funding assistance for entrepreneurs as well as publications, seminars, and workshops. Ask for the brochure "Business Loans from the SBA."

10. Foundation Center in New York
    79 Fifth Ave.
    New York, NY 10003-3076
    (212) 620-4230

    The center collects, organizes, and disseminates data on foundations and corporate philanthropy.

11. Council on Foundations
    Washington, DC
    (202) 466-6512

    Call or write for information on grant-making foundations and corporations.

12. Securities and Exchange Commission

    Write the Commission for a copy of Regulation D, governing private placements.

13. Forum Publishing Co.
    383 Main Street
    Centerport, NY 11721
    (516) 754-5000
    Publication: *Venture Capital Directory*

    This publication includes over 400 members of the Small Business Administration and Small Business Investment Companies that provide funding for small and minority-owned businesses.

14. Venture Economics
    Wellsley Hills, MA
    Stanley Pratt, author
    Publication: *Pratt's Guide to Venture Capital Sources*

    This publication contains information on more than 700 venture capital companies and lists the type of companies in which they invest.

15. Security and Exchange Commission

    SEC keeps information on corporations with publicly traded stock. To obtain copies of their documents, go to one of their public reference rooms, maintained in New York, Chicago, and the Washington, D.C., headquarters.

9 Selecting the Best Business Advisers

9-1 Overview

Hiring outside advisers and utilizing members of the entrepreneurial infrastructure are key strategies for operating a successful venture. Too many times such personnel are chosen because they are friends or relatives of the owner. This is one of the biggest mistakes an entrepreneur can make. Those selected should balance out the management team, bringing in expertise that the owner lacks and the business strongly needs.

Entrepreneurs give equally little thought to selecting members of the infrastructure—lawyers, accountants, and other management professionals. Again, they usually choose people they know, regardless of their expertise and reputation. Because most start-up ventures cannot afford to take on additional employees to handle various management functions, infrastructure contacts become especially critical. They must be seasoned professionals, chosen solely on the basis of their expertise. This is the only way to build a strong management team besides hiring one. On an informal level, friends, associates, suppliers, and vendors, can be good sources of outside advice.

Establishing a board of directors and an outside board or council is one of the best investments entrepreneurs can make to strengthen the stability and growth potential of their ventures. An outside board gives a fresh perspective and objective feedback about the operation and its strategic direction. Unfortunately, few founders seek enough of such advice. Often they neglect to establish a board of directors or advisory council because they think no one would want to serve on a board or that setting one up is too much work.

9-2 Smart Strategies for Using the Infrastructure and Business Professionals

1. Find a lawyer experienced in small business and establish a working relationship before you ever need to hire counsel.
2. To save on legal fees, complete as much up-front work and information gathering as possible before meeting with your attorney.
3. Never talk to another party's attorney without having your own attorney present.
4. To reduce legal costs, use standardized forms of conducting routine business, but always have your attorney review them before implementation.
5. To avoid surprises with legal bills, estimate the number of billable hours for your legal project and then negotiate a cap or ceiling on the total fee.
6. Select an accountant who is also a good business adviser—one who is familiar with your industry, knowledgeable about tax planning, and committed to building and managing a sound cash flow.
7. If you are considering raising venture capital or going public, contact an accounting firm that has a track record working with promising smaller businesses.
8. Before you begin a small to mid-size venture, obtain a business-owner's policy to cover all your major property and business liability exposures.
9. Ask your local or national professional and/or trade association if it has a group insurance arrangement with specialty brokers or insurers.
10. Avoid "I can do it all" consultants.

11. Use a written consulting agreement that specifies work assignments, responsibilities, and compensation.
12. Assemble a board of directors to add credibility to your venture, enhance your corporation's assets, and obtain management expertise and advice.
13. Establish an advisory board to serve as your in-house management consulting team.
14. Look for advisory board members or board directors who have the specialized knowledge and skills you lack.

9-3 How to Find a Lawyer for Your Business

Guidelines for Hiring a Lawyer

QUESTION

I am in the process of selecting an attorney to assist me with some legal matters in starting my new business. How do I find a good attorney who is reasonably priced and specializes in small business?

ANSWER

In this highly complex legal society, entrepreneurs need competent legal advice. Ironically, this can be the most difficult assistance to find. Simply contacting your local legal society is not the solution. In most cases, it will not recommend an attorney. Instead, pay attention to the lawyers used in your industry. Who represents local entrepreneurs in your field? Who seems to win the court cases? Ask your fellow entrepreneurs to describe their experiences in working with local lawyers.

Accessibility should be a key factor in your decision. Remember that the demand for legal services is unpredictable. Rarely will you know in advance that you are going to need legal advice. For example, you have an opportunity to purchase a business on particularly advantageous terms, but a memorandum of agreement needs to be drawn up immediately. You cannot begin your search for a lawyer now and then wait several days or weeks to meet at his or her convenience. Evaluate how quickly an attorney can or will respond to your requests.

The size of the firm is another important consideration. The legal profession is dominated by several very large firms with dozens of partners. Many of these firms have substantial political power and many contacts. A large legal firm offers certain advantages to the entrepreneur. First, it can call upon expertise in many different fields.

If you have a tax problem, it has tax experts. If you have a problem with the Securities and Exchange Commission, it has specialists in the field. If you are taking your company public, having a large, prestigious law firm behind you can add significant credibility to your venture. Thus, with one legal connection, you have rented yourself expertise in just about every area in which you will be operating.

However, the big firm presents disadvantages as well. If you operate a small business, you may not be an important enough client. Your concerns may be ignored or else assigned to a rookie, just out of law school, who has little experience in small business concerns. Second, the legal fees may be prohibitive. A large firm might easily charge you $3000 to $5000 for incorporating your business, whereas a smaller firm might charge $300 to $500. For these reasons, some entrepreneurs use smaller firms that are more eager for their business.

Start by asking your friends and business contacts for their recommendations. Perhaps your banker or accountant knows a competent attorney with considerable and practical experience in small business affairs. After you establish a list of potential business lawyers, set up a series of interviews. Ask for referrals of other entrepreneurs they currently represent. Find out how many years of experience they have had working with entrepreneurial companies. Determine what their particular small business expertise is. Describe a routine legal matter to take care of and evaluate how they would handle it.

Lastly, determine how well you relate to each lawyer you interview. Is there some chemistry between the two of you? In the end, selecting a business lawyer is a personal decision.

> ➪ **Courtney's Smart Tip**
> **It is paramount that you and your business attorney get along and have a similar business philosophy.**

Remember, this is an age of specialization and there is far too much for any legal consultant to know. There are legal specialists in taxes, patents, securities, and so on. You will most likely select an all-around business attorney and then use specialists when the need arises.

Guidelines for Controlling Legal Expenses

QUESTION

I am starting a bakery business. Several friends have recommended different lawyers for me to use as legal counsel. Do you have any advice on how to choose the best lawyer for my bakery?

ANSWER

Before deciding on the right lawyer for your business, evaluate the scope of services you are likely to need in your new venture. Decide whether you are looking for a one-time legal service or seeking a long-term relationship to handle various legal problems. Find a lawyer who is familiar with your business—you will get better and more appropriate legal advice. Make sure the candidates you are considering have extensive experience in small business affairs.

Next, consider what size law firm would be the best for you and whether it would be beneficial for you to retain more than one firm for specialized needs. For example, if you want to obtain a trademark logo or a patent, you'll need to find lawyers with special expertise. Remember that whatever the size and reputation of a law firm, your ultimate success depends on the lawyer with whom you are working.

Check the references of lawyers recommended by your colleagues. Contact their firms and ask for résumés or brochures that describe their practices. If this material is not available, ask for some representative clients to contact. Find out if those clients have legal concerns similar to yours and if they have been satisfied with the services provided.

Then go to your public library and consult various directories on lawyers and their credentials. The most comprehensive is the *Martindale-Hubbell Law Directory*, which lists law firms nationwide and provides detailed information on the background of the firm, its areas of specialization, and in some cases its major clients. The directory also gives "ratings" for legal ability, ethical standards, professional reliability, and diligence. These ratings are based on confidential recommendations solicited from other lawyers.

Other directories include *The Lawyer's Register by Specialties and Fields of Law*, the *Attorney's Register*, the *U.S. Lawyer's Referral Directory*, the *Directory of the Legal Profession*, and state-by-state blue books of lawyers. In addition, most local bar associations publish lists of local lawyers with some basic information about credentials and expertise.

There is a useful checklist of interview questions for lawyers in *100 Ways to Cut Legal Fees and Manage Your Lawyer*.[1] This excellent publication runs the gamut from how to choose a lawyer to how to act as your own. The book costs about $12.00 and can be ordered by calling (800) 638-6582 or by writing the National Chamber Litigation center, 1615 H Street NW, Washington, DC 20062.

Schedule interviews with the lawyers you are most interested in retaining. Many lawyers offer an exploratory session free, so ask if there will be a charge. If so, find out how much. Will the fee be credited toward initial services? Try to get a sense of how you relate to the lawyer during the interview. The right chemistry is extremely important.

> ➪ **Courtney's Smart Tip**
> **Credentials are important, but the lawyer-client relationship is critical.**

Choosing a lawyer is a time-consuming process, but it is well worth the effort you spend.

Controlling the Cost of Legal Services

QUESTION

I am in the process of negotiating a licensing agreement for my product. How can I control my legal costs and best utilize a lawyer?

ANSWER

There is an art to using a small business lawyer advantageously. Legal advice is another form of outside expertise which must be managed effectively. Below are some guidelines to follow when contacting a small business attorney.

1. *Assist your attorney by conducting a preliminary investigation and obtaining all necessary information in advance.* The more legwork, investigation, and information gathering you accomplish on your own, the more money you will save. Give your attorney all the important documentation required to aid in the decision-making process. Use your lawyer's expertise to review the issues surrounding the legal matter and to bring up potential risk factors.
2. *Use standardized forms for conducting routine business.* Entrepreneurs use many different forms in operating their business—legal forms for organization and incorporation, lease forms, tax forms, intellectual property forms, and so on. Using standardized forms can save you expensive legal fees as well as time. Be sure to have your attorney review the forms you will prepare so they can be tailored to fit your particular needs. Reliable form books include the *Complete Book of Corporate Forms*[2] and the *Basic Book of Business Agreements*.[3]
3. *Decide when to involve your business attorney in negotiations.* When you are trying to buy or sell something, do not involve a business attorney until you have established some common ground of agreement. Both the buyer and the seller must have an initial contact—in

order to discover whether an agreement is possible. Use your business attorney to review the situation, point out risk factors, and then draw up the legal documents to finalize the deal. The ultimate business decision has to be yours.

4. *Listen to your attorney's recommendations.* There may be some instances when tax or technical problems in the deal require resolution. You may not be able to judge the true impact of the deal you are considering entering into. Good counsel should clearly tell you what you are about to agree to and its implications. Lawyers are experts at pointing out the risk factors associated with a business deal.
5. *Beware of lawyers who are in court all the time.* Although litigation is a cost of doing business, it is also expensive. Many entrepreneurs have discovered that the only winners in a court case are the lawyers. A competent lawyer should do everything possible to keep you out of court. Litigation is time-consuming, frustrating, costly, and hazardous to your health, both mentally and physically.
6. *Beware of lawyers who refuse to go to court.* On the other side of the coin are the attorneys who lack the necessary skills or motivation to represent you in court and who will do everything possible to avoid it. They will suggest settlements and compromises, sometimes giving away your position to the adversary to avoid litigation. At times, you will have to draw the line: "Okay, this is the way it is going to be, or we'll sue." Your posture has to be that you are perfectly willing to go to court to secure your justice.
7. *Never talk to another person's attorney by yourself.* Always have your lawyer present when the other side brings counsel. Lawyers have superior knowledge about the law and may try to bluff you. An ethical attorney would never speak with you directly without your attorney present. Never let the adversary's lawyer talk with you alone. Once you have retained legal counsel, all correspondence should be handled through your attorney.
8. *Discuss fee arrangements with your attorney up front.* Determine the costs associated with representation in all legal matters at the beginning of the lawyer–client relationship. Many entrepreneurs negotiate a written fee arrangement with their attorneys before any services are rendered.

In summary, select a lawyer with the experience and expertise that fits your needs. Do all the legwork first and collect all necessary information. Prepare in advance of meeting with your attorney to minimize your legal fees.

Reducing Legal Fees for Patent Applications

QUESTION

My colleagues and I developed a software product that is ready to go to market. Because of its unique features and the lack of current competition, we decided to patent this product and contacted an attorney friend of ours for assistance. He has just completed the patent search and is beginning to prepare our patent application. Our current bill for this work is $2000, and the attorney has informed us that it will cost considerably more to apply for the patent. Are these fees reasonable and is there any way to ensure that we are not paying too much for this work?

ANSWER

Acquiring a patent is quite often an expensive project. It depends on how complicated your patent application is. Costs will increase with the complexity of the invention. Also, if your patent lawyer is required to file one or more amendments in responding to a patent examiner, the cost will increase accordingly. A patent will normally be issued 1 to 2 years from the date of the filing of the application.

Legal fees are usually charged on a straight hourly basis according to the specific time devoted to your project. It is important to monitor the various patent services you receive under this hourly fee arrangement. To begin, find out your lawyer's exact hourly rate and the rates of other members in the law firm who will be doing work for you. Today rates may vary from $50 to $250 and more per hour depending on the staff member's specialty, experience, and status. For example, partners charge more than associates because they have more experience. At the lower end of the fee scale are paralegal workers, hired by many firms to do research, review files, or prepare drafts of simple documents.

It is common to have a paralegal or new associate perform routine services like conducting a patent search, and you should be billed accordingly. Otherwise you have paid an unnecessarily high fee. If an associate can perform the service for about the same amount of time as the partner, the partner should assign it to the associate.

Discuss with your lawyer the overall strategy of applying for your patent and the level of expertise and essential skills needed to handle it. Give your lawyer some flexibility in selecting other personnel in the firm to handle parts of your patent application. Find out about the minimum billing time for your lawyer's firm. Some bill for a quarter-hour minimum; others bill for shorter periods. A 3-minute phone conversation may cost you 15 minutes of one lawyer's time and only 5 minutes of another's. Some lawyers don't charge for phone calls under 5 minutes.

Ask for an estimate of the number of billable hours and find out which lawyers will work on the project. Try to negotiate a cap or ceiling on the total fee, whenever feasible. At least, ask for a threshold which would require your lawyer to notify you that your fees are about to exceed that point. Ask for a bill which details the service performed, the name and hourly rate of the person who performed the service, the amount of time spent, and the date on which the service was performed. Request that you be informed in advance if there are any hourly rate changes.

In applying for a patent, a combination of fees might be most advisable. Since a patent search is fairly routine, you probably could request a fixed fee for that service, whereas an hourly fee might be appropriate for completing the patent application. Ask your lawyer to describe the various ways in which your account might be handled and to recommend the fee structure most appropriate for you. In the end, you will probably save on legal fees if you hire a top patent lawyer who is already working in or familiar with your industry. To locate such an expert, examine key patents in your field and contact the lawyers who wrote them.

> ➪ **Courtney's Smart Tip**
> **Consider paying your lawyer with products, services, or stock instead of cash.**

Whatever route you choose, if your business is like most start-ups, you will probably be short of cash. You could offer your lawyer services or a financial interest in your company as compensation for legal assistance. Be cautious, however, about exchanging stock for legal services.

One last point: software-related products are usually protected under a copyright, which costs very little to obtain. Consider getting a second opinion as to whether in fact your software is patentable.

9-4 How to Choose an Accountant for Your Business

QUESTION

Over a year ago I started a small retail store featuring baby furniture. Since I am not a wizard with numbers, I hired a bookkeeper to set up my books, reconcile my bank statement, prepare monthly financial statements, and fill out tax returns. Now I am thinking about expanding and opening another store. How can I find a reputable accountant to help me?

ANSWER

You need an experienced accountant who specializes in small business and works with other owners like yourself. As your business grows, the duties of the accountant will become more numerous and demanding and will ultimately involve designing customized accounting systems for your business. This member of your management team should be a good business adviser as well as a skilled tax planner. He or she should understand the importance of building and managing sound cash flow documents, should be able to provide assistance in securing loans, and should become a good source of business contacts as your venture grows.

Shop around for a competent accountant and consultant. This member of your management team will become one of your most trusted and most frequently used advisers. Ask other business owners in the retail trade about accounting people they would recommend. Call your banker, lawyer, or trade association for additional recommendations.

> ➪ **Courtney's Smart Tip**
> **Find an accountant who has experience working with clients in your industry.**

If you are planning a significant expansion of your business, seek out an experienced certified public accountant (CPA). If you think you might be a candidate for raising venture capital or going public, contact an accounting firm with an established track record in initial public offerings or private placements. Typically, these firms search for new small ventures that will become the leading businesses of the future. If they are interested in your business, they will most likely charge less than their usual fee until you become more profitable. Then their charges will rise accordingly.

Hiring a nationally recognized firm will lend credibility to your financial statements and enhance your chances of attracting growth capital. Also, major accounting firms have a number of professional manuals, books, and other programs to assist new founders. These materials are usually available free or at very low cost, since accounting firms want your continued business as you grow.

If you do not feel that you need a national accounting firm, look for an experienced independent accountant or retired accountant who could work part time. Local colleges and universities with accounting departments are another source for referrals. Finally, contact the society of certified public accountants in your state. Most have referral banks.

After collecting a list of potential accountants, interview each one. Check the chemistry and make sure you are compatible. Ask about services and fee structures. Fees will vary significantly according to the experience level of the accounting expert and the size of your venture. As with other members of your infrastructure, do the routine work yourself and use your accountant for professional expertise.

Setting up and maintaining your books at the beginning is critical to successfully managing your venture as it grows. Many entrepreneurs hire bookkeepers to perform the routine accounting work and then utilize a CPA to review their financials on a monthly or quarterly basis.

You need to become familiar with the day-to-day numbers associated with managing your business. Don't just wait for the prepared financial statements at the end of the month or quarter. You must have a feeling for the money going out and the money coming in—your cash flow. Carefully track your sales and expenses, and how much money you are owed and owe. Do not delegate this function to your accountant.

9-5 How to Find a Reputable Insurance Agent

QUESTION

I have been running a small alterations business from my home for the last 10 years. Because my business has grown steadily, I have decided to move into a neighborhood shopping center. How do I find a good insurance agent to help me buy business insurance and what kind do I need to obtain?

ANSWER

Many business owners do not give much thought to risk management until they or one of their friends encounter a disaster. You need to have business insurance to cover unexpected and unpreventable events—fire, theft, lawsuits, severe weather conditions, and so on—whether you operate out of your home or in a separate location. You can work with either an independent agent who represents many different insurers or an agent who represents one company.

To begin, contact your personal insurance agent or company and ask about the types of business insurance available and the costs. Describe your business needs and determine the best form of coverage. Then shop around for both the best price and the best level of service. Select an agent or broker who fits your needs and specializes in your industry or particular type of business. An alterations business has very different needs from a restaurant or construction business.

Ask other business owners who have similar needs to recommend an agent. Contact your local or national trade or professional association for recommendations. Find out if the organization has group insurance arrangements with specialty brokers or insurers. Call your local chamber of commerce as well as your banker, lawyer, and accountant for additional recommendations of agents with experience in your industry.

Interview several agents and ask for their opinion on the kinds of insurance your business needs. Ask what you should do if you need to file a claim. If they respond by giving you the insurance company's telephone number, be wary. The correct response is "Call me first." Request a list of customers you can call and then contact these references.

Make sure the chemistry is right. It's important that you feel comfortable with an agent and confident that he or she will be there to assist and represent you if a claim must be filed. Ask about the various coverages available and seek out advice in reducing your exposure to potential losses. Effective agents are experienced in risk management. Check to see if your candidates recommend any particular safety devices for theft protection or fire detection, and find out if you can receive credit for installing them.

Before making a final selection, call your state's insurance department to determine if any complaints have been filed against the agent or company you are considering using. Don't make your decision solely on price. Balance that important criterion against the agent's expertise and, once again, the chemistry.

If you determine that your business needs several policies, you might end up with several different agents—one for property or liability insurance, another for benefits coverage, and so on. An excellent resource on this subject is Sean Mooney's *Insuring Your Business.*[4] The book covers property insurance, liability insurance, boiler and machinery coverage, workers' compensation, and other critical areas that business owners need to consider. To order a copy, call (800) 331-9146.

9-6 How to Select and Use Management Consultants

QUESTION

I am starting a new retail computer supply business and need assistance in finding a location, negotiating a lease, and setting up my records and bookkeeping systems. I do not have the experience to do all this myself and I am thinking about hiring a consultant. Where should I look for one?

ANSWER

For many entrepreneurs, consultants are less expensive than hiring staff, especially when a specific problem must be solved or a project calls for expert assistance.

Choosing a consultant is a very important decision, and should be made only after carefully researching and interviewing potential consultants. Many skilled consultants can provide invaluable services—if you can find them. Nowhere are the options so abundant while the quality is so variable. The price you pay for consulting services varies tremendously. Proceed with caution.

First, consider whether you want a generalist or a specialist. You may need several different consultants to help you. The person with expertise in finding a location for your business most likely will not have the skills you need to set up your books. Be wary of "can do all" types. Second, consider the consultants' track records. Whom else have they worked for and what services did they render? Obtain references from other entrepreneurs so you can verify performance.

The best way to find consultants is through referrals from your banker, lawyer, accountant, and fellow entrepreneurs. The government is also a good resource and sometimes provides consultants at no charge through the Small Business Administration (SBA). Some of these consultants are paid by the government; others volunteer their services. College and universities are a source for both private consultants and those working under federally funded programs. You might also look in the Yellow Pages under management consultants and shop around.

In the beginning, founders are short of cash and often try to find low-cost educational programs or government-funded management assistance programs such as those offered by the SBA. Typically independent consultants charge anywhere from $100 to $1000 a day. Well-known consulting firms usually charge higher fees. Unfortunately, it is difficult to judge consultants solely on the basis of the fees they charge.

Narrow your selection process down to a few consultants and interview them in depth. Ask about their expertise and approaches. Be sure that you are comfortable with and can communicate with them. Evaluate their enthusiasm and openness. Try to determine their interest level in your project. Ask for sample proposals based on your needs. Evaluate their proposals by looking for outcomes and objectives they intend to accomplish. Inquire about their fee structure. Is it hourly, daily, or a fixed fee? You want to hire a consultant who works fast, but effectively.

> ➪ **Courtney's Smart Tip**
> **When you decide on a consultant, work out a written agreement specifying the consultant's responsibilities, objectives, and compensation.**

A good book on hiring consultants is Herman Holtz's *Choosing and Using a Consultant.*[5] Ask your librarian for reference books or articles on consulting. Don't underestimate the amount of time it will take to find a consultant who has the expertise and enthusiasm you need.

9-7 Recruiting and Utilizing a Board of Directors

How to Assemble a Board of Directors

QUESTION

I am interested in starting a dry-cleaning business and plan to incorporate. Do I have to have a board of directors for my new company? If so, where do I find people to serve?

ANSWER

Your decision to incorporate your business is a wise one, especially if financial risk and personal liability are involved. You might look into the possibility of starting your dry-cleaning business as an S corporation. Check with your accountant about the potential tax advantages of this type of corporate structure.

Every corporation is required by law to have a board of directors. Whom you choose for the board is up to you. Many entrepreneurs give little thought to this task. Instead, they take the easy way out and appoint family members just to meet state requirements. Inside boards rarely contribute solid business experience or reliable advice to a venture. Board members should be looked upon as resources who can make a significant contribution to the new corporation. They should be able to bring in business, make introductions to potential customers, and influence members of the business community.

> ➪ **Courtney's Smart Tip**
> **An active and effective board of outside directors is one of the greatest resources an entrepreneur can have.**

Board members who have extensive entrepreneurial experience, especially with problems similar to yours, can be invaluable. Retired executives make excellent choices, as do influential community or business leaders. They will strengthen the management team as well as impress potential lenders or investors. Most investors and lenders prefer to see outside board members participating—not family members, unless those relatives happen to have direct experience in the industry.

The purpose of a board is to set overall company policy and to ensure that policies are administered by the owners. Board members are responsible to the shareholders and must see that management carries out its responsibilities. The management team should look to board members as in-house consultants. Sometimes management gets too close to the operation, and board members can offer more objective analyses and place problems in proper perspective. However, the board should not be involved in day-to-day operations.

New entrepreneurs need all the management expertise they can tap into. Most founders appoint at least five board members. A well-qualified board can improve strategy, stimulate planning, and provide emotional support. Often, entrepreneurs flounder around trying to obtain credit from vendors, get goods shipped on time, and so on. One phone call from a board member can accomplish all that in minutes. Board members can act as sounding boards for new ideas and as references for banks, investors, and lawyers.

The downside of appointing an outside board is that busy executives and business leaders may not have sufficient time to devote to your venture. Or they may be reluctant to serve because of the personal liability assumed in becoming board members. Many founders try to secure board liability insurance to protect their members. This is an additional budgetary expense, but in the past few years has become less costly.

Lastly, it is a common practice to pay board members a nominal fee for attending monthly meetings—or to compensate them with stock options. Your strategic operating plan will dictate whether appointing an inside board will suffice or whether an outside board would enhance your venture.

The Value of Directors to a Small Business

QUESTION

I operate a small landscaping business and my banker has suggested that I recruit a board of directors. Does this make sense, since my company is so small?

ANSWER

Recruiting a small board of outside directors is a smart entrepreneurial strategy for any business. Yet most entrepreneurs neglect this resource. Studies show that less than 10 percent of medium-sized private companies have outside boards.

Do not feel that because your business is so small, no one will want to serve on your board. Whenever one entrepreneur approaches another for assistance, the response is most often favorable. First, serving on a board is flattering to the ego. Second, board members usually find the experience rewarding and learn not only from you and your business but also from other board members. It helps them better manage their own ventures. Consider how your own expertise in landscaping could help another entrepreneur who faces "seasonal" sales.

If you are thinking about expanding your business, an outside board will be especially valuable. Don't think that it is simply too much extra work. Expansion is exactly the time when you need a board of directors to provide outside expertise, direction, and advice on planning your growth strategies. Board members can brainstorm different ideas, opportunities, and approaches. They are not concerned about day-to-day operating details. They provide an objective analysis and will give honest feedback about the business. Fast-growing companies desperately need good board members who can anticipate potential problems and develop solutions.

Finally, don't fall prey to the objection that recruiting a board of directors will cause you to lose control over your business. Control lies with the shareholders, not necessarily with the board. Assert your position by limiting the terms of your board members to 2 years so you can more easily replace a director. If you are still hesitant about assembling a board of directors, start out with an advisory council—a group of advisers who have no voting rights or legal presence.

The advantages of establishing an outside board invariably outweigh the disadvantages. Being a business owner is often a lonely profession with few people available to exchange ideas with and plan new directions. By having an outside board, you will find yourself more confident to take new risks. It is the best investment you can make in the future of your business and its continued success.

An excellent publication for recruiting outside boards is John Ward's *Creating Effective Boards for Private Enterprise.*[6]

9-8 Establishing an Advisory Board

QUESTION

I have just started a new consulting company and I am thinking about putting together an advisory board. Is this a good idea for my type of business? If so, how should I select board members and how can I best utilize them?

ANSWER

Using an advisory board instead of a board of directors can be most helpful, especially when starting a new venture. An advisory board is easier to establish and can be converted to a board of directors later. Many business advisers are reluctant to serve on a board of directors because of the potential legal liability involved. This is not the case with an advisory board.

Like directors, board advisers should be selected because of their business acumen and their ability to generate new business, make introductions to potential customers, and influence business leaders in your industry. Members of an advisory board should have a healthy mix of talent and related business experience. Look for people who have specific knowledge and skills you lack. Your relationship with an advisory board can be enhanced by involving it thoroughly in the early stages of your venture.

An advisory board serves a very different function from a board of directors. The mission of an advisory board is to provide guidance and feedback about the venture's goals, objectives, and directions. Unlike a board of directors, advisory board members have no voting rights or legal liability. They are there primarily to provide counsel and make recommendations for operating and growing your venture.

Where should you look for qualified members? Retired executives, entrepreneurs who run noncompeting companies, business school professors, members of the infrastructure, and key users of your products or services are excellent sources. Check to ensure that potential board members have no ethical or legal conflicts with you or your business.

One of the advantages of establishing an advisory board is that members have no legal power (or legal liability) and can easily be replaced. Another advantage is the relatively low cost to assemble and maintain such a board. Rarely are advisory board members paid for meeting expenses. You can show your appreciation by taking them out for a group dinner or some type of entertainment.

Avoid making your advisory board a rubber stamp by limiting membership to insiders and relatives. An advisory board of outside directors can legitimately help young ventures grapple more effectively with the many challenges of growth.

> ⇨ **Courtney's Smart Tip**
> **Include a half-page biographical sketch of each member of your board in the appendix to your business plan. Investors and lenders like entrepreneurs who know that outside boards strengthen the management team and build new business.**

Overall, advisory boards and boards of directors enhance the organization's management team and can bring sound business knowledge and expertise to your venture. They can give you a valuable edge over your competition and can assist in obtaining working capital for expansion.

9-9 Pitfalls to Avoid

1. Selecting a consultant without interviewing and checking references.
2. Consulting with a business attorney without first preparing for the meeting and completing as much work as you can yourself.
3. Failing to establish an agreed-upon price for consulting services.
4. Ignoring the need for business insurance until you are involved in a loss or disaster.
5. Failing to utilize an advisory board for your business.
6. Using family members or friends as directors or advisors when they lack the requisite skills and business contacts.
7. Hiring a generalist when you need a specialist.

The Good News. Entrepreneurs can call upon many experienced and skillful members of the infrastructure and other professionals to help plan, manage, and operate their ventures. They need to network the business community and balance their team by selecting people who have the expertise they lack.

9-10 Entrepreneurial Resource Checklist

References

1. Krasnow and Conrad, *100 Ways to Cut Legal Fees and Manage Your Lawyer,* National Legislation Center, Washington, DC, 1988.
2. Ted Nicholas, *Complete Book of Corporate Forms,* Finance Dearborn, 1994.
3. *Basic Book of Business Agreements,* Irwin, 1990.
4. Sean Mooney, *Insuring Your Business,* Insurance Information Institute Press, New York, 1992.
5. Herman Holtz, *Choosing and Using a Consultant,* Wiley, New York, 1989.
6. John Ward, *Creating Effective Boards for Private Enterprise,* Jossey-Bass, 1992.

Library Reading

Martindale-Hubbell Law Directory

The Lawyer's Register by Specialties and Fields of Law

Attorney's Register

U.S. Lawyer's Referral Directory

Directory of the Legal Profession

Contacts

1. Society of Certified Public Accountants

   Check with your state society of certified public accountants for referrals of accountants who specialize in small businesses.

2. National Association for the Self-Employed
   P.O. Box 612067
   DFW Airport, TX 75261
   (800) 232-6273

   The self-employed members of this association have access to a business consultant hotline. Group health and disability insurance is also available.

3. Young Presidents Organization (YPO)
   451 S. Becker Dr., #200
   Irving, TX 75062
   (214) 541-1044

This is an international group of presidents with strong local chapters. It has strict age requirments and company qualifications for membership.

4. U.S. Chamber of Commerce
   Center for Small Business
   1615 H. St., N.W.
   Washington, DC 20062
   (202) 463-5503

   The Center for Small Business is actively involved in representing small business concerns before our government. It also provides issue reports, the Small Business Update, and other publications.

5. Service Corps of Retired Executives (SCORE)
   409 Third St., S.W.
   Washington, DC 20416
   (202) 205-6600
   (800) 827-5722 Answer Desk

   SCORE, part of SBA, is an organization of retired businesspeople who provide free advice to entrepreneurs. The answer desk provides information on all government agencies.

10 Franchising

10-1 Overview

Franchising is a growing industry and currently accounts for nearly one-third of all retail sales. Approximately 300 businesses are franchised annually. In 1990, there were over 3000 franchise companies representing over 500,000 outlets doing over $600 billion in sales. It has been estimated that there will be over 9000 franchise companies by the year 2000, which is a growth rate of 500 franchise start-ups per year. The following shows the breakdown of types of franchise businesses.

Type of business	Percent of all franchises
1. Restaurants	10.7
2. Auto products and services	2.0
3. Auto and truck dealers	50.5
4. Nonfood retailing	4.0
5. Business aids and services	2.7
6. Convenience stores	2.0
7. Gas stations	16.1
8. Lodging	3.3
9. All others	8.7

Adapted from International Franchise Association, *Franchising in the Economy, 1988–1990* (Washington, DC, International Franchise Association, 1990).

NOTE: Ted Rice, co-founder and former chairman of the board of T.J. Cinnamons, contributed many ideas to this chapter, sharing his experiences in building a worldwide franchise of retail and wholesale bakery stores. Ted is currently the CEO of Big Bob's Carpet and is building yet another franchise organization. He is an adjunct professor at Wichita State University and several other colleges and universities in Kansas City (Missouri) teaching entrepreneurship. He is also a Price-Babson College fellow.

Franchising is an excellent strategy both for successful entrepreneurs who want to expand their markets and for potential entrepreneurs who are considering purchasing a franchise as a business entry strategy if there is an innovative, proven business concept and system to replicate it. This chapter addresses the questions from both entrepreneurs who want to purchase a franchise operation and those who are thinking about franchising their business concept.

The reason franchise operations are more successful than new start-ups is that their concept has been proven and an operating system has been established. Most franchises are designed to be somewhat of a "turnkey" operation for launching and operating the venture. That is, the owner can begin operation with a complete planning, management control, and operational system in place which includes ongoing support and training. The turnkey concept was developed around the idea that the franchisee has only to turn the key in the door and be open for business. In reality, however, the franchisee must undertake much investigation and up-front work, including locating a site, negotiating the lease, finishing the space, obtaining the equipment, and hiring the staff. Potential franchisees who think this is a "slam dunk" way of doing business have been misled.

The survival rate of franchised businesses is far superior to that of entrepreneurial ventures. Approximately 4 percent of franchised businesses fail during the first few crucial years, while other new ventures suffer an 80 percent failure rate during the crucial period. Because not all franchises are successful, it is imperative that potential franchisees perform "due diligence" and investigate everything, including the industry, the market customer base, and the track records and background of both the franchisor and other franchisees.

Ask for all information available from the franchisor: the franchise package, year-end financials, a list of existing franchisees, disclosure documents, and so forth. It is also important to determine potential profitability and to consider whether the franchise could reach the financial returns you expect. Unfortunately, most people don't want to spend the time and effort to investigate and make an informed decision.

> ➪ **Courtney's Smart Tip**
> **Potential franchisees need some type of entrepreneurial experience obtained from working, from taking seminars or courses, or both.**

Potential franchisees must have sufficient funds to invest in the business and the commitment to run the operation. Entrepreneurs who truly want to be their own boss may be disappointed with buying a franchise because of the restrictive requirements to follow a standardized operation and use only authorized products. Some franchises are more restrictive than others.

On the other hand, franchising is an excellent expansion strategy for founders who want to grow—provided their product or service is franchisable. Franchising can open the door to low-cost financing not available through traditional money sources. But franchising a new concept takes considerable up-front money that must be spent before collecting any fees. Whether you are considering franchising your business or purchasing an already established franchise, considerable thought, investigation, and evaluation are essential.

10-2 Smart Franchising Strategies

1. Proceed carefully by gathering all available information about franchising opportunities, including the franchisor and a list of the franchisees.
2. Experience the product or service first hand, if possible.
3. Determine whether there is a continuing market for the franchised product or service.
4. Visit typical franchisees and ask them about the franchisor, profitability, market potential, long-term commitment, and other factors.
5. Ask about the training and support, both initial and ongoing, that the franchisor will provide.
6. Ask the franchisor how many franchisees have closed and for what reasons.
7. If you do not have any small business experience, enroll in a seminar or course on entrepreneurship and running a franchise.
8. Open several locations and evaluate the capability of your business to be franchised to different locations.
9. Determine if you have enough money, patience, and management capability to franchise your concept.
10. Investigate potential franchisees, evaluate their entrepreneurial capability, and always look for an owner-operator.
11. After performing all of the "due diligence," rely on your intuition in deciding whether to become involved with a franchisor or to sign up a franchisee.

10-3 How to Research and Buy a Franchise Business

QUESTION

I am interested in starting a used-car rental agency along the lines of Ugly Duckling or Rent-a-Lemon. What would it take to open such a franchise business, and where would I begin?

ANSWER

Purchasing a franchise can be a good entry strategy for entrepreneurs. It eliminates many of the headaches associated with starting a venture from scratch. It is also an opportunity to benefit from the experience, knowledge, expertise, and support of a franchisor who has successfully tested and proven a business concept in the marketplace. Proven franchises offer lower risks of failure than unproven franchises or new start-up businesses.

Often the franchise offers an established trade name and reputation along with instant recognition in the market area. These favorable aspects will not guarantee success, but can certainly give you a head start. For example, *Inc.* magazine reported that 38 percent of start-up businesses fail within the first year compared with less than 4 percent of franchises.

Warning: Considerable due diligence is required before entering into a franchise agreement. To begin with, ask yourself whether you would enjoy working with a parent company that will most likely require you to follow certain policies and procedures in operating your business. Joining any franchise involves a loss of freedom for entrepreneurs who must abide by the stipulations contained in the franchise agreement.

Are you willing to pay a franchise fee along with a monthly royalty to the parent company? All franchise companies receive an up-front fee when the franchise agreement is signed, and then collect monthly royalty fees. This fee is based on a percentage of gross sales before taxes, usually 5 percent. If you feel comfortable with these conditions, then thoroughly investigate the franchise by following the steps below.

First, select at least three franchises that offer the same product or service. Before contacting these franchises, visit the business section of your local library. Consult the various franchise handbooks that contain information about existing franchises and their parent companies. Look up articles that have been written about the franchise in newspapers, journals, and magazines.

Write for a copy of the *Franchise Opportunity Handbook,*[1] published annually by the Superintendent of Documents, U.S. Government

Printing Office, Washington, D.C. It is extremely helpful and probably contains more extensive information on franchises than any other publication. It costs about $10.

Next, ask the librarian to assist you in accessing one of the many electronic databases that contain financial information and disclosure statements on franchises. It is critical that you evaluate the financial strength of the parent company. These databases contain annual reports, quarterly financial statements, and other detailed financial information. While at the library, consult INFOTRAC, another database that lists published articles in many different magazines. Get copies of anything written about the franchise. Also, several magazines publish annual listings of franchise opportunities.

Visit a couple of franchise locations in your area. Check out the location, examine the exterior and interior, and observe the customers. Try the product or service. Talk to the managers and ask them about their operations and their relationship with the franchisor. What problems have they encountered with the parent company?

You are now ready to contact the parent company and indicate your interest in joining the franchise. Ask the franchisor if you can come out and visit the corporate headquarters. Inquire as to whether they provide training on how to produce and market their product or service that you may not understand well. Question whether they have established training manuals available for franchisees.

Ask what type of management expertise the franchisor has in producing, marketing, and financing the product or service. Ask how many franchises there are in the company and how long they have been in business. How many franchises have closed and why?

Request that the franchisor send you a disclosure document. It will reveal information about the franchisor, including educational background, experience (what types of businesses he or she has been involved in), and any pending litigation. Sometimes, franchisors are reluctant to provide a disclosure document early on. Be persistent. They are required by law to provide you with a copy. If you are not satisfied with the answers to these questions, pursue other potential franchisors.

10-4 How to Evaluate a Franchise Agreement

QUESTION

I am interested in opening up a weight loss franchise business. The franchisor just sent me the franchise agreement. How do I evaluate it?

ANSWER

Most franchise agreements are written for 5 years with an automatic renewal. Determine the exit, or how you can get out of the franchise agreement. Can you sell your franchise and do the potential buyers have to qualify as franchisees? Under what circumstances can the franchisor terminate the agreement?

What are your obligations to the parent company and the franchisor's to you? How far from your business can another franchise be located? How are royalties determined? Are your royalty payments subject to audit by the franchisor? If yes, how much notice will they give you before the audit?

The franchisor will probably ask you what locations you are considering.

> ➪ **Courtney's Smart Tip**
> **Never lease or rent property until you have signed a franchise agreement.**

The franchisor must find out whether the territory you are interested in is available. Most franchisors have site locators that directly work with them and provide the franchisee with considerable location assistance. What, if any, arrangements have you made with the landlord?

During your initial conversations, decide whether you feel comfortable with the franchisor. Buying into a franchise situation is akin to entering into a marriage. There must be good chemistry between both of you, or you'll end up at each other's throat or in court, or out.

If you are still interested in pursuing the franchise opportunity, ask for all the available information about the franchise. Because it costs the franchise about $15 to send out a complete informational kit, it may first try to qualify you as a potential buyer. Usually, the franchisor will send out an initial questionnaire that asks for certain information about your financial condition, including your net worth and your source of money for opening the business.

After receiving the questionnaire, the franchisor will ascertain whether you are capable of purchasing. Then, the franchisor will probably send out a formal application package. This package contains detailed information about the company's operations and history, including brochures, flyers, and sample marketing and sales material. Remember, it is the sales tool for the franchisor. Don't take anything at face value; investigate everything. The application packet will ask you to provide biographical data and complete financial information. It will include a copy of the franchise agreement and available territories for purchase.

Consult an attorney who specializes in franchising before signing the franchise agreement to ensure that you fully understand all the terms and conditions of the contract. Guard against having your attorney rewrite the agreement—it is a waste of your money. Instead, ask the attorney to review the franchise agreement and look for any major flaws or inconsistencies. Although most of the terms are standard, you may be able to negotiate some items that are important to you.

Decide whether the franchisor is reputable and whether the required investment will give you the financial returns you are looking for. The franchisor must determine whether you are a viable purchaser and whether you will be able to operate a successful venture. In most instances, the franchisor is looking for an owner/operator versus an absentee owner.

Finally, it's time to review and evaluate all the information you have gathered. Then, ask the franchisor for high and low financial ratios for the typical franchise operation, including gross revenues and net earning for the franchisees. You might be able to obtain this information from existing franchisees. In general, if the business is a restaurant, ask for the average ticket price. If it is a retail operation, ask for the average sales per square foot.

At each step of your investigation, determine whether the franchisor is fair, honest, and reputable. Will you get the essential assistance you feel is necessary to operate a successful venture? Does the franchisor have related industry experience? What has been its track record to date? Try to visit as many franchise locations as possible.

During the evaluation process, you will most likely eliminate some of the various franchise alternatives. Compare the different front-end fees, royalty payments, expenses, and so on. Franchisors can offer an easier alternative to starting a new business, but entrepreneurs must carefully assess and analyze each opportunity.

10-5 Purchasing an International Food Franchise

QUESTION

Since I came back from an overseas vacation, I have been entertaining the idea of opening a specialty restaurant or franchise fast-food business in another country. I feel this could be a good opportunity for a small family enterprise. How can I find the capital needed to start such a venture? What advice would you offer for pursuing this idea?

ANSWER

Launching a specialty restaurant or fast-food franchise overseas could be difficult, expensive, and time-consuming. In a foreign country it will be easier to open a fast-food franchise, since you will not have all the headaches associated with starting a business from scratch. Not only will the franchisor provide a plan for operating the business, but also, it will furnish key management advice, tax information, and other business consulting. An international franchisor has valuable contacts providing expertise on operating a franchise abroad. More important, franchises have an already established name providing immediate recognition, and have a proven fast-food concept that has already demonstrated success in the marketplace.

However, there will be some risk involved, since you might not know whether the concept you choose will be successful in another country. The fast-food market may be quite different from its success in the United States. In addition, it will probably be more costly to start a franchise in another country, since the policy of most franchisors is to sell rights to an entire country versus a specific geographic location. Generally, franchisors require a multi-unit commitment to open several locations within a certain period of time. Usually, they sell the franchise rights to a national of that country.

There are several important factors to consider before becoming involved with an international franchise. First, determine if you can open a business within about 90 days. If it takes longer than that, look for another country. Ask if you are required to make a joint venture with a citizen of that country who must own some percentage of your company. Can you take a profit out of the country? Some franchises require that any money earned must be reinvested in that country. Also ask how much of the raw product or materials must come from that country. Most important, ensure that all money exchanged shall be in U.S. currency at the exchange rate the first of the month and fifteenth of the month at 12 noon Greenwich mean time. Lastly, obtain legal counsel from an attorney in that country to help you understand requirements and customs for conducting business there.

Research which fast-food franchisors have international locations and whether you would be able to purchase the rights to a foreign country. The *World Wide Franchise Directory*,[2] available in most libraries, is a guide to franchise opportunities around the world. The library would also have *Doing Business In. . .*[3] published by Price Waterhouse. This is a series of books focusing on how to operate ventures in many different foreign countries.

While at the library, access the National Trade Data Bank (NTDB) on CD-ROM. This is a database about marketing and doing business abroad developed by the U.S. Commerce Department. Or contact one of the Commerce Department's regional offices of the International Trade Administration for additional information. The office will conduct customized market research for a fee in areas where the government has a foreign office.

Another good source for gathering information concerning international franchises is to attend the annual International Franchise Trade Show sponsored by the International Franchise Association located in Washington, D.C. You can contact the IFA about its shows at (202) 628-8000. There are also international franchise fairs held abroad that feature how to start a franchise business in various countries. Contact the Trade Show Bureau in Denver, Colorado, at (303) 860-7626 to obtain further information.

As a rule, franchisors do not provide funding for opening a franchise business. They can assist you with leasing agreements for obtaining necessary equipment. Franchisors can also refer you to preferred lenders that they have worked with. Consult a copy of the August, 1991 issue of *Nation's Business.* It contains a directory of lending sources, for people and groups interested in owning franchises, that provides beneficial funding contacts.

10-6 Franchising a Successful Venture

QUESTION

Several years ago I started a fast-food restaurant that sells a new kind of southwestern taco made with a special machine that I designed. Because of its success, I opened another restaurant in January. This restaurant has been equally successful. Several of my friends have suggested that I franchise my business, which I am seriously considering. What is your advice?

ANSWER

Franchising is a sound business expansion strategy for you to consider if you have an innovative, proven concept and business system that can be replicated with repeated success. Entrepreneurs have been franchising their ventures at increasing rates for the past decade. Currently franchises account for nearly one-third of all retail sales. On the average, about 300 businesses are franchised annually. As stated earlier, in 1990, there were over 3000 franchise companies representing over 500,000 outlets doing over $600 billion in sales. It has been estimated that there will be over 9000 franchise companies by the end of the century—a growth rate of 500 franchise start-ups per year.

There are a couple of reasons why franchising has been so popular as well as a successful means of expanding a business. It is an excellent way to quickly expand your business, if in fact, you can prove that your concept works, your product is widely recognized and accepted, your business has a steady record of success, and you can establish that it could be disseminated to other locations.

The franchisor must provide the franchisee with a predictable way of doing business—that is, a business that is completely assembled so the franchisee can begin operation with complete planning, management control, and operational systems that include ongoing support and training. Facilities are duplicated and equipment is purchased in bulk and installed. Inventory is provided through established procurement systems.

But is this the strategy for you and your business? It is extremely important for you to evaluate whether you should get involved in this expansion strategy. Does it make sense for you to franchise? Do you have the expertise and *capital* to franchise? Will you be getting the value you want from franchising? Are you giving value to potential franchisees through your experience, knowledge, and continual support? To be successful, you must have productive restaurants that provide a steady stream of income to you.

There are several different types of franchises. They include trademark and brand-name franchises, product distribution franchises, business format franchises, and affiliate or conversion franchises.

- In a *trademark and brand-name* franchise, the franchisee pays for the right to use the franchisor's established trademark or brand name usually for marketing purposes. By marketing products or services under a well-known trademark or brand name, the franchisee can gain market visibility and market share more quickly by capitalizing on the credibility and recognition of the franchisor.
- In *product distribution* franchises, the manufacturer of a product establishes a distribution network by contracting with dealers who distribute the product. The manufacturer stipulates how the franchisee will operate. For example, the distributor may not be allowed to sell competitive products or purchase parts or supplies not expressly authorized by the franchisor. The franchisee receives support in terms of capital, advertising or discounts on purchases, and managerial support.
- In *business format* franchises, the one you are considering, the franchisee pays a fee, and in most cases, a royalty to receive the entire business format—trademarked products or services, operations systems and manuals, site selection, training, accounting, and other

managerial support services. This type of franchise operation is attractive to the individual who is not familiar with business or does not want to take the time to launch a new start-up. It is the fastest growing segment of the franchise industry today.

- In an *affiliate* or *conversion* franchise, franchisees ally themselves with like ventures. This often occurs in a fragmented industry where there is little opportunity for large-scale visibility. By forming such a system under one name, individual affiliate franchises pool funds for marketing and advertising campaigns that are designed to capture greater consumer attention and recognition for their businesses. Many real estate companies are organized this way.

10-7 Franchising a New Concept

QUESTION

I am thinking about franchising my leadership training business. What key factors should I consider in making this decision? Wouldn't franchising be an excellent way for me to expand my business?

ANSWER

Whether to franchise a successful concept is a difficult decision. Many entrepreneurs think they have a great idea, and therefore should franchise it. After all, franchising only involves signing a contract and selling to potential franchisees. Franchisors just sit back, count the royalty checks, and deposit them in the bank. Many entrepreneurs have no idea of the legal constraints, contracts, and operating criteria that are required to franchise a concept.

Before franchising a business concept, consider whether you have a product or a service that can be franchised. Does it have a proprietary ingredient, a distinctive manufacturing or operational system, or a unique service delivery system that can be franchised? Having at least one of these ingredients is key to launching a successful franchise business.

Even if your concept has one of the above characteristics, you must consider the partnership arrangement where each party has a close and continuing legal relationship over time—like a marriage. It is a constant give-and-take relationship.

There are several attractions and pitfalls in franchising a successful business concept. The major attraction to the franchisor is the extensive and rapid expansion without borrowing or taking significant financial risk for growth capital. Most franchise systems require the franchisee to put up a significant amount of money in the beginning—the initial fee—which reduces the total investment of the franchisor in the system. This allows for faster growth on a limited capital base. Many lenders are reluctant or unwilling to provide capital for expanding new businesses. Franchising may open the door to low-cost financing not available through traditional money sources.

Franchising provides another financial attraction with the income from franchisee operations. This revenue is derived from three major sources: (1) royalties on ongoing sales, (2) profits from sale of supplies and equipment, and (3) management fees. This income can provide both a healthy ongoing profit stream and an exit strategy to the franchisor.

> ⇨ **Courtney's Smart Tip**
> **Franchising a new concept takes considerable up-front money that must be spent before collecting any fees from potential franchisees. It is not an inexpensive expansion strategy to implement.**

In addition, to become successful, the franchisor must stay close to the operation, its customers, and the problems of the franchisees. This means that much time and "sweat labor" must be spent in the trenches learning about typical problems and challenges faced by your franchisees—not behind a big desk. It is critical to keep tabs on both the direction of the industry and your individual franchisees. Also, continual innovation is an essential ingredient in maintaining market share.

Another attraction is that it is usually easier to find competent franchisees than to hire competent managers and staff to expand the business. Many businesses, especially fast-food, experience a high turnover of personnel. The franchisee has an investment in the venture and is more likely to be motivated to work hard and manage the unit successfully.

Pitfalls of franchising include finding a fragmented market with limited demand, expanding nationally before building recognition regionally, and maintaining quality, as follows:

Many entrepreneurs overestimate market penetration and embark on a large-scale expansion strategy only to find there is a limited demand and fragmented market for the product or service. Expanding to these types of markets will cause franchisees to become disgruntled and antagonistic. If your image is no better than your competition, then you have to stimulate demand through more advertising and promotion—which is an expensive proposition.

Many franchisors make the mistake of trying to expand nationally before penetrating regional markets thus, strengthening name recognition and image. Building a strong regional identity first allows the franchisor to better penetrate other regional markets with the capital needed for more sophisticated marketing programs.

The maintenance of quality is one of the most challenging aspects of franchising when you cannot personally oversee each franchisee's operation. The pitfall is in assuming that putting out a product or service is a routine matter. Many customers may have already lost faith in your operation causing sales to decline.

Be leery of catching the franchise expansion fever unless you have considered and evaluated these factors. Many entrepreneurs fall in love with their product or service and assume that everyone else will too. Remember, it is not realistic for average products or services to be readily accepted in every market. But, innovative concepts with established operating systems can succeed in the franchising world.

10-8 Pitfalls to Avoid

1. Failing to gather the information needed to make an informed decision before signing a franchise agreement and paying the required fee.
2. Signing up with a franchisor that does not have a track record of multiple locations and a profitable bottom line.
3. Purchasing a franchise that does not complement your skills, work experience, or interests.
4. Thinking that if you purchase a franchise, you will make a lot of money.
5. Thinking that if you franchise your product or service, you can sit back, collect checks, and make a lot of money.
6. Selling a franchise to an absentee owner or letting the owner's family operate the business.
7. Expanding a franchise nationally before successfully penetrating regional markets.
8. Failing to adopt strict quality-control standards and ways to measure them.
9. Franchising an average product or service in a highly competitive industry.

The Good News. Franchising can be a smart business strategy to enter the world of entrepreneurship if you perform "due diligence" in searching for the right franchise opportunity for starting your business and thoroughly investigating this business opportunity. It can also be an excellent expansion strategy if you have a proven and innovative concept that can be replicated and enough capital to franchise it.

10-9 Entrepreneurial Resource Checklist

References

1. *Franchise Opportunity Handbook*, published annually by the Superintendent of Documents, U.S. Government Printing Office, Washington, DC 20402-9325.
2. *World Wide Franchise Directory*, Gale Research
3. *Doing Business In . . .*, published by Price Waterhouse, is a series of books focusing on how to operate ventures in many different foreign countries.

Further Reading

Arden, Lynie. *Franchises You Can Run from Home*, Wiley, New York, 1990.

Bond, Robert E. *The Source Book of Franchise Opportunities*, Business One, Irwin, 1993.

Evaluating Franchise Opportunities, Small Business Administration, publication MP 26.

Justis, Robert T., and Richard J. Judd. *Franchising*, Van Nostrand Reinhold, 1990.

National Trade Data Bank (NTDB) (on CD-ROM), a database about marketing and doing business abroad, developed by the U.S. Commerce Department.

Sherman, Andrew. *Franchising and Liscensing: Two Ways to Build Your Business*, AMACOM, 1991.

Starting and Managing a Small Business of Your Own, vol. 1, available from Superintendent of Documents, U.S. Government Printing Office, Washington, DC 20402-9325.

Magazines

Nation's Business, Inc.
1615 H St. N.W.
Washington, DC 20062
(203) 463-5650

Entrepreneur
P.O. Box 58808
Boulder, CO 80321

Contacts

1. American Franchise Association (AFA)
   (800) 334-4232

   This is a national organzation aimed at improving the investment climate for potential as well as existing franchisees. AFA publishes a quarterly newsletter.

2. International Franchise Association
   Washington, DC
   (202) 628-8000.

   This association is one of the best sources for gathering information concerning international franchises. Ask about the $15 "Franchise Opportunities Guide" as well as about other books and tapes at (800) 543-1038. Attend the annual International Franchise Trade Show.

3. U.S. Commerce Department's regional offices of the International Trade Administration.

   This association conducts customized market research for a fee in areas where the government has a foreign office.

4. Program Adviser
   Franchise and Business Opportunities Program
   FTC, Washington, DC 20580
   (202) 326-3128

   This agency provides information to people who are considering investing in franchise businesses.

5. Pilot Books
   103 Cooper Street
   Babylon, NY 11702
   (516) 422-2225
   Publication: *Directory of Franchising Organizations and Franchising Investigation and Contract Negotiation*

   This source supplies a list of titles on franchising.

6. Entrepreneur
   3211 Pontius Avenue
   Los Angeles, CA 90014
   (213) 477-1011
   Publication: *Franchising Directory*

   The publication of this organization is an annual directory of franchises.

11

The 10 Questions Entrepreneurs Should Ask But Don't

As you have noticed from reading the previous chapters in this book, I have received many questions from readers across the United States about both starting and growing entrepreneurial ventures. The range of their letters has been varied, indicating that they are groping for basic entrepreneurial knowledge and skills. I have noticed a void—there are certain questions that entrepreneurs are not asking but which are critical to operating and growing successful ventures.

Therefore, I have developed "The 10 Questions Entrepreneurs Should Ask But Don't," which should be considered by all business owners. Too often, these questions crop up at later stages in the venture's development when the owner encounters problems. The high failure rate experienced by every type of new venture and reported by Dun & Bradstreet, illustrates that many of these questions should have been asked at the time of start-up. In 1992, *USA Today* reported that 88 percent of business failures can be attributed to internal causes such as inadequate leadership, poor business planning, insufficient management experience, and excessive debt.

Since most entrepreneurs experience the same business problems, if these questions had been considered earlier, the novice entrepreneurs could have greatly increased their chances of operating more stable and profitable ventures. This chapter provides important insight into the typical areas overlooked by founders that can jeopardize their chances for success.

The 10 Questions Entrepreneurs Should Ask But Don't

1. How do I go about writing a feasibility plan to determine if my idea for starting a new business could turn into a profitable business venture?
2. What kind of legal structure should I consider for my new business?
3. How do I design a plan for financing my business?
4. How can I put together a budget that will measure my start-up costs as accurately as possible?
5. How can I distinguish my business from others and increase my sales?
6. How do I put together a winning management team when I can't pay high salaries to attract and retain a talented staff?
7. How do I find a corporate strategic partner to assist me in bringing my invention to the marketplace?
8. What kind of business insurance should I get to protect my business?
9. How can I strengthen my sales skills as well as those of my staff?
10. What skills should I develop to keep pace with the growth of my business?

QUESTION 1

How do I go about writing a feasibility plan to determine if my idea for starting a new business could turn into a profitable business venture?

This is an excellent question that budding entrepreneurs should be asking before investing any money into a new venture. Usually, the opposite is true. The entrepreneur gets all wrapped up and excited about a new venture idea without thoughtful consideration, research, and evaluation of its potential and pitfalls. Several years later, the entrepreneur realizes the idea was sound, but finds that the market was saturated, the profit margin was too narrow, the management team was not in place, there was an insufficient amount of capital, or a myriad of other reasons why the venture failed.

If entrepreneurs thoroughly researched new venture ideas and wrote feasibility plans before starting, many failed businesses would have never been launched in the first place. That is one of the fundamental reasons why so many new businesses fail during the first tenuous years of operation. Most statistics show that 40 percent of new start-ups fail during the first year and, by the fifth year, 80 percent fail. This failure rate could be significantly reduced if properly structured research and planning was conducted in the beginning.

Starting a new venture takes time, market research, seed capital, financial forecasts, and a sound feasibility plan—all of which entrepreneurs are reluctant to do. Entrepreneurs are doers who want to take their ideas to the marketplace quickly. They know that the window of opportunity will probably be there only for a short period of time. Consequently, they avoid taking the necessary time to research and strategically plan their ventures, identifying problem areas and formulating plans to prevent potential problems. When this is done, they have time to formulate solutions before encountering problems.

Astute entrepreneurs understand the importance of writing feasibility plans which indicate whether ventures are likely to succeed. While writing the plan, you can identify which areas pose the greatest threats and develop alternative solutions if a problem should occur. If the feasibility plan demonstrates that the venture idea has potential, the next step is to write a business plan.

Many entrepreneurs think that if they have a great business opportunity which matches their experience and expertise, the venture will be successful. In reality, finding the right business to start comprises 10 percent of the work involved before opening up for business. The next step involves writing a feasibility analysis to determine if the venture idea could be profitable. This consists of researching its workability, marketability, profitability, and your capability as well as identifying any potential danger signals.

Writing a feasibility plan forces you to consider every facet of your business opportunity and write the results on paper, where you and others can objectively evaluate its potential. Since every venture has both risks and opportunities, what are the risks compared to the opportunities? What are the potential problems? Could the potential problems be either eliminated or minimized? Developing a feasibility plan addresses these questions and allows for trial-and-error testing before any dollars are spent.

Feasibility plans explore whether venture ideas have potential to succeed. It is a gateway that must be passed through on the way to developing a detailed business plan to prove the venture idea. There is no reason to waste your efforts on pursuing a business opportunity if it does not have a growing market, and the potential to earn a healthy profit.

I suggest that you use the following outline for developing a feasibility plan which specifies the scope of information that should be researched and included in the plan.

Entrepreneur's Feasibility Plan Outline

Executive summary
Product or service
The market
Price and profitability
Plan for further action

The *executive summary* is a brief, concise overview of the venture idea and key dimensions contained in each section of the plan. The *product or service* section covers the stage of development, limitations, liabilities, proprietary rights, production, and related services and spinoffs. The *market* section looks at the size of the market, growth potential, industry trends, customer profile, customer benefits, target markets, and market penetration methods. The *price and profitability* section measures what customers will pay for the product or service. It is critical that the venture be able to maintain a sufficiently high gross margin to cover expenses and still yield a healthy profit. This section examines the cost of the product or service, sales estimates, gross margin, operating expenses, and start-up costs. The last section, *plan for further action,* focuses on the future, identifies likely pitfalls, strong points, needed capital, license potential, potential corporate partners, infrastructure members, the entrepreneur's role, and whether to proceed with the new venture idea and write a business plan.

Many entrepreneurs use their feasibility plan to show to potential investors, bankers, friends, personal business advisers, and strategic partners. Feedback from these groups will produce useful information and help better focus the venture idea. Remember, the main purpose of writing a feasibility plan is to test the venture idea to determine if it should be further developed. If the answer is yes, you should proceed to write a detailed business plan.

➪ **Courtney's Smart Tip**
Market research and business planning are critical to launching profitable and successful ventures.

Entrepreneurs who plan carefully are more likely to succeed than those who do not. Planning minimizes risks and gives you better foresight for identifying potential problems. Spending time on writing a feasibility plan is time well spent. Writing everything down on paper allows you to encounter and solve many problems before they jeopardize the venture. Business planning skills will maximize your potential for success and minimize your chance of failure.

QUESTION 2

What kind of legal structure should I consider for my new business?

Many entrepreneurs just start their ventures without giving any thought to what kind of legal structure would be best for the business and the entrepreneur. Owners discover too late that the legal structure of their ventures is crucial to strategic planning, raising capital, and potential success. When you start a business without declaring a legal structure, the law assumes that your business is a sole proprietorship. This means that you and your venture are legally one and the same. This type of legal structure is usually not the best for ventures, especially those that need to raise outside capital and have high growth potential. Instead, the corporate structure is usually the best legal structure for entrepreneurs.

Before choosing a legal structure, consider tax implications as well as how to limit your business liability. Establishing a sole proprietorship involves only obtaining required local, state, and federal licenses. While there are few formalities and legal restrictions, you have unlimited personal liability. This means you and you alone are responsible for the full amount of your business debts. This liability extends to your home, car, stocks and other personal possessions. All the profits from the business are yours, but so are all the losses. The only way to limit the liability risk is to obtain proper business insurance.

A sole proprietorship is the most difficult legal structure for raising capital since you and your business are one and the same. If anything jeopardizes your ability to run the business, investors or lenders could lose their investments. There are also some tax drawbacks. Although you avoid the problems of double taxation with the corporate structure, sole proprietors cannot deduct many expenses that corporations can, such as a defined benefit pension plan, insurance expenses, health benefits, and other corporate expenses.

Overall, the sole proprietorship has some fatal flaws besides personal liability, tax drawbacks, and limited ability to raise capital. First, the life of the business terminates with the life of the proprietor, which poses severe problems to estate planners, not to mention difficulties with the disposition of the business.

Second, existing options are hampered. It is much easier to sell a corporation than a sole proprietorship. Growth is restricted because of financing difficulties. Lastly, it is more difficult to attract good management and staff to work in a sole proprietorship, which limits growth and performance.

> ➪ **Courtney's Smart Tip**
> **Incorporate your venture to protect against liabilities and to enhance your ability to raise capital.**

The corporate shield can protect you personally from creditors' claims except for personal negligence, civil wrongs, or torts—when you are acting as an employee of the corporation. For more detailed information about different legal structures, including partnerships, corporations, and S corporations, refer to Chapter 4, Legal Structures.

In summary, when deciding on the legal structure for your venture, consider the cost, stability, risks, liability, and your personal taxation situation. Consult with a small business attorney and tax accountant for expert advice on legal structure.

QUESTION 3

How do I design a plan for financing my business?

When starting out, most entrepreneurs neglect designing a plan for financing their ventures through various stages of growth they will encounter. Instead, they search for capital, often not knowing how much money they need, if they can raise it, and how they will use it.

Typically, entrepreneurs contact the wrong money source for financing their ventures. This is evidenced by the many letters I receive from entrepreneurs who ask advice in finding venture capitalists who might provide seed money for new ventures. In the majority of cases, venture capitalists are not an appropriate money source for new start-ups.

From my experience as Board Director for a Denver bank specializing in small business and professional and business loans, I learned that most entrepreneurs have no idea how much money they will truly need to run their businesses. Few give much thought to how debt and equity financing will affect their business, ownership, profitability, and ability to grow.

Another financial consideration is that the capital you raise must be obtained at a cost that is affordable. One basic entrepreneurial principle to follow is *you cannot make money if you pay too much for what you buy.* Further, your capital structure should be flexible enough so that changes can be easily made to accommodate rapid expansion or contraction of operations. Your capital structure should not block you from pursuing attractive business opportunities. Finally, your legal structure should provide the control you want, while giving your investors and lenders the protection they demand. The balance you should maintain between selling equity in your venture or incurring debt will change depending on your stage of growth.

Before designing a financial plan for your venture use the following checklist to help you formulate your financial strategy.

Entrepreneur's Financial Plan Checklist

1. What stage of development is my business in now?
2. What are my immediate dollar needs?
3. What are my immediate dollar needs in 6 months? 9 months? 12 months?
4. What are my future dollar needs?
5. When will my venture need an injection of capital?
6. How many rounds of financing will I need over the next five years?
7. What type of balance do I want between debt and equity financing?
8. How much debt am I willing to tolerate?
9. How much ownership am I willing to give away for equity financing?
10. What type of financial terms would I be comfortable with and want to negotiate?

QUESTION 4

How can I put together a budget that will as accurately as possible measure my start-up costs?

One method of determining how much money you will need to start your business is to do a mental "walk-through" of what your business will look like. Use the following Entrepreneur's Start-up Cost Checklist as a basis for estimating your start-up costs.

Entrepreneur's Start-up Cost Checklist

1. Where would the business be located?
2. What size will it be initially?
3. What will the office or retail space look like?
4. What type of walls and fixtures will it have?
5. What type of equipment will I need? (Consider computers, furniture, carpet, copy machine, shelving, etc.)
6. What type of signage will be required?
7. How much of an opening inventory will the business need?
8. How will inventory be paid for?
9. What kind of deposits will I be required to make? (Consider telephone, utilities, rent—first and last month, etc.)
10. What city codes must I comply with and are there any costs involved?
11. What type of government (local, state, federal) business licenses will be required?
12. What types of supplies will I need? (Consider cleaning, office, shipping, boxes, etc.)
13. What kind of marketing costs will be incurred before opening? (Consider brochures, advertising, stationery, business cards, etc.)
14. What type of staff training is necessary before opening for business?

When estimating these expenses, be as realistic and accurate as possible. Entrepreneurs always discover hidden costs that are incurred, but not planned for. Ask other owners in a similar business what their start-up costs were and how much money they suggest you have in reserve before opening your doors for business.

Most lenders recommend that entrepreneurs should plan on having a minimum of 3 months operating capital on hand. Ideally, they prefer 6 months of operating capital in the bank. Operating capital is defined as all expenses incurred that will be direct cash outlays during the first 90 to 180 days of operation.

➪ **Courtney's Smart Tip**
Build a pad into your budget to allow for surprises.

Guard against forcing the budgeting process or trying to underestimate start-up costs. Let the budgeting process indicate how much money the business concept really needs. The purpose of estimating start-up costs is to determine if you can raise enough money to start the venture and if your business opportunity can earn a profit.

For example, one entrepreneur wanted to launch a venture that involved purchasing a submarine and selling underwater ocean tours in the Hawaiian islands. The idea seemed to be feasible. There was a growing market for these types of tours similar to the helicopter rides that tourists purchase on their Hawaiian vacations. At the time, there were no other competitors.

He began his research, analyzed the market, created a market niche, and then located a 12-seat used submarine in Houston, Texas that he could remodel for the tours. After estimating his start-up budget he discovered that he needed about $1.2 million for operating capital to launch the venture. He could raise only about $10,000. After estimating start-up costs, he determined there was no way he could start this business himself. Several years later, a couple of other entrepreneurs started the same business and, today, have a profitable venture.

There is no lack of ideas for launching new companies, but your venture ideas must match your personal and business criteria as well as your pocket book. Problems like running out of money or realizing that you cannot raise enough to launch your venture idea can be avoided by accurately estimating start-up costs and preparing an initial start-up budget. This exercise is one that entrepreneurs cannot avoid before spending more time on a venture idea.

QUESTION 5

How can I distinguish my business from others and increase my sales?

Many "me-too" or run-of-the-mill businesses fail because they do not distinguish their product or service from competitors. Successful ventures carefully carve out a distinctive marketing niche by doing something different. The following Marketing Tips Checklist will help you design your marketing niche and increase sales.

Marketing Tips Checklist

1. Know what your customers want.
2. Make your product or service the best it can be.
3. Analyze your competitors and capitalize on their weaknesses.

4. Establish a complete customer profile database.
5. Give your good customers a little extra.
6. Use direct marketing to discover how to improve.
7. Stay in close and constant communication with your customers.
8. Get your customers to sell for you.

Each of the preceding tips are discussed below.

1. *Know what your customers want.* When it comes to marketing and distinguishing your product or service, it is vital to know exactly what your customers want and expect. Often their wants are significantly different from what you think they want and expect. One thing you can be assured of—your customers always want more and expect better.

To understand your customers, put yourself in their shoes and see things from their perspective. Look at your venture from their viewpoint and make any changes that are needed. Do whatever it takes to get insights into your customers' thinking. Talk to them often and listen closely to what they say. The most important question you can ask them is "why?" Also listen for what they don't say. Look for patterns and be responsive to their needs and wants.

2. *Make your product or service the best it can be.* Many entrepreneurs think they offer the very best product or service. Just ask them and they'll tell you. Or ask their staff and they'll say the same: "We offer the very best." What makes a difference is when your *customers* tell you that you offer the very best. It is extremely important that you obtain continual customer feedback about quality.

3. *Analyze your competition and capitalize on their weaknesses.* Your competition can provide you with a wealth of information, if you become a good detective. Evaluate your competitor's strengths and weaknesses. Then concentrate on offering what your competitors don't do well. Expand your marketing niche by offering speedy delivery, more convenience, better service, faster turnaround time, more value, or offer specialized services that your competitors don't offer. Do whatever you can to rise above your competitors.

4. *Establish a complete customer profile database.* You need good, up-to-date, and accessible customer records which contain information about your customer's business, its history, purchasing habits, special needs, and so forth. A good customer database provides indispensable statistics and patterns which will suggest ways to market your product or service more effectively and at reduced cost.

5. *Give your good customers a little extra.* Have you ever purchased a dozen cookies but instead received 13; i.e., the "baker's dozen"? If so, you will most likely remember that vendor and purchase from it again. Being generous and thoughtful is a wonderful way to show your customers how much you appreciate their business. For example, a very successful neighborhood shoe repair store gives a sample size of shoe polish with every major repair job; it outsells its competition by 2 to 1. What could you do to give your customers a little extra? Think creatively. Could you offer discounts, small gifts, or extra services to make your best customers feel needed and appreciated?

6. *Use direct marketing to discover how to improve.* Follow up with your customers to find out how their purchase experience went. Call and ask your customers about their purchase experience or send them a short questionnaire on a postcard. Ask them how they liked your product. Ask if it met their expectations. Ask what you could do to improve and do things better next time. Ask if there is anything else that you could offer.

7. *Stay in constant communication with your customers.* Keep in close contact with your current and/or prospective customers on a routine basis. Send them an informal newsletter, promotional letter, or a "for your information" memo about industry trends or new products or services you plan to offer. Send a newspaper or magazine article about a new idea or trend to help your customers' business. Send a postcard or fax about a special sale you are running. Keep your customer relationship alive and full of benefits.

Using the above checklist will assist you in developing effective marketing strategies. You will be able to better carve your marketing niche and increase sales. It is easy to operate as a "me-too" business, but it takes time, effort, research, and planning to be really effective. Remember, the greatest profits come from the sales you've already made.

8. *Get your customers to sell for you.* Give your customers referral cards and offer them a discount on their next purchase for completing the card. Then thank your customers for having taken the time to do this. Run contests among the staff for those collecting the most customer referral cards. Ask your customers to write testimonial letters. Feature key statements in your promotional material. Develop a customer list of your top and most recognizable customers and use it to legitimatize your business and solicit new customers.

QUESTION 6

How do I put together a winning management team when I can't pay high salaries to attract and retain a talented staff?

Entrepreneurs put together a management team differently from professional managers working in large organizations. Such organizations have the luxury of hiring a multitude of professionals such as lawyers, CPAs, marketing experts, controllers, insurance experts, and other consultants of all types. Entrepreneurs cannot afford such luxury, although they need such highly specialized and technical advice.

Entrepreneurial ventures are a tale of teamwork of key management team members, each of whom plays a critical role in the evolving enterprise. Professional lenders and investors are well aware of the importance of the management team to building a profitable venture. Practically all of them consider your team the most important factor to make a venture profitable. Early in your planning, identify the key management roles and think of what kinds of employees you would like to recruit. Examine your strengths and weaknesses and look for management team members who complement your skills.

One key management trap for entrepreneurs is placing close friends and family in key positions. Generally this is because you know them, they are convenient to hire, and/or you feel obligated to them. The new venture graveyard is littered with founders who hired inept friends and relatives.

> ➪ **Courtney's Smart Tip**
> **Team up with only the best qualified and most highly motivated people who can prove their talents in their track record and who have the training, experience, and skills to do the job you need.**

Professional lenders and investors become immediately suspicious when you hire friends and relatives. Be prepared to defend your selection of people who will play key roles in your venture. You should have good reasons to support your selection of each management team member.

Once you determine which positions are critical to your venture, you are ready to assemble your team. There are two ways to put your management team together—contract with professionals or hire staff. The selection of your management team members is of critical importance to your success.

Generally, entrepreneurs are big users of independent professionals to provide technical advice. By contracting with such professionals, you can reduce your labor costs, use only the best, and pay them only when you need them. For further details on the best way to select contract professionals, refer to Chapter 9—Selecting the Best Business Advisers.

Most entrepreneurs cannot match the pay scales of their larger competitors for members of their management team. As a consequence, you must use tactics other than high wages to compensate your employees, such as establishing a winning incentive program.

Your incentive program could include stock options, stock warrants, phantom stock, profit-sharing programs, deferred compensation plans, perquisites, time off, and the like. Astute entrepreneurs establish several varied incentive plans for different members of the management team. Be very cautious about the tax aspects of your incentive programs and how employees can eventually cash out.

A creative incentive program is key to motivating your management team. Recognize, praise, and reward their efforts. Share with your people the success they have helped create. The only way to attract and retain highly qualified people is to make it worthwhile for them.

QUESTION 7

How do I find a corporate strategic partner to assist me in bringing my invention to the marketplace?

Many entrepreneurs do not think about teaming up with a corporate strategic partner to fund and/or bring their invention or idea to the marketplace. Today, finding a corporate partner is one of the better ways to tap money sources. A corporate strategic partner can provide the capital resources, credit, management expertise, distribution channels, and/or manufacturing services to successfully market your product or service. A corporate strategic alliance can provide needed funds for research, development, and marketing your product or service.

There are several advantages to partnering with large corporations. First, a corporate partner is usually willing to wait longer to receive a return on its investment than traditional lenders or investors, such as bankers or venture capitalists. *The return on the investment is not as important as the potential of establishing new divisions.* If corporate partners are interested in taking an equity position in your business, you probably will give up less ownership than working with a venture capitalist.

Corporate partners can contribute more than capital to your business. They may offer good business advice, moral support, and provide state-of-the-art technology. Establishing a corporate strategic alliance can also provide valuable contacts in the business and financial community.

The disadvantages of corporate strategic alliances include loss of control or making demands that you are opposed to. For example, you could be required to share your research results in exchange for use of their facilities. Also, your affiliation with one corporation may affect your ability to sell your product to its competitors. Or, corporate mission and goals could change, causing your corporate partnership to sour.

To identify a potential corporate partner, look for corporations searching for complementary products to distribute through their existing channels. The key is to find a corporation with the resources, but not the time, commitment, or creativity to pursue the product or service you provide. Remember, corporations are mainly interested in building and strengthening their basic business. Therefore, your output must fit their mission and goals.

Focus on corporations who are interested in early-stage ventures and have already invested in your industry. Also look for a corporation that might be interested in the right to license your invention.

An excellent resource for structuring corporate strategic alliances is *Winning Combinations* by James W. Botkin and Jana B. Mathews. This highlights the new wave of entrepreneurial partnerships between large and small companies. Refer to Chapter 8, Financing Your Venture, for more detailed information on finding and forming corporate strategic alliances.

QUESTION 8

What kind of business insurance should I get to protect my business?

Business owners are exposed to a number of different risks but rarely seem to think about these risks when starting a venture. There are two major risks that owners need to insure against: property loss and liability for injuries. Entrepreneurial ventures frequently purchase packaged policies that cover both types of exposure.

The most popular package is a *Businessowner's policy,* frequently referred to as a "BOP," which covers all the major property and liability exposures in a single policy. The biggest advantage of purchasing a BOP is that the founder generally receives broader coverage at a much lower price than if he or she were to buy each type of insurance separately.

Even if you qualify for a BOP package, you may have inadequate coverage for a disaster. For example, loss of business income due to business interruption occurs when vital business equipment or other business property is unusable because of fire, an explosion, or other property peril. If ever there was a case for business interruption insurance, it was the recent explosion in the World Trade Center, forcing nearly 350 companies to conduct business elsewhere. Experts estimate that over 50 percent of small business owners do not have business interruption insurance.

Ask your insurance agent about business interruption insurance coverage. Make sure such coverage covers your company for more than just a few days. Most tenants in the World Trade Center disaster were shut out for at least a month or longer. Depending on your type of business, consider buying "Extra expense" insurance to pay for temporary relocation of people and machinery so you can get back in business fast.

> ➪ **Courtney's Smart Tip**
> **The right type and degree of business-interruption insurance can keep your business alive if disaster destroys your company or if thieves walk out the door with your equipment.**

You may be able to play the odds and survive without this type of insurance, but you will probably be in debt for a long time. Whether you purchase a BOP or separate policies, it is critical that you adequately cover your disaster contingency needs. The rule of thumb is to carry enough insurance to get you back into business without impairing your cash flow. This amount is usually equal to what your property is worth.

For further information about business insurance, call the Insurance Information Institute, Inc. (III) in New York at (800) 331-9146. It is a nonprofit educational organization that provides information about the property and casualty insurance business and has many helpful publications. Ask them about getting a copy of their publication, *Insuring Your Business,* by Sean Mooney.

QUESTION 9

How can I strengthen my sales skills as well as those of my staff?

Most entrepreneurs do not think about the sales function or its importance to their survival. In addition, they often don't think about or practice how to close a sale. Since many entrepreneurs work alone when starting a business, they perform all the jobs themselves and often don't obtain sales training to strengthen their bottom line. However, you don't have a business without customers and you cannot attract customers without a strong sales effort and plan.

Many owners make the mistake of thinking that because they have a superior product or service, customers will flock to their business and sales will automatically happen. Others do not see themselves as salespeople since they may not be directly involved in contacting and selling to their customers.

The truth is that all entrepreneurs are involved in sales from the inception of their business. Entrepreneurs are always selling—themselves, their business, and their products or services. They may infrequently call on customers themselves, but they must continually interact with various members of the infrastructure, such as bankers, accountants, lawyers, and investors, to obtain support and advice for their business. During each contact, owners must constantly sell and resell their venture, its concepts, and its potential.

Developing entrepreneurial sales skills is one of the more neglected areas of operating a business. Entrepreneurs should assess their selling skills and take steps to strengthen them. This is especially true for founders who have not had prior selling experience and formal sales training.

Sales are generally gained or lost in the first minutes of an encounter. Therefore entrepreneurs must get attention and interest during the first few minutes of the meeting by highlighting captivating or "sexy" features and benefits of your product or service. It is critical for owners to sharpen their sales skills towards becoming expert salespeople. The following are three tips for improving your sales skills.

1. First, recognize that it is not what you say but how you say it. Research has shown that logic, i.e., the perceived value of the product or service, does not play as great a role in a persuasion transaction as voice inflection and body language. In fact, body language plays the biggest role and accounts for 55 percent of the buying decision, followed by voice inflection, which accounts for 38 percent. Logic only accounts for 7 percent in making a buying decision. Therefore, it is not what you say, but the way you say it that makes the difference. Both conviction and enthusiasm displayed in body language and voice inflection are critical to making the sale.
2. Second, sales are dependent on relationships. People buy from people they like, know, and respect. Therefore it is key that entrepreneurs contact customers and establish relationships with them whether or not they have their own sales staff.
3. Lastly, use mental imaging to practice your selling skills. Imagine and then walk yourself through a sales call. See yourself being successful as well as handling resistance. Positively comparing your company to your competitors, closing the sale, and the like. This exercise is similar to what successful athletes have done for years to improve their golf swing, pass a football, or land an intricate skating jump.

Access your sales skills and those of your staff. Provide sales training for your entire team, and especially your sales staff. Everyone in your organization should be constantly selling. The good news is that selling skills can be learned and enhanced if the person has a genuine desire to succeed at selling. It just takes a little time, effort, and some sales training.

QUESTION 10

What skills should I develop to keep pace with the growth of my business?

Often entrepreneurs find out that their business has significantly grown, but their skills haven't. They have not had time to devote to personal professional development. Yet continual enhancement of entrepreneurial and leadership skills is needed. Important entrepreneurial skills to continually develop include business planning, goal setting, problem solving, financial management, marketing, human resource management, and motivational skills. Other important leadership skills are visioning, coaching, influencing, negotiating, delegating, and listening. Both sets of skills are pivotal to the continued success of any venture.

Experts say that over half of all business problems originate with the perceptions, attitudes, and practices of the owner. The other half come from poor hiring. Both types of problems can be overcome.

It is important to plan how your business will grow, how fast a pace you can handle, and how this growth will affect your staff. Invite your staff to participate in the planning stages rather than hearing about the growth after the fact. Point out areas of vulnerability and develop strategies to strengthen weak areas. Consider what additional skills and training you and your staff will need to prepare for growth.

> ➪ **Courtney's Smart Tip**
> **Success doesn't continue forever—markets will change continually, making it necessary to develop new strategies and tactics.**

Index

Aburdene, Patricia, 7
Accountants:
  as business adviser, 236
  certified public accountant, 236
  firms, 236–237
  as tax planner, 236
Advertising:
  disadvantages of, 37
  and going public, 2
  television, 162–164
  word-of-mouth, 145
  (*See also* Market penetration)
Advisory council, 228–229, 242–244
Alternative money sources, 186–188, 207–215
American Home-Based Business Association, 7
Americans with Disabilities Act (ADA), 16–17
Angels, business, 184, 211
  (*See also* Investors)
Angel networks, 32
Attorneys:
  finding, 229–230
  firms, 229–230
  intellectual property, 128
  legal expenses, 230, 232–235
  patent, 111, 122, 124–125

Banks:
  commercial, 27, 189
  investment, 190, 206–207
  lending checklist for, 30
  loan policies, 183
  questions to ask, 31
  relationship to, 30, 192
Berle, Gustav, 47
Beta test, 153
Blechman, Bruce, 212
Blue, Martha, 34
Blue-sky laws, 204
Board of directors, 228–229, 240–243
Botkin, James W., 213
Brabec, Barbara, 29
Brand name, 109
Brokers:
  business, 102, 209–210
  informational, 113–114
  licensing, 122
  mortgage, 189
Budget, 268–270
Business cards, 138, 164
Business plan:
  consultant to, 44
  method, 156
  outline, 58–60
Buy-sell agreement:
  leveraged, 202
  provision for, 83
  "shoot-out-clause" for, 83
Buyout agreement (*see* Buy-sell agreement)
Buyout entrepreneur, 95
Bygrave, William D., 32

Certified development companies (CDC) (*see* Small Business Administration)
Certified public accountant (CPA) (*see* Accountants)
Charitable organization (*see* Nonprofit organization)
Collaterial:
  and factoring, 219–220
  as loan guarantee, 188–189
Commercial financing companies, 184, 189, 208–209
Compensatory damages, 108
Competition:
  and business plan, 139–140
  and market research, 146
  and new product, 153
  and start-up-factors, 50–52

Consignment merchandise:
advantages/disadvantages of, 168–171
marketing strategy for, 139
Consultants:
business plan, 44
financial, 209–210
management, 238–240
Contracting:
service business, 2, 4
with former employer, 7
Cooperative Research and Development Agreement (CRADA) (*see* Small Business Administration)
Copyright, 33–34, 109, 118–121
Corporate partner:
finding, 113, 274–275
establishing alliance with, 212–214
option, 184
Corporate refugees, 2, 39, 95, 101
Corporation:
articles of incorporation, 85
bylaws, 85
choosing a, 266
corporate structure of, 77–78
and double taxation, 77–78, 86
(*See also* S corporation)
Council on Foundations, 222
Credit Cards:
charge-backs, 196
merchant's, 195–197
personal, 184, 187, 214–215
rates, 196
Credit unions, 189
Customer base:
cultivation of, 35–37
database, 157–159, 262
list, 126–127
demographics, 159
profile, 159, 271
focus group, 147
Customer complaints, 148, 150
Customer mailing list, 36, 138, 160
Customer referrals, 138, 158, 272
Customer service, 148–151

Databases, 39, 138, 251
Direct marketing, 158, 272
Disabled entrepreneurs:
opportunities, 15–17
Disabled entrepreneurs (*Cont.*):
trends, 2–3, 7
Disabled workers, 16–17
Disadvantaged business enterprise (DBE), 2, 11–13
Disclosure agreement, 110–112, 120–122, 125
Displaced workers, 19–21, 39
Distributors, 170–171, 208
Dychtwald, Ken, 157

Edwards, Paul and Sarah, 56
800 number, 139, 165–167
80/20 rule:
sales, 35
time management, 56
Employee agreements:
confidential information, 126–127
noncompete, 126
and trade secrets, 125
Entrepreneurial myths, 47–49
Entrepreneurial traits, 44–47
Entry strategy, 39, 248–250
Ethnic businesses, 4
Exclusivity rights, 123
Executive entrepreneurs, 18–19
(*See also* Corporate refugees)
Existing business, 98, 103–105
Exit strategy, 204, 252, 258
Expansion strategy, 8, 255, 258

Factoring, 184, 218–221
Feasibility plan, 53, 57, 263–266
Federal Laboratory Consortium (FLC), 218
Federal Trade Commission, 35
Female entrepreneurs (*see* Women business owners)
Financial ratios, 104
501(c)(3) (*see* Nonprofit organization)
Focus groups, 138, 146–148
For your information memo, 158, 272
Foundation Center, 222
Foundation for Ongoing Revitalization of Competent Executives (FORCE), 16
Foundations (*see* Nonprofit organization)
Franchising:
agreement, 253
application package, 252
consulting company, 3
disclosure document, 248

Franchising (*Cont.*):
entry strategy, 39–40
fees, 250
and franchisors, 253, 256–258
international, 254–255
site locators, 252
types of, 256–258
Friendly money, 183–189, 210
Fund raisers, 209–210

Gaston, Robert J., 212
General partnership, 79, 82
Godfrey, Joline, 15
Going concern (*see* Existing business)
Going public (*see* Initial public offering)
Goodwill, 197–198

Holtz, Herman, 240
Home-based business:
contracting, 3
opportunities, 6–8
quiz, 28–29
regulations, 54–56
service, 2
time management, 56–57
Home delivery, 3, 5–6

Iannarelli, Cynthia, 14
Incubators, 61–63
Industry trade association, 141–142
Infringement, 108, 117–118
Infrastructure, 199–200, 227
(*See also* Accountants, Attorneys, Banks)
Initial public offering (IPO), 188, 201–205, 234
Insurance:
benefits, 238
business owner's 79, 275
finding agent for, 237–238
key employee, 83–84
liability, 78, 238–241, 275–276
life, 81–82
Intermediaries, 209–210
International business, 2–3, 8–9
Invention:
and beta test, 153
licensing, 121
log book, 114
patent, 110–111
protection, 108
Invention marketing company, 34–35, 109, 128–133
Investors:
foreign, 201
private, 32, 184–186, 211

Job Accommodation Network (JAN), 17
Joint venture, 210, 212
(*See also* Corporate partner)

Kaiser, Leland, 5
Krasner, Jay, 15–16

Lease negotiation, 69–73
Leasing company financing, 190
Lenders, hard-asset, 208
Levinson, Jay Conrad, 37, 212
Library (*see* Market research)
Licensing agreement, 121–124
Limited liability company (LLC), 78, 88–89
Limited partnership, 77, 82, 202
Line of credit, 184, 193–195, 214–215, 220
Luxton, Larry, 16

Management team:
balance, 82
board of directors, 244
importance to investors, 200, 206
infrastructure, 227
retired executives and, 241
selection of, 272–274
Margolis, Don, 108*n*.
Market penetration:
costs, 137
image, 167, 207
targeting, 152
tools, 39–40
(*See also* Advertising, Media)
Market research:
competition, 139–151
current customers, 40
customer wants, 271
demographics, 137
Market segmentation, 152
Marketing mix, 152
Marketing plan:
development of, 151–153
importance of, 37–39

Marketing tips, 36, 270–272
Mathews, Jana B., 213
Media, 161–164
Merchant's credit card (*see* Credit cards)
Mestin, Robert, 168
Mezzanine financing, 202
Mini-billboards (*see* Business cards)
Minority Business Development Center, 13
Minority business owners, 2, 10–12
Minority Enterprise Small Business Investment Company (MESBIC), 215
Mooney, Sean, 238, 276
Mystery shoppers, 138, 148–149

Naisbitt, John, 7
National Association of Women Business Owners, 15
National Business Incubation Association, 62
National Center for Policy Analysis, 7
National Education Center for Women in Business (NECWB), 14
National Executive Service Corps, 222
National Factoring Services, 221
National Minority Supplier Development Council, 13
National Venture Capital Association, 31
New product:
- consignment, 171
- development, 153
- and invention marketing, 129
- patent, 112
- research funding for, 218
- trade show, 176–177

Newsletters, 138, 158, 272
900 number, 139, 167–168
Nonprofit organization:
- forming, 78, 89–92
- funding, 221–222

Novelty search, 110, 112–114, 125, 132
(*See also* Patents)

Offering memorandum, 203–204

Partnership, 77–78, 80–82
Patent:
- application for, 110
- benefits of, 108

Patent (*Cont.*):
- and "examiner's action," 116
- fees, 116
- obtaining, 33–34
- prior art, 114, 116
- rights, 115

Patent attorney:
- advice, 111
- choosing, 231
- fees, 234–235
- process, 113–114
- trade secrets, 124–125

Patent depository, 113–114
Patent, foreign, 115–116
Patent pending, 113, 121, 125
Personal criteria, 27, 49, 104
Personal professional development, 278
Personal savings, 183–184, 186
Peterson, C.D., 105
Phantom sales, 138, 155
Physically disabled entrepreneurs (*see* Disabled entrepreneurs)
Pitzak, Avery N., 165
Postcards, sales, 138
President's Committee on Employment of People with Disabilities, 17
Pressman, David, 33
Private placement, 190, 202–204
Privately held companies, 140
Procurement opportunities:
- corporate, 2
- federal, 10
- government bidder's list, 3

Procurement Technical Assistance Centers (PTACs), 10
Promotion, 160–162
(*See also* Media)
Proprietary rights, 124
Publicity:
- difference from advertising, 162
- free, 138–139, 142
- as part of marketing mix, 152
- (*See also* Promotion)

Publicity held company, 140, 205

Regulation D, 203–204
Register mark (*see* Trademark, Service mark)
Research Institute for Special Entrepreneurs, 15
Retail location, 63–68

Rice, Ted, 247*n*.
Right stuff (*see* Entrepreneurial traits)
Risk management (*see* Insurance)
Royalties, 108, 121, 123, 130

S corporation:
  articles of incorporation, 87
  choice of, 78
  common stock, 87
  different from regular corporation, 86–88
  double taxation, 78, 87
Sales:
  contest, 150
  forecasting, 154–156
  increasing, 35
  leads, 159–160, 174–178
  skills, 276–278
  training, 277
Sales representatives:
  commissions, 172
  finding, 172–173
  and house accounts, 174
  and marketing tool, 138–139
  problems, 126,128
  sales meetings, 174
Securities & Exchange Commission (SEC), 203, 205–207
Seed capital, 188, 209–210
Seed money:
  different from seed capital, 188–189
  launching, 183–184
    founders, 186
  venture capitalists, 267
Self-financing, 186
  (*See also* Personal savings)
Seltzer, Michael, 90
Senior business owners, 7
Service business:
  marketing, 156–157
  trends, 2–4
Service marks (SM), 33–34, 109, 117
Site location (*see* Franchising, Retail location)
Small, Samuel, 19
Small Business Administration (SBA):
  business loan, 184, 190, 192, 215–217
  certified development companies, 217
  consultants, 239
  contract finance program, 217
  cooperative research and development agreement, 218
Small Business Administration (SBA) (*Cont.*):
  8(a) program, 10–12
  exporting, 9
  guaranty loan program, 215–216
  procurement, 8
  small business innovation research program, 218
Small Business Development Center (SBDC), 9
Small Business Foundation of America, 9
Small business investment centers (SBIC), 190, 217
Software programs, 33, 234–235
Sole proprietorship:
  advantages/disadvantages, 84
  establishing, 79–80
  option, 77
  without declaration, 266
Spinoff products, 37
Small business innovation research program (SBIR) (*see* Small Business Administration)
Start-up:
  capital (*see* Seed capital)
  considerations (*see* Personal criteria)
  factors, 50–52
State departments of commerce, 9, 217
Strategic alliances (*see* Corporate partners)
Subcontractors, 146

Target markets (*see* Market penetration)
Technology, 122, 218
Telemarketing:
  charge-backs, 196
  marketing strategy, 138
  process, 165–168
Television:
  cut-rate spots, 162–164
    preemptible time, 138–139
  talk show, 160
10K form, 140
10Q form, 140
Testimonial letters, 138, 153, 158
Time management, 56–57
Timmons, Jeffry A., 32
Trade credit, 208
Trade dress, 109
Trade journals, 142, 161

Trade secret:
definition, 33–34
different from copyright, 120
laws, 111–112
process, 124–128
protection, 114–115
types, 109
Trade show:
marketing strategy, 142
types of, 175–180
Trade Show Bureau, 132, 145
Trademark (TM):
definition, 33–34
fees, 117–118
process, 125
types, 109
Tuller, Lawrence, W., 32
Turnaround artist, 96–97, 103
Turnkey operation, 248

Underwriter, 207
U.S. Copyright Office, 112, 119
U.S. Department of Commerce, 9
U.S. Department of Defense, 10
U.S. Department of Transportation (DoT), 12–13
U.S. Government Printing Office, 39
U.S. Patent and Trademark Office, 108, 112–113, 132

Venture capital:
attracting, 198–202
finding, 184–186
firms, 32
funds, 32
requirements, 190
Venture capital clubs, 212
Venture checklist, 27
Venture ideas, 26, 43–44, 47–49
Venture opportunities, 1–21, 49

Ward, John, 243
Women business owners, 2, 7, 10–15, 91

Zoghlin, Gilbert G., 20